Charles Bannon

AUSTRALIAN PRINTMAKER

Charles Bannon

AUSTRALIAN PRINTMAKER

An Aspect of Australian Art

1968–1982

David Dolan

Angus & Robertson Publishers

For my girls

ANGUS & ROBERTSON PUBLISHERS
London ● Sydney ● Melbourne

This book is copyright. Apart from any fair dealing for the
purposes of private study, research, criticism or review, as
permitted under the Copyright Act, no part may be reproduced
by any process without written permission. Inquiries should
be addressed to the publisher.

First published by Angus & Robertson Publishers, Australia, 1982

© Charles Bannon and David Dolan, 1982

National Library of Australia
Cataloguing-in-publication data.

Bannon, Charles.
   Charles Bannon.

   Bibliography.
   ISBN 0 207 14779 5.

   1. Bannon, Charles. 2. Printmakers —
Australia — Biography. I. Dolan, David.
   II. Title.

769.92'4

Typeset in 13pt Cheltenham Light Condensed by Savage & Co. Pty Ltd
Printed in Hong Kong

Acknowledgements

Thank you John Bannon for suggesting to your father that he invite me to write this book. I have enjoyed doing it, and gained much from working with him.

Suzanne Roux organised the initial business side of the project, and gave good commonsensical advice on many occasions.

Linda Waters, a former student of mine, carried out the basic research, clerical and cataloguing work, and I depended on her throughout. A grant from the South Australian Government made her task possible.

I should like to acknowledge the Master of Kathleen Lumley College at the University of Adelaide, where I retreated to do the writing; and Helen Keene who typed the text.

DD

List of Prints

Charles Bannon

One-man Exhibitions

1956	Royal Society of the Arts, Adelaide.
1957	Athenaeum, Melbourne.
1958	Royal SA Society of Arts, Adelaide.
1959	Blaxland Galleries, Sydney.
1962	Royal SA Society of Arts, Adelaide.
1965	North Adelaide Galleries. Gallery A, Canberra.
1966	Darlinghurst Galleries, Sydney. Kennigo Street Gallery, Brisbane.
1969	Strawberry Hill Gallery, Sydney. North Adelaide Galleries.
1971	Lidums Art Gallery, Adelaide.

Commissioned Works

1955	Displays for Royal Show.
1957	Pectoral Cross, Episcopal Rings for Archbishop of Adelaide.
1961	Designed and executed for the Church of England, complete interior of church at Largs Bay, Adelaide.
1962	Designed and executed fountains for Royal Agricultural Society, Adelaide.
1981	Series of paintings for Ayers House restaurant, Adelaide.

His commissioned works also include many stage settings, heraldic crests and murals.

Awards

1954	Blake Prize for Religious Painting.
1955	Barmera Prize.

Chapter One

The Man and the Time

The 1960s were boom years for Australian art. The economy was strong, there was a hump of young people in the demographic curve, we were shaking off our feelings of inferiority in all matters — particularly art — to "overseas", and there was plenty of that sixties optimism, now sadly missed, to go around. The full impact of Vietnam had not been felt, nor was it obvious what price the technologically advanced nations were going to have to pay for their determination to get rich at the expense of the environment and the rest of the human race. No one knew the initials OPEC; and inflation was running at four per cent in a bad year. Unemployment happened in other places.

It was a good time to collect art. Art was vigorous and colourful, not very intellectually intimidating, and even a bit controversial (like the bikini), and evidence of the collector's standing as a progressive and enlightened human being. With the economy on a steady rise, it was also a good investment.

Australian art definitely looked like a good thing. Thanks to Dobell it was respectable. Thanks to Whiteley it was lively. Thanks to Nolan and his friend Ned Kelly it was nationalistic. Thanks to the glossy American magazines it looked international. Thanks to the stock market it appeared likely to be lucrative.

The sixties were good years in which to be an artist or a dealer in Australia. It was possible to survive without the aid of government grants, then almost unknown. Young artists came out of the art schools (many of them relatively small and independent, for the era of the polytechnic colleges of advanced education was but dawning) and arranged exhibitions and sold work with ease.

The strength of Australian art in the early sixties was painting, traditionally the premier mode of expression in the western world. Paintings could achieve the scale and brightness and show the marks of physical vigour which were highly prized.

Sculpture was gesturing towards freeing itself from the confines of the physical object, but it had not then generally freed itself from the pedestal or from the limitations of formalist abstraction. Most Australian sculptures of the sixties were harmless little things, if they were not tired old things. The exceptions to that generalisation were indeed rare exceptions.

One of the real surprises of this bubbling episode in Australian art was provided by a development in the printmaking area. The present writer, then an eager undergraduate discovering simultaneously the sober pleasures of art history and the heady joys of contemporary art, remembers his first encounter with products of the Paddington Print Studio as an ecstatic moment. Prints were not all colourless brown-grey-black scratchy little things! It was possible to get your hands on signed originals by the national culture heroes — Blackman and Boyd and Dickerson and Crooke and others — for sums as low as fifty dollars! (To establish a sense of relative money values, I was working in a pub to put myself through university, and I could earn fifty dollars for a Friday night and Saturday noon-to-midnight.) That was in 1968.

The introduction to Paddington Print Studio art was also, for me and no doubt for many others, the first encounter with the term "serigraphy". The use of this term, rather than the more familiar "silkscreen" or "screenprint", was being encouraged by Charles Bannon, the driving force behind PPS.

Although the Australian public was hungry for art, it was not educated or discriminating. Photography was not popularly regarded as an art form, and the differences between artists' original prints and commercial reproductions were not widely appreciated.

Bannon decided that if artists' original prints, produced by the screenprinting process in limited editions, were to be accepted for what they were, the term "silkscreen" with its industrial overtones had to be avoided. The term "serigraphy", which suggests, quite properly, a kinship with lithography and other graphic arts media, would give the prints a chance.

His choice of terminology was not a matter of pretentiousness, but rather of public education. The press coverage of PPS from 1967 to 1970 has one major theme: a serigraph is an original print which is not the same as a mass-produced or photographic reproduction. Bannon had laboured to impress this upon the journalists who were in turn trying to impress it upon their readers. The 1969 PPS Travelling Exhibition included a photographic display showing how the prints were made.

One of the major achievements of PPS was to educate the Australian public about original prints. The acceptance of prints and printmakers, in all media, in subsequent years, is largely due to Bannon's pioneering efforts in the late sixties. Working in a parallel direction and at times linked to PPS, was the Print Council of Australia, established in 1966.

In retrospect, it seems inevitable that Bannon should have played a part in the artistic education of the Australian public. A successful artist in his own right, he devoted much of his life to education, not only in the schools.

He was born in Edinburgh in 1919, and came to Australia in 1927 with his parents and a brother, to join another brother who had gone ahead. The family settled in Bendigo, Victoria.

His early life was erratic, with his father often absent; there was not a lot of money, but there was always enough for young Bannon to have tuition from a local private teacher, Ada Jackson, who charged sixpence and a meal for a three-hour lesson. Bannon cannot remember a time when he was not interested in art, particularly drawing.

As a youth he worked as a message boy and later as a shoe salesman in Ezywalkin at Bendigo, for a maximum of seven shillings and sixpence a week: at that time the average pair of shoes he was selling was priced at about one pound. He continued his art education as best he could at night at the Mechanics Institute, the School of Mines and the Bendigo Art Gallery.

His interests in religion and politics developed early. He has always been a Labor supporter; but his spiritual path has been less distinct. In his mother's house he was exposed to many and diverse brands of Christianity, for she flitted from one denomination and sect to another in search of . . . something.

A considerable influence on his artistic development was a friendship, in his early teens, with an elderly local amateur painter named Woodward. Young Bannon carried the old man's paintboxes and easels, and was rewarded one day with an introduction to the local collector Dr Neptune Scott, in whose home he saw paintings by Corot, Courbet and others of the French mid-nineteenth century, which the doctor had acquired as a student in Europe. They are now to be seen in the Bendigo Art Gallery.

The Bendigo Art Gallery was crucial in Bannon's development. Along with the movies (illegally entered over a fence, when he lacked the admission price) it provided the only way to spend the Saturday afternoons for a lad who did not want to run with the larrikin pack. Bannon has always been something of an outsider (hence the resentment of the academic art establishment), and this role was adopted in his youth when he was a "little pommy bastard". Art became the centre of his life.

While still in his teens, Bannon was recruited into the Light Horse in

Bendigo; and then joined the Darwin Mobile Force with which he went to Darwin as a soldier in 1937. It was the beginning of a continuing relationship with the Northern Territory and its people.

War came in 1939 and with it a transfer to the 2/3 Field Regiment, in which he was a bombardier. He moved around during the war, doing a stint at the POW camp at Cowra, visiting the UK, and seeing active service in Libya, Syria and Lebanon. He held the rank of Warrant Officer 2 when discharged in 1945.

What did he do in the army? He "worried about Judas", and re-evaluated Christianity. Judas Iscariot became the subject of the painting which won him the Blake Prize in 1954.

From 1945 to 1948 he studied at the Melbourne Technical College (now Royal Melbourne Institute of Technology) and the National Gallery School, and completed a Teacher's Certificate and an Art Teacher's Certificate. Among the artists, both teachers and students, with whom he was associated at this time were Ambrose Dyson, Vic Greenhouse, John Rowell, William Rowell, Murray Griffin, Rees Williams, Kenneth Jack, Eric Smith, Leonard French, and the late Geoff Barwell.

Upon completing his training he took a position as art master at the Collegiate School of Saint Peter, the prestigious Adelaide college operated by the Church of England with a history going back to 1847, making it the oldest school on the Australian mainland. He remained on the staff at St Peter's until 1963, and achieved a number of pioneering advances in art education, including a television programme on art for children.

His first marriage, at the end of the war, produced four sons. The eldest, John Charles Bannon, became the leader of the Parliamentary ALP in South Australia in 1979, following a brief term as the minister responsible for the arts in the Dunstan and Corcoran governments.

While at St Peter's, Bannon painted continuously and experimented with a variety of print media, and held at least twelve one-man exhibitions as well as participating in many mixed shows. The highlight of this period was the Blake Prize for Religious Art in 1954, when its credibility was at its peak.

He was also actively involved in theatre and church design in South Australia, producing stage sets and theatrical posters, ecclesiastical silver, stained glass and murals.

In 1964 he took up an appointment as art education director for the Commonwealth government in the Northern Territory, and was the first art adviser to Aboriginal special schools. He took the opportunity to make a study of Australian Aboriginal art during the two years he spent travelling around the Top End.

Writing about a dispute over Aboriginal bark paintings, in the *Australian*, 22-23 November 1980, Max Harris, well-known poet and social commentator said:

"I chose to consult Charles Bannon, who is thought of largely as the artist who has led Australia's revival of printmaking. But Charles Bannon has had seventeen years' experience out in the vastness of the bush, first as an adviser to the federal government, and secondly as Project Officer in South Australia to the Aboriginal Resources Branch. He is not an office expert. His connection with artifacts has been on a man-to-man basis.

"He has been able to explain how genuine confusions can have arisen. Bark paintings are totemic and expressive of one man's dreaming. But one man's dreaming is not relevant to another man. It is his own dreaming. And he may do what he wishes with it. Aboriginal tribal life is not as rigidified as we tend to believe. Indeed individualism is integral to their way of life. As is humour. As is an indifference to personal property."

Bannon developed a creative relationship with Aboriginal culture unequalled by any artist in the history of modern Australia, not forgetting such figures as Sir Russell Drysdale or William Ricketts, a fact not widely known.

Bannon's "aboriginality", if we may call it that — his extraordinary ability to empathise with others and enter into their creativity — was the basis of his success in working with artists of so many different personalities and persuasions at PPS.

So when he went to New South Wales in 1966, Bannon was a rarity among Australian artists of his generation — educated in Victoria, with experience in South Australia and the Northern Territory, he was not a man with a one-state reputation, like so many who aspire to become national figures but remain always provincial.

In Sydney he tutored in graphic communication at the University of New South Wales, and taught at several small private art schools, including Mary White's. Paddington Print Studio grew out of this situation.

After the demise of PPS in the early seventies, Bannon returned to Adelaide with his second wife, Anne. While lecturing part-time at the Salisbury College of Advanced Education, in the art department, he established a small studio at the rear of his home in the suburb of Prospect, from which he issued the second series of Australian artists' prints produced from a Charles Bannon studio.

Chapter Two

Printmaking in Australia

During the late 1940s when Charles Bannon was an art student, printmaking in Australia was far from thriving — in fact, it might almost as well not have existed at all. For a number of reasons, there had been only a few times in the past when printmaking in Australia had taken its place as a medium of artistic expression equal to but distinct from painting.

Although the first European artists to depict Australia were sketchers (usually in watercolour) it was through the print media that their images became widely known at home. These artists were the topographical draftsmen attached to seaborne and overland explorers. In the days of imperialist and missionary exploration, which had a strong scientific component, no leader would be bothered setting out without an artist in his team to document its discoveries. In the pre-camera era, the artist was as essential to a voyage of discovery as are the television cameras on the spacecraft of today.

But the full value of the images of newly discovered lands could not be realised while they remained sketches or paintings which existed in the form of one-off originals. They had to be multiplied for dissemination (often there was a strong propaganda purpose involved, such as the encouragement of the migration of a working class). The means used were steel engraving and lithography, but the making of these prints by journeyman printmakers took place in the old homeland. Often the result of the hack printmaker's total unfamiliarity with the subject matter is hilariously obvious to modern eyes: under his hand, the carefully observed Australian flora and fauna were (unconsciously, most often, no doubt) metamorphosed into hybrid European-looking flora and fauna.

A particular instance which can be cited is the work of George French Angas, who came to South Australia in the colony's first decade and made meticulous studies of Aborigines, landscapes, and vegetation. But when these were reworked as illustrations for *South Australia Illustrated* in 1847, the lithographers tidied up, distorted and even censored them.

So to refer to the printmaking which was generated by the interest in the antipodes in the late eighteenth and early nineteenth centuries as "merely reproductive", which sounds scathing, is in fact often giving it too much credit: it was derivative and conventionalised, and it was English rather than Australian.

There were many printmakers — more often journeymen than artists — among the convicts who comprised so large a portion of the first Europeans to live in Australia. In many cases they were transported for forgery. It was always a temptation for the engraver who found himself short of ready money to *make* money, literally, himself. One of the most famous of the convict-artist-forgers was Thomas Griffiths Wainwright, who included murder in his repertoire, and is the subject of Oscar Wilde's essay "Pen, Pencil and Poison".

Another artist who came to Australia as the guest of the British government was John Eyre. He was convicted not of forgery but housebreaking, and he was a watercolourist of limited talent. His images were produced as prints by Absalom West in Sydney in 1812. West was an emancipated ex-convict, and his first edition of 1812 made history because it was the first to be printed here (rather than back in England).

Despite the limitations imposed upon them by the market, there is all the variety one might expect in the works of printmakers of such diverse personalities and backgrounds. Among this first generation is the meticulous botanical illustrator Sydney Parkinson, the topographer William Westall (whose "Cape Wilberforce Australia, Discovered by Captain Flinders in HMS Investigator" is one of two Australian scenes printed by George Baxter of Baxter Print fame), the birdwatcher J. W. Lewin, the surveyors Evans and Light, the professional artist-teacher Edward Dayes, the soldier James Taylor and the convicts Lycett and Wallis.

Topographical sketching was part of the training of many naval and military officers at the time, and as well as Taylor there were military artists named Dale and Hext, who depicted Western Australia and Sydney respectively. Among others transported for their crimes was Charles Rodius; and it is also worth noting the presence of women artists at this time, including Elizabeth Hudspeth.

Not surprisingly though, it was from the ranks of the professional artists and architects and scientist-illustrators that the major works came: Augustus Earle (friend and colleague of Charles Darwin), Benjamin Duterrau, John Lhotsky, Samuel Jackson, John Skinner Prout, Joseph Fowles, John Gould and Samuel Calvert.

Finally, we ought to note that not all of the early artists whose work became a basis for prints and illustrations were British: Louis Sainson, Louis Breton, Charles Lesueur and Nicholas Petit were French artists attached to naval expeditions in the first third of the nineteenth century, before France relinquished interest in this part of the Pacific.

There are several reasons why, even after West began his publishing enterprise in 1812, most of the prints after these artists were made in England. There was a limited amount of printing equipment in Australia, but even more, a limited local market. The demand for Australian images was strongest in England, and so it made sense to take a few sketches there and print the editions there, rather than print them here and transport the bulkier full print editions back. Furthermore, the editions were for the English publishers, who wanted the work and the profit for themselves — they were not interested in stimulating the development of printmaking in Australia.

By the middle of the nineteenth century things were changing, as the local market increased. Among the outstanding artists who came to Australia and whose work was turned into prints were Eugène von Guérard, Conrad Martens, S. T. Gill, and Nicholas Chevalier. All of them helped shape Australia's self-image, and it was because their work was published that it had its effect. Paintings could be seen by relatively few people, especially before the era of the "national" galleries in the state capital cities, but cheap multiples (prints) democratised art.

Samuel Thomas Gill was a scientific illustrator by training, but versatile, and after his involvement in the tragic Horrocks exploration expedition to the Flinders Ranges in 1846, he became the recorder of the mining era. He worked underground as well as above at Kapunda and Burra in South Australia, but it was his involvement in the great gold rushes of the 1850s in Victoria which made him famous. His sense of humour, best described as an "ocker" dis-respect for authority, propriety and snobbery, accords exactly with a dominant aspect of what has become regarded as the traditional Aussie attitude.

Martens (like Earle) had worked with Darwin, and had learnt much from him and the *Beagle*'s commander Fitzgerald about nature and weather. His tropical yet Turnerian images of Sydney and Queensland herald the high romantic era in Australian art.

Von Guerard (from Austria) and Chevalier (French-Swiss) took an even grander view of Australia. They sought out alpine spectacle, and there is a new "think big" approach to the landscapes in their paintings, and in the prints after their paintings.

Chevalier often added elements of the colloquial and picturesque to his scenes, while von Guerard had a cosmic moral vision, seeing God's hand in all Nature.

Another devotee of the big landscapes was W. C. Piguenit. Active in the last years of the nineteenth century, he is of special interest as the first Australian-born painter to reach the highest technical and aesthetic level; and we may regret that he made so few prints.

Artists at this time often entered into worker-capitalist relationships with publishers of their prints, and lost control, in many instances, of their images. We do not have any evidence that any Australian publishers of editions became as wealthy as some of the most successful in Europe and England at the time, and nor do we know what the artists usually earned for their efforts. Independent individual artist-printmakers were a rarity, partly no doubt because of the cost of the equipment required for making lithographs or steel engravings, particularly if it was not to be used on a steady basis, and also because the hack work involved in printing large editions did not appeal to creative artists.

In the nineteenth century the woodblock had been an important medium for illustrating newspapers and other cheap publications. It was made redundant by photographic engraving and printing processes, but it was to make a comeback as a fine art printmaking medium in the early-mid twentieth century.

The only print medium to continue in use with artists from the nineteenth century into the twentieth century was etching, which had a vogue, particularly amongst amateurs, from the 1880s on. Engraving (and lithography, but to a lesser extent) became a thing of the past. Lithography was to make its comeback too, but engraving — a harsh linear medium, however well it is handled — seems to have gone forever.

The trickle of late Victorian-era etchings turned into a flood in the years around the First World War. Etching is a medium which allows, even demands, fluidity and spontaneity. It has an intimate quality, revealing to the full the artist's personal style; and the process permits only relatively small editions before the plate breaks down.

In later nineteenth-century England etching was a favoured print medium, with the aesthetic-movement works of Alphonse Legros and J. McN.

Whistler setting the standard of taste. The major figures in the Australian etching school of the subsequent generation were John Shirlow, John Mather, Sydney Long, Jessie Trail, Henry van Raalte, Harold Herbert and Lionel and Norman Lindsay.

Several famous painters of the time also experimented with etching, among them Hans Heysen, Elioth Gruner and Penleigh Boyd; but they made few editions, some only one or two.

Etching and the associated techniques of aquatint and soft-ground (for particular effects of texture) required a press, but it did not have to be big; and artists could share presses and studios and help one another print. Etchings were usually signed and numbered, unlike lithographs or steel engravings (which were sometimes signed "on the stone" but not individually by hand). No publisher or other intermediary was needed with the small editions, and artists could sell direct from their studios or to their dealers. The market for prints, in particular etchings, was stimulated by the magazine *Art and Australia*, edited by Sydney Ure Smith, himself an etcher, although more prolific than inspired. There was no national marketing system, and in fact very few dealers, for the commercial gallery system as we now know it was in its infancy.

The little groups of etchers who worked in the major cities were generally unknown outside their home towns, and their market was largely home-town, unless their work was favoured by *Art and Australia.*

Perhaps because of the reaction which always sets in against the fashions of the previous generation, etchings went rapidly from their high point of popularity to almost a joke: "Come on up and see my etchings", with its overtones of seedy lechery, for instance.

The best Australian etchings of the decades on either side of the First World War were frequently sensitive responses to light and shadow in the landscape, often touched with nostalgia (old buildings were a favourite motif), and reflected, although they never led, the best art of the era. Sydney Long's "Pan" and "Spirit of the Plains" are perhaps the most famous of these works, and it is interesting to note that he produced them almost twenty years after his paintings which are regarded as the peak of Australian art nouveau. In the interim he had lived and exhibited in England.

The other body of Australian etching which has a large crowd of devotees came from Norman Lindsay, whose wife did most of his printing for him. Lindsay's vision of life — a schoolboy's wet dream of fancy-undress in a multi-racial nudist colony (with zoo) — is as preposterous as it is repetitive and derivative. People who like that sort of thing like that sort of thing. Whether it was a help or a hindrance in the war against the wowsers and puritans, who can say?

The most exciting chapter in the history of Australian printmaking, prior to recent years, was the development of interest in relief printing in the decades between the World Wars. Relief prints — meaning that the mark is made by ink carried on raised areas rather than in grooves — is an old process, but it was little used in Australia until the advent of a cautious modernism in the twenties. (The necessary qualification here is the use of woodblock illustrations in early newspapers, as mentioned before.)

The flat areas of colour which this process permits, and the bold thick lines, were ideally suited to the new ideas about form and design and self-expression. There were two main materials used, linoleum and woodblock, with occasional experiments into perspex and other modern substances.

At this time Australian printmakers were ahead of the practitioners of other art forms in Australia, although it must be remembered that many of the leading painters were printmakers too. Among the artists whose names are associated with the mild modern relief printmaking of the twenties and thirties are Margaret Preston, Dorrit Black, Rah Fizelle, Ludwig Hirschfeld Mack, and Eric Thake. When it is taken into account that the traditionalist Mervyn Napier Waller and the social realist Noel Counihan also made many important relief prints, it becomes apparent that this episode was not a by-product of modernism in Australia, but something which transcended it. A true arch-conservative, both in art and in his view of the world, was Lionel Lindsay. Yet he contributed some of the finest, best designed and executed woodblock prints of birds and flowers that have come from any of the international multitude of artists who have chosen such subject matter.

Nor did the relationship between relief printing and book illustration remain dormant; in the hands of Christian Waller, whose style may perhaps be designated "art deco", it had a brief but significant resurrection. Ethel Spowers used relief prints to create decorative works especially for children; Thea Proctor, for adults.

One of the advantages for artists in the relief printing process is that it requires a minimum of equipment — no press is necessary, for prints can be made by hand-rubbing of the paper on the block of wood or lino. Cost would thus be reduced, for only cutting tools and ink were needed. The artists could work, if necessary, in isolation and without assistance.

The impetus of this era was lost with the Second World War, and then in the post-war years Australian printmaking was at its lowest ebb. There was little follow-on from the achievements of the twenties and thirties, although

Eric Thake and Noel Counihan persisted in their efforts to stir our sense of humour and social conscience respectively. The teaching of printmaking in art schools was rare; it was the "heroic age of Australian painting" (in Alan McCulloch's phrase), and so it was painting which dominated Australian art.

In 1946 an exhibition of screenprints by Allan Sumner in Melbourne gave advance warning that that process was to come rapidly from nowhere to the forefront of Australian printmaking within two decades or a little longer.

In fact it did not come from nowhere, but rather from industry, where stencil printing processes of various kinds had long been used for labelling and otherwise marking all sorts of surfaces. Just as particular aspects of other techniques had been appropriate to the artistic concerns of other generations — etching for intimacy, relief prints for their boldness — so screenprinting was to be found perfectly adaptable to the artistic concerns of many in the 1960s and beyond.

The process is a simple one, and can be performed with very little equipment if a rough result is acceptable, as on posters which will have only a short life, or T-shirts being embellished with slogans of a topical nature. For the best results, and for consistency in a large edition of fine art screenprints, good equipment is necessary; and the more complex the print (in terms of the number of colours, and thus the number of screens to be perfectly aligned) the more important equipment and expertise becomes.

During the sixties increasing numbers of artists turned to screenprinting, among them Alun Leach-Jones, Bea Maddock and Jan Senbergs, but there was only a limited public acceptance of the process as one of the options available to artists who wished to produce original prints. Its past was held against it for more than twenty years after Sumner's pioneering exhibition.

Another important development in the sixties was the establishment of artists' workshops where facilities were available and expertise could be shared.

At Gallery A in Melbourne a lithographic workshop with Janet Dawson had a brief but distinguished flourishing, and in Sydney in 1963 a similar workshop-studio operated under the auspices of the Workshop Arts Centre.

The relationship between the individual artists and the master printmaker is the crux of these workshop situations, and to a great extent that depends on the personality of the master printmaker, who must be able to submerge his or her own ego in the creative expression of the artist with whom he or she is working. The master printmaker must be more than a mere technician. Like Dawson at Gallery A or Bannon at PPS, he or she must be capable of entering into the artistic vision of the artist on an equal but not a competitive level.

Different artists are involved to different degrees in the production of a print in a workshop. Some do almost every action themselves, under the eye of the master printmaker. Others stand back, giving clues and instructions, supervising and approving every stage of the process, but keeping their hands clean. Yet others have very little direct involvement, and may spend next to no time in the workshop. These long-distance operators just send in a folder of drawings with annotation and the instruction, "Turn these into a print for me"; and then the various efforts of the master printmaker are shuttled back and forth through the mail, until the artist is satisfied and says go ahead. The common factor in all cases is that the artist designs and directs, whether or not he or she ever touches the paper until it is time to add the signatures.

A comparison with practices in other fields of the visual arts should reassure those for whom this seems a dereliction of the principle of involvement. The mistake such people are making is to confuse art with cottage crafts, and assume that artistry lies more in the hands than in the brain.

Consider the case of a sculptor working on a large public commission — for example, Herbert Flugelman with his huge stainless-steel forms in Adelaide, Sydney and Canberra. He makes a little model, a maquette, no more than one hundredth the size of the final piece, and hands it over to a fabricator with an industrial workshop. No one imagines that Flugelman makes twenty metre steel towers with his own two hands, or attacks him as a non-artist because he does not.

The nature of the screenprinting process is relevant here. It does not have the immediacy and personal qualities of etching, where the thickness and flow of every line reflect the artist's hand movement. It is a more premeditated process, allowing for trial and error, and it is not to imply any aesthetic shortcoming to say that in that way, and that way alone, it always reflects its industrial ancestry.

The production of the screen or screens comes first, after the image to be achieved has been finalised, either in the artist's mind or as a sketch or maybe a painting, usually annotated.

It is in the interpretation of the artist's instructions, however they are expressed, that the printmaker's ability to empathise is crucial. One of the areas in which the limitations of our vocabulary are most constricting is the choice of colour of the inks which are forced through the screens to make the image.

Bannon recalls working on Charles Blackman's "Girl on a Beach", and spending hours trying to find the combination of ink layers which would get the right yellow-brown background colour, but repeatedly failing to satisfy Blackman.

Eventually he exploded in frustration: "Well, what colour do you want, for God's sake?"

"Bloody wet sand colour," was Blackman's reply. "Why didn't you say that in the first place?" asked Bannon, who then worked through the night and produced the exact colour required by morning.

The ink is forced through the open sections of the screen(s), by a rubber squeegee — a device like a giant windscreen wiper — and goes on to the paper, which is stretched on the vacuum press. The matter of registration, that is the precise lining up of the images produced by each screening, is crucial to the achieving of a coherent image, and is the most tedious and time-consuming part of the total process.

Each time a new layer of ink is added to the paper, in the progress towards the finished print, it must be inspected and dried. A mistake in applying, say, the ninth layer of ink, renders all that has already been done on that sheet of paper spoiled and useless. Mistakes are irreparable and total.

When both the artist and the printer are satisfied with the completed edition, the screens are scrubbed out, and the edition signed and numbered. The scrubbed screen, like the cancelled etching plate, means the end of the edition; but the screen can be re-used when another image is drawn on it.

The technical difficulties and the dangers of wasted effort increase in geometric proportion to the number of screens used on an edition. It is possible for a single artist, in isolation, to produce serigraphs which involve many screens, but it must be a good way to risk insanity. Few Australian artists who worked alone on serigraphs in the sixties tempted fate by aiming for difficult colour effects with numerous screens.

Chapter Three

Two Studios: Sydney and Adelaide

The technique of serigraphy, alias silkscreening (or screenprinting as it is often called nowadays: few screens are made of silk), was not exploited for fine art printmaking in Australia in any sustained or concerted way until Bannon established the Paddington Print Studio in 1967.

Like so many important developments in the arts, PPS came about slowly and almost by accident. One of Bannon's students at Mary White's School of Design wanted to learn screenprinting, and there was equipment at the school for the purpose of printing on to fabrics. At the same time the Old Tote Theatre Company asked Bannon, who had a reputation as a stage designer, to create a poster for them, and he said that he would not only design it but he would print it too.

At this time he also produced posters for NUAUS Travel, a student travel service then operating charter flights at low fares to Europe and Asia.

Bannon extended the printmaking facilities of his own studio and hired a shop, where he did the Old Tote commission, and some Aubrey Beardsley reproduction posters which (surprisingly in view of the art nouveau craze of the late sixties) did not sell well. To pay the rent he made Christmas cards and wrapping paper.

Artists often dropped by and worked in the studio, one of the most frequent visitors being Rodney Milgate, who was another tutor at the University of New South Wales. Milgate's "Human Image", in an edition of sixty, produced in collaboration with Bannon, was the first serigraph in the sequence which led to the establishment of PPS.

The potential of serigraphy was becoming obvious. In the economic climate of the sixties art boom in Australia, the time was right. Bannon was the man who could make it happen because he had experience as a painter as well as the knowledge of screenprinting techniques.

It must be appreciated that few of the artists with whom he was to produce editions at PPS had any previous printmaking experience, and certainly none had experience of the serigraphic technique. He was not merely helping artists make serigraphs, rather he was helping *painters* render their sort of visual images into *prints which worked as prints*. Only someone who could relate to the artists as their equal as a painter could expect success in this venture. No matter how thorough his technical grasp of screenprinting, a non-painter could not have done it.

Bannon made the decision to concentrate on producing serigraphs in collaboration with other artists. (He also intended to make some of his own, but he became so busy that none of these was ever finished, although four were begun.) He quit Mary White's school, and also withdrew from the Bakery School, which he had been helping John Olsen to run.

He moved to new premises in Little Oxford Street, and invented a device for registration of the prints. While at that address he produced Charles Blackman's "Butterflies", Francis Lymburner's "Dancer Resting" and several prints by Cedric Flower. On the side, there was also some wallpaper made.

The artists who made prints at PPS were offered more than a master printer's skill and the labour of his assistants. There was the plant, the vacuum presses and associated equipment, which represented a considerable capital investment, and one which few artists could have made for themselves alone, unless they were confident that serigraphy was for them. PPS provided an opportunity for an artist to try extending into a new medium without risking too much time and money on the unknown. The financial terms on which editions were produced were extremely favourable to the artists, who required no capital. PPS supplied everything down to ink and paper; and asked half of the wholesale proceeds.

Bannon advised artists on such delicate matters as pricing and the ideal size of editions (sixty and a hundred were most usual), and established contact with dealers for those artists who did not have their own outlets in every state.

Herein lies the most important single contribution PPS made to Australian art *as a professional practice*. There was a national marketing network for artists, such as there had never been in Australia before. The artist who produced a PPS edition knew that his work would be seen and sold in galleries from the Gold Coast in Queensland to Salamanca Place in Hobart, Tasmania.

This amounted to nothing less than the chance for a beginning of pan-Australian art, for everything before was regional. The old Sydney versus Melbourne rivalry, which had been behind the antipodean manifesto and exhibition in 1959, was not then over, but PPS brought artists from several Australian states to Sydney to work on editions which were assured of nation-wide exposure.

It is impossible to exaggerate the significance of this; and we can only regret that after the demise of PPS no other art studio also served as a national promoter, although the Print Council has continued its annual touring exhibitions.

Australian artists have always travelled to Europe, and often in recent years to the United States, to further their experience, but few have made any impact on the wider art world. One part of Bannon's vision was the international promotion and distribution of PPS work, and this vision was well on the way to being realised when PPS ceased operation.

The art export drive was announced in the Australian press in mid-1970, and articles appeared explaining the serigraphic process and the history of PPS in *Austral News*, the international trade journal, in September that year, and agents were sought. This publicity extended to New Zealand, the Pacific Islands, Canada, South-east Asia, the Middle East, Japan, Europe, the USA and Africa.

Responses indicating interest were received from the USA, England, Africa (Lagos) and Canada. The *South African Printer*, a journal serving the graphic arts, sought information on the technique, in particular the new method of registration Bannon had developed.

A parcel of prints was sent to the Stockholm Trade Fair in July 1970. They were proof prints from the PPS entitlement, not numbered prints from the edition in which the artists retained a fifty per cent interest; and the cost of freight was met by the authorities which were organising the fair. However, return freight was not offered, so Bannon decided to present the prints to the Australian government's agencies in Stockholm, to remain on permanent display in their premises.

Plans were prepared to display PPS prints at trade fairs in Hong Kong, Kuala Lumpur, San Francisco, Singapore and Tokyo and negotiations were begun with the Vincent Price Galleries, San Francisco. In London PPS prints were sold by Enchel's Print Shop.

These schemes represented an unprecedented opening-up of opportunities for Australian artists to show their work to the world. They also differed, fundamentally and in an important way, from the worldwide distribution schemes operated by such dealerships as Marlborough Fine Arts or Pallas and Soho Galleries. The artist who worked at PPS retained a share in the value and control in the fate of his creations throughout the marketing process. If their value increased, so did the value of his stake. The London dealers mentioned above, and others like them, paid an artist to make an edition and assumed total control of it thereafter, having bought him out completely.

Other promotional schemes within Australia included the production of three special editions which the World Record Club sold to its members; and before the sudden closure of PPS the club had taken options on another eight editions, for 1970-1971. The *Home Journal* was negotiating for two editions to be offered to its readers. These were to be commissioned from Pro Hart and Cedric Flower.

The value of such schemes was not just that they put money in the artists' pockets and kept the studio going. They helped to break down the intimidating image of high art as something pure and untainted by commerce or the real world. They were a part of the process of educating the public to an acceptance of the low-priced multiple image as a valid work of art, and an alternative to both the exclusive, expensive one-off painting and the mass-produced mechanical reproductions of junks in the sunset and Chinese ladies with green faces (in fancy frames) sold in the furniture shops.

Perhaps because of the industrial connections of the screenprinting process, there was a momentary hesitation before PPS serigraphs were accepted in the high art fastnesses where prints had always meant reliefs or intaglios, woodblocks or etchings. But in October 1969, when three PPS serigraphs were on show at the Art Gallery of South Australia in the Print Council's annual exhibition, the director of the AGSA, John Baily, wrote to Bannon: "I am full of admiration for the job you are doing with your print studio and hope that on some future visit to Sydney I may be able to pay you a visit."

Among the major collections which acquired PPS prints were the Gold Coast Gallery and Art Centre, Queensland University and the Art Gallery of South Australia. David Boyd's "Bull Effigy" was included in his 1970 retrospective exhibition in London, Manchester and Edinburgh. It was based on a painting over a metre square which at first it had been intended to copy closely. However, the peculiarities of the screenprinting process asserted themselves, and it evolved into a distinctive work in its own right.

The commercial success of the individual prints was related largely to the popularity their makers had previously earned as painters. Charles Blackman's "White Cat's Garden" sold fifteen in one night at the Bonython

Gallery in Sydney. PPS was not in existence long enough to establish any new careers.

By early 1970 arrangements had been made for their first PPS edition by Charles Bush, Ian Fairweather, Leonard French, Tom Gleghorn, Jon Molvig, John Olsen, Clifton Pugh, Stanislaus Rapotec, Jeffrey Smart, Udo Sellbach, David Strachan and Fred Williams. Sir Russell Drysdale had indicated interest, and many artists who had already made a PPS edition were planning another.

The premature demise of PPS was a tragedy for Australian art, as can be appreciated when what might have been achieved in the serigraphic medium by the artists mentioned above, and others, is contemplated.

The difficulties began in mid-1969 when Bannon's "sleeping partner" who had put up some of the original capital, and who was involved in many other ventures, decided to end the partnership for personal reasons. Bannon could not afford to buy him out, so an agreement was reached to divide the assets; Bannon kept the equipment and work continued with the loyal staff, Dimity Martin, Juliet Schlunke and Julian Halls.

The next year Australia's first ever Papal visit inspired the biggest edition to be made at PPS.

On 14 October 1970, Bannon wrote to Pro Hart: "At the moment we are flat out producing a 5000 run of a portrait of Pope Paul by Eric Smith for the Papal visit. And it is all nearly driving us mad. But it is good to be working again and particularly on something which could be quite lucrative for the studio and for Eric."

PPS had been reorganised as a private company in early 1970, and moved to new premises in Brisbane Street. Overheads were much higher than they had been in Little Oxford Street, and difficulties resulting from the terms on which the partnership had been ended plagued the finances.

In 1971, PPS went into liquidation, with devastating suddenness, and although Bannon did all he could for them, several artists sustained losses of prints in which they had a substantial equity.

Kevin Connor had just finished signing fifty sets of his seven-print "Andalusian Portfolio", the fruit of a working trip to Spain. He lost all 350 prints, without any recompense.

Bannon went back to his work with the Aborigines.

The studio which he founded several years later, with the help of his student Alex Campbell, in the Adelaide suburb of Prospect, is a tiny operation in comparison with PPS in its heyday. It is a small wooden structure, which as well as the screenprinting room has facilities for potting, painting, carving and other arts and crafts. In a small way, Bannon has here realised the

Bauhaus dream of integration and coexistence of the arts.

The prints which are made here have the embossed symbol of a brolga, surrounded by the words "Charles Bannon South Australia".

The business contract between Bannon and the artists varies, often involving a flat fee for service and facilities.

Whereas there was a staff of four at PPS in 1971, Bannon now works alone with the artists. It harks back to those early days in Sydney, in 1967, when Rodney Milgate and Bannon worked together in a small studio after their teaching at the University of New South Wales.

Chapter Four

The Prints

Four important contributions to Australian art from PPS can be identified. The education of the public to an acceptance of prints as originals, and of serigraphs in particular. The opening-up of a new means of expression for artists who were primarily painters. The injection of new life, exemplified by new colour, into Australian prints. The establishment of the first national exhibiting and marketing network which Australian artists could "plug into", and the moves towards greater international exposure (the latter cut off before they could be developed).

All of these relate to the practice of art as a profession, and are important quite apart from any question of the aesthetic merits of individual prints.

Any critical assessment of the prints which have come from the two Charles Bannon studios must be tempered by the consideration that PPS was cut off before its artistic prime, at a moment when prospects looked like surpassing what had already been achieved. We are not seeing an episode in the history of Australian art which was allowed to run its natural course, but rather one truncated by difficulties.

But between the years of 1967 and 1971 fifty editions came from PPS, and there is a cross-section of the concerns of Australian artists in those years, with examples of figuration both expressionistic and decorative, lyricism, nostalgia-tripping, hard-edge abstraction, and of course a variety of approaches to the landscape.

It is pleasing and apt that the print which began it all, Rodney Milgate's "Human Image" of 1967, is a work which has stood the test of time. It embodies two of the aspects of the Australian art of the late sixties which, although they could be derided as "old-fashioned", provided a bulwark against international sterility: the conviction that mankind was still the most proper study of man, and the realisation that the border territory between abstraction and the figurative is the most fertile field in which to cultivate the artistic expression of that study. Milgate's image has connections with the European early modernists, including in particular Andre Breton, while it also parallels much of the work of Ian Fairweather.

The human image and the human condition was the subject of the sole PPS edition by Francis Lymburner, the dramatic details of whose dying in a restaurant a few years later made him better known to the general public in death than he had been in life. Lymburner was a master of the academic nude, which he handled with flair and verve; and he was not above demonstrating his technique, step by step, for a popular girlie magazine.

His "Dancer Resting" (1968) is in the tradition of Degas only in that it shows the dancer as a tired working artist, beautiful perhaps, but in no sense glamorous. The difference between Lymburner's treatment of this subject and that of Degas' Australian followers (like Daryl Lindsay) is most of all in his calligraphic drawing, as personal as handwriting, which balances the strong blocks of low-key colour.

Charles Blackman's association with Charles Bannon, both at PPS and at the South Australian studio, is the longest and most productive of any of the artists. The poetic sensitivity of the best of Blackman's paintings established him as a leading Australian artist in the late fifties, and he has produced prodigiously ever since.

The garden theme, with variations involving flowers and cats and clouds, is embodied in Blackman prints from the early days of PPS and again more recently from South Australia. These prints are a celebration of simple beauty, restfulness, domesticity, life and energy, and are among the artist's most popular creations. They strike a happy nerve in the home-loving Australian suburbanite or trendier town-house dweller. The art historian is reminded, by the subject matter and mood, of those post-impressionists of turn-of-the-century France who found all the world they needed within their garden walls or even the papered walls of their drawing rooms, but there are no stylistic similarities.

The odd work out on the garden theme is "Paradise Garden" of 1976, which is distinctly biblical with its reference to Adam and Eve before the fall, and austere in its reliance on *faux-naif* drawing without colour.

Cedric Flower (who himself printed two editions with PPS) includes Blackman in his book *Erotica: Aspects of the Erotic in Australian Art* on the strength of "The Embrace" of 1969. It is not an erotic work in the usual sense, inasmuch as it is not titillating despite a hint of voyeurism. Unlike most of the twentieth-century images in Flower's selection, it has a spiritual dimension, and deals with people making love, not a mere clashing of sexual organs.

The erotic frenzy of young girls — who were always a favourite subject for Blackman — is captured in "I Love Tom Jones", also dating from 1969, after the Welsh pop singer's Australian tours had established him as a teenybopper idol here.

Also erotic in mood is Paul Delprat's "Discotheque" of the same year which has similarities of style as well as subject to Delprat's "Artist's Studio", his other PPS edition of 1969.

Critics are, and always have been, divided in their estimation of the work of David Boyd, who has been accused of over-dependence on his brother Arthur, and vehemently defended by no less a writer than Professor Bernard Smith, who knocks the knockers in his *Australian Painting* volumes.

Although his work is uneven, David Boyd is capable of powerful poetry, and his sole PPS edition "Bull Effigy" shows him at his best.

Reminiscent occasionally of Gauguin, but carrying no such heavy load of symbolism, Ray Crooke has made the people in shady interiors, the lush green growth and the bright colours of clothes and brighter blue seas of the Pacific region into a distinctive *oeuvre*. His work is an often underrated aspect of the waking-up-to-our-neighbours which was central to the changes in Australian foreign policy in the sixties and seventies, an awakening which came too late. It is also reflected in Donald Friend's loving Balinese Sketches and Dobell's New Guinea mannerism.

"Mining Town, North Queensland" is typical of Crooke, and is one of a series of images — the rest in paint — in which the Australian landscape is tackled with the same colouristic apparatus as Crooke uses for his Pacific region images. It is not only a distinctive rendition of the Australian environment but also one which suggests, in its context, our links with the other nations in our part of the world.

Robert Dickerson, like David Boyd, is in the forefront of the artists of his generation, although he has laid himself open to some hard criticism for repetition and softening of his imagery over the years.

"The Orange Ball" typifies his style of figure drawing, with which he communicates his understanding of the lives and limitations of some of the less privileged in our community — poor children, workers tired by routine, the old and the lonely.

The antipodeans and their manifesto have already been mentioned in the context of Sydney-Melbourne rivalry. It is significant to note that three of the group — Blackman, Boyd and Dickerson — made editions with PPS, and that others were contemplating doing so, bridging that absurd and insidious gap in the Australian art community.

Two of the most powerful figurative painters who operated close to the abstract, John Olsen of Sydney and Jon Molvig of Queensland, were the subjects of forceful portraits by Eric Smith, printed at PPS in 1969. The technique of breaking the face into ragged areas as in tonal dropout photographs, but colouring those areas for formal and expressionistic purpose rather than description, was again used the following year, for the Papal portrait which received official Vatican recognition.

Pro Hart began his association with PPS in 1969, at a time when he was moving away from his early folksy primitivism. "The Blade Shearers" of 1969 and the Captain Cook series of 1970 may be regarded as among the very last works in which the qualities which originally drew attention to Hart can still be seen.

Charles Blackman's 1970 PPS editions explored the butterfly motif, a development from the garden theme, which was of course to be revisited later. They are the most unpretentiously decorative works Blackman has produced, in any medium, at any time in his career.

Two other series of exceptional interest came out of PPS in 1970: the "Andalusian Portfolio" of Kevin Connor, and the four editions on the urban beaches of Australia by John Aland.

Aland used bold colour patterns with clever drawing to convey heat and cool, blinding light of noon and delicate light of dawn and dusk, in works which continue the preoccupation with sun and sand which has been a feature of Australian art from at least Tom Roberts and his colleagues through Lindsay and Meere in the early twentieth century (not to mention the digger's rising sun badge, and the lifesaver cult) until the present.

Kevin Connor's "Andalusian Portfolio", developed from a series of drawings he had made while travelling in that corner of Europe, must stand as one of the most important works to come out of PPS and a highlight of Australian graphic art of the later twentieth century. The wiry drawing, the extraordinary tensions conveyed in black and white, make this a potent folio which needs to be surveyed as a whole (seven prints) to be fully appreciated. It must be regretted that since the demise of PPS, Connor has not returned to the screenprint medium. The Australian National Gallery in Canberra has the artist's proofs of "Andalusian Portfolio".

The last edition to be completed at PPS was Michael Nicholson's serial work based on a theory of colour intervals, "Modular Strip Art-oons", in 1971.

The first editions to come from the Prospect, South Australia, studio included David Dridan's "Mundoo Channel", and an unusual pair of abstracts for Frank Hodgkinson: "Genesis" A and B.

Western Australian landscapist Robert Juniper, and Mervyn Smith of Adelaide whose usual medium is watercolour, also worked with Bannon in 1977-1978; but it was Blackman again who produced the major pieces — a pair of large oval-format prints, "Alice in Wonderland" and "Alice Through the Looking Glass". The real subject of these is distortion of perception, and they have a seriousness missing from Blackman's nursery rhyme theme etchings on perspex of the following year.

Former UK painter-etcher Basil Hadley made his move into screenprinting with Bannon in 1978, with the aid of a grant from the Visual Arts Board to enable him to experiment with combining different printing techniques.

The first fruits of the Hadley-Bannon collaboration was "Skipping Girl Wall", based on children's drawings and graffiti. The edition was embossed by means of un-inked intaglio on the presses of the South Australian School of Art, and then screenprinted at Prospect. The combination of processes meant that a variegated textured pattern produced by the dry plates controlled the way the screened image took to the paper: this is the basis of the remarkable wall surface effect. This print won the Townsville Prize in 1979.

Next came "Wall Theme VII" (the numbering relates to earlier wall theme prints in all-intaglio media), a straight serigraph; and then another mixed media edition "Wall Theme VIII" which combines etching, aquatint and screenprinting. The latter received the George Gatton Memorial Print Prize at Maitland, New South Wales, and the Fremantle Prize, both in 1979.

"Wall Theme IX" used the same process as its predecessor, with the addition of gold leaf, applied by screen. Gold leaf was also used for the ear-rings of "Girl with Ear-rings". The last edition for 1979 was a straight screenprint, "Smile".

Hadley's success, measured in terms of three prizes of national importance with six editions, involving excursions into media not previously used by him, would not have been possible without the facilities and techniques available through Bannon's Prospect studio.

During 1979-1980 Bannon expanded the studio to broaden the range of arts and crafts he can practise himself, but he intends to sustain the flow of new editions of artists' serigraphs into the eighties.

In 1981 John Aland, who had worked at PPS in 1970, came to South Australia and together with Bannon produced a new print, which was different in style but similar in colourings to his PPS editions, entitled "Midsummer Night's Dream". Also inspired by the theatre was Max Mastrosavis's "Beckett on Love". Early in 1982 Keith Cowlam, recently graduated from the SA School of Art, worked with Bannon on "A Man and his Dog", an unpretentious park scene in the vein of his recent paintings. Plans for late 1982 included several new editions for Basil Hadley.

Bibliography

Ballarat Fine Art Gallery: "Outlines of Australian Printmaking" (a catalogue), Ballarat, 1976

Deutsher, C. and Butler, R. A.: "Survey of Australian Relief Prints, 1900-1950", Melbourne, 1978

Draffin, N.: "Australian Woodcuts and Linocuts of the 1920s & 1930s", Melbourne, 1976

Engen, N.: "Victorian Engravings", London, 1975

Flower, C.: "Erotica", Melbourne, 1977

Kempf, F.: "Contemporary Australian Printmakers", Melbourne, 1976

Smith, B.: "Place, Taste and Tradition", Melbourne, 1979

AFTERWORD

Afterword:
An Autobiographical Note by Charles Bannon

Rereading David Dolan's concisely written pages, which were born out of long discussions under backyard gum-trees, glasses of wine in the studio, and much patient digging for detail by him, I have become acutely aware of how frustrating it must have been for him to have been told from time to time, "No, skip that now, I'll write about it in detail at a later date."

With the benefit of hindsight, I understand how difficult it must have been to work, with me skating over a variety of details and ineptly curtailing information which was by right David's.

However, I was not being bloody-minded, self-conscious or spuriously evasive. It had something to do with self-deception, emotional insulation and the preservation of an illusionary character in the saga that, in all seriousness, I felt was me. At the time I found it damned hard to get my act together without appearing to have an axe to grind or lacing it with recriminations, bitterness or sentimental dross.

Further to this, I held a predisposition to fantasise about a book I was going to write in the future, a book that would explain it all away when age, living and place provided a starting point for a nostalgic back-glance at five or six decades retreating into the distance.

It stemmed in general from mixed emotions and painful memories linked to some periods of the past, and in particular the more recent disappointments and frustrations associated with the short life of Paddington Print Studio.

Time and the equanimity inherent in David's writing have winkled me out of my mental bolt-hole, propelling me backwards in a retrospective world of sensations, sounds of old music, conversations, sights and smells . . .

There was a smell about Edinburgh. A smell which matched its metallic greyness.

Number Two, Salisbury Street, was an apartment on the second floor in a line of grey, five-storey tenements. It appeared to be part of a soot-encrusted, glacial-scarred, basalt escarpment, squeezed narrow and vertical between and facing dozens of its clones. The tenements were cast-iron railed with white-washed front steps and basement flats, whose windows were permanently in shadow and shaded against inquisitive glances over the railings into gas-lit, wallpapered rooms. Its smell was of leaf dampness, wallpaper paste, washing hung to dry on ropes near the ceiling in the kitchen, coal fire soot, gas lights and verdigris, grilling kippers, and the mustard plasters I wore back and front throughout the autumn and the winter. It was one of codliver oil, embrocation and whisky toddy.

During the season we called summer, the excited voices of other children would float up to our second-storey window from the street, "The sun's out, the sun's out." I'd be overcoated, scarfed and rugged up — "don't forget your galoshes" — and bundled hurriedly down the stairs through the all-pervading smells, now laced with the aroma of cabbage and potato water from the other apartments and the strong smell of urine coming from somewhere at the bottom of the stairwell, to join them in our only play area, the Muddy Green, a narrow cleared block that once had housed a tenement similar to our own and which had either been gutted by fire or had crumbled and died of shame.

Perhaps I am only remembering the disappointments of those days, as it seemed to be the exception rather than the rule that I experienced the sun. With great perversity, it seemed to hide behind the overcastes as I appeared, leaving all of us in a bleak, windy, cobble-stoned street in the hard, unyielding cityscape that was home to me.

It seems to have been a period of interminable confinement to a coal fire warmed bedroom. Hours in isolation on a large sofa, window-watching life in the street below. Kids playing hopscotch on the pavement, or throwing a wooden diabolo high into the air and catching it dexterously on a string held taut between wooden handles. The lamplighter with his long pole lighting the street gas lamps high on their cruciform cast-iron posts in the evenings and extinguishing them the following morning. Fishmongers with baskets of fish, tinkers with barrows, whet stones and pots, rag and bottlemen calling up the stairs. Coalmen, hooded in spiked jute bags, like black-faced Ku Klux Klansmen, shoulder-hoisting bags of coal from the bottom of the stairs to the kitchen coal bunkers. There were melodeon players, singers, mouth organ buskers; there were clog dancers and sand dancers rattling a lone penny in a tin mug, or standing over an inverted ragged tweed cap which made an inviting circle on the cold gutter curbings.

I remember the windows themselves were an endless source of fascination to me. I watched for hours fine sleety mist turn to water drops and slowly slide down the other side of the pane whilst I urged one or another to race the rest to the bottom sill. Or the inside of the window misting over, enabling me to finger paint pictures and words on the opaque steamy surfaces. Or sometimes just clearing a round eyehole to see what was going on outside without being seen.

Apart from frequent visits to doctor this or professor that at the clinic for tuberculosis of the Edinburgh Royal Infirmary — with x-rays or a change of dressing for my skinny throat from which they had removed a gland, or the occasional pneumonic crisis I seemed to have just recovered from — life was not altogether as thoroughly depressing as the milieu that housed it.

In those early years we were a well-knit family. There were two elder brothers and a younger sister, a grandfather and two grandmothers, uncles and aunts, lots of relations and friends. Weather permitting, there were family picnics in the King's Park or on the pebbly beach of the Firth of Forth; there were holiday trips to Yorkshire, London and southern England, Loch Lomond, and the occasional sight-seeing bus or train day trip to country villages surrounding the city.

There was Drummond Street Primary School with hot water pipes under the wooden seats which I enjoyed attending (unfortunately all too infrequently); Grandfather's garden allotment outside the walls of Holyrood Palace where we were allowed to dig for potatoes and turnips; slates and slate pencils, coloured crayons and plenty of white paper to draw on; books and more books; street processions; Punch and Judy shows at the Mound near Sir Walter Scott's monument in Princes Street; theatre and silent films — "Felix the Cat" — on some Saturdays; the Savoy Orpheans heard through earphones of a crystal set all the way from London. There was warmth and affection from a caring extended family.

Towards the end of 1927 conditions changed dramatically. It was a time of quiet dank melancholia.

It may have been the aftermath of the British general strike, as well as the effects of the sudden death of my sister and my eldest brother John's departure for Australia under the auspices of the Big Brother Movement.

Brother Harry was sent to a special skin school for treatment for a scalp infection, coming home at weekends with a large-sized cap pulled over his shaven head. Father seemed to spend less time at home, and when he was there he was quiet and preoccupied. My mother wept frequently at odd times, while I spent more time listlessly in bed swallowing with indifference beef tea, codliver oil and the occasional whisky toddy. The house was never without relatives or friends consoling and comforting.

It was then that Canada and my father's relatives in Winnipeg, or Australia where my brother and uncles were, were introduced into endless conversations.

Early winter gales flushed choking eye-stinging coal smoke and wet soot back down the chimneys, causing windows and doors up and down the stairs to be hurriedly opened in panic, leaving apartments colder and smelling like deserted railway yards after the smoke had cleared. There was a waiting list for the services of chimney sweeps.

Sleet and snow whipped at the windows as a bleak biting wind savaged the low cloud rack, rooftop high, flinging it down the narrow funnel of Salisbury Street to engulf the hills of the King's Park at the bottom of the street in an impenetrable bruised gloom.

These are not memories to sharpen, polish or treasure. Although even now they are as sharp and bleak as the wind that blew around every corner of Old Reekie. But from this point of time they certainly are not as bitter.

At last the decision was made. We were going to Australia! Huge boxes, wicker panniers and cabin trunks were packed with books, linen, clothing, candles and bric-à-brac.

Despite the weather outside, there was much fairytale speculation of long sunny seashores, blue skies, fresh fruit to be had for the picking, freedom and perhaps fortune. Australian books, maps and atlases were examined and discussed at length. Letters from John and my uncles were read and reread aloud many times over. Despondency and bereavement gave ground slowly in the face of a growing, excited optimism.

The resilience of my mother and father infected brother Harry and myself to such an extent that we felt and displayed in our home-bound games that we were the chosen Livingstones, Mungo Parks and even Vasco da Gamas of the twenties. Explorers completely irrelevant to Australia, they gave us a peg to hang our play caps on when the anticipation of the great adventures ahead became impossible to bear with quiet patience.

My mother was born in Whitby and moved to Edinburgh at the age of thirteen when her father left the *Middlesborough Gazette*(?) or *Times*(?) to work on the *Weekly and Daily Scotsman.*

Her grandfather had been chief officer of the Whitby Coastguard, her great-uncle a master of a clipper on the China Sea run, a great-grandfather a ships' architect, and a whole host of male relatives seafaring men, while she herself seemed to have spent her happiest times living or holidaying in Yorkshire. Thus, without blinking an eye, she stepped into the role of an authority on the continent Captain Cook had discovered, claiming, in a mood of sheer romanticism, that she was a distant relative of the great explorer, a statement she embroidered with many anecdotes which fired our imaginations and fuelled our impatience, making time between the decision and the act of departure almost unbearable for two small boys.

I don't think the weeping and the sad goodbyes of my parents and grandmothers and uncles touched me very much. I was impatient to be off on a long voyage to the land that Captain Cook had discovered.

Even the bleakness of Tilbury Docks could not dampen my sense of excitement and exploration when we boarded the P & O liner, the *Beltana.*

Having in mind that my brother John affectionately called me Sparrow, claiming I was as strong as a sparrow's fart, how can I start to describe my first feelings of wellbeing?

Fogs, sleet, cold and rough seas were left behind in the Bay of Biscay. Las Palmas in the Canary Islands, our first port of call, presented us with blue almost tropical skies, sun and balmy scents of spices and other odours that I had never experienced in my life. Dark-skinned boys dived around the ship for pennies dropped overboard, and their adult counterparts pulled baskets of fruit, curios, perfumes and silks on a long jute line they had attached to the ship's rails as a two-way funicular from boat to deck.

My parents relaxed and laughed together again, played cards and made new friends, and my mother, during a ship's concert, sang a lament, "My Ain Folk", to an entranced audience of passengers and crew. It was magic.

From there it was to Freetown in Sierra Leone and then on to Cape Town and around the Cape of Good Hope on the last leg of a seven-and-a-half week voyage to Australia. And there I was, filled with the wonder and joy of it all — mustard plasters back and front were a thing of the past, and a cough that had plagued me since I first could remember had disappeared.

The dullness of Melbourne docks, though disappointing, did not seem in any way to reduce my sensations of joy and expectation, even though Victoria was suffering a heatwave and the temperature had been over a hundred degrees for at least a fortnight.

The 150-kilometre trip to Bendigo took a lifetime for both my brother and myself. In fact, it was six or seven hours, with the train stopping and shunting and being held up from time to time by the bushfires that swept across the tracks of Woodend, Mount Macedon and other stations dotted through the Dividing Range. But we made it to swelter all night in a weatherboard, tin-roofed, four-bedroomed house that my uncle had rented for us and lived in prior to our arrival.

I cannot remember with any certainty how my parents coped with the heat, the new country, and the two of us. I do remember quite vividly, however, following my mother into the kitchen and being startled by an inordinate buzzing sound, and running into the yard after my mother, who was calling to my father, "Quickly, there's a swarm of bees in the kitchen." The man from next door ran in banging a kerosene tin, hoping to catch the hive *in toto*, disappointedly saying to my mother, "They're no bees, missus, they're blowies. Your brother didn't put his meat in the Coolgardie safe before he left last week."

Settling into the Australian way of life, as "new chums", during the Christmas of 1927, was not all beer and skittles. There were so many novel situations and pathetic incidents, ranging from the facetious to the burdensome. Bendigo was to be my own new world. A world of cicadas, sun, sandhills, peppercorn trees, gums, acacias and mines. Fresh fruit, milk in a billy can from the milk cart out in the street. The vitally essential Coolgardie safe, with wetly dripping streamers of flannel hung from the water-filled top along its four sides to slake the thirsty hessian of its walls. There were white pipeclay coolers for rich, golden butter, and elegant kerosene lamp light.

I put on weight, grew and was brown and barefooted, free in the sun, clad only in short pants for the first time in my life, following the water cart laying the dust in a spray of cold water.

There were buggies, jinkers and gigs. Cabs and heavy drays of milky quartz, with horses that ranged from Palaminos to huge Clydesdales, all smelling of hot steamy hay and manure. Even the jibes or the bullying of my larger, healthier and more aggressive school associates, whose attitudes stemmed from their parents' apprehension with the onset of the Depression and fears that pommies would take the bread out of their mouths, did not blunt my sensations of wellbeing and *joie de vivre*.

Admittedly, there were times of acute trepidation as I waited through long summer school days to be faced with yet another black eye, a bruised rib or lip for protesting to a group in the playground that I wasn't a pommy, I was a Scot.

All of which seems to have been a process of toughening me up, building suspicion and a healthy aggression. It enabled me to devise means of retaliation with wooden pickets, bats or cricket stumps, for if I was going to survive the hours I was thrown into contact with a peer group whom I was certain were "out to get me", I had to emulate their behaviour patterns, and with as much speed as possible give measure for measure.

As I grew and became more proficient with fists and tongue, I was finally left in peace and I could continue to live in my exciting private world of sights, sounds and exploration.

In a country where it seemed the seasons almost ran into each other without the precise definition we had been used to in Edinburgh, winter was unexpected.

School mornings of blue skies and hoarfrost draped like white blankets of salt on wooden railings, black buggy hoods and paddocks.

It was back to woollen coats, scarves, gloves and chilblained ears. Legs stung red raw where the serge of short pants chafed the skin on the tender inside surfaces above the knees.

With gloves, I indulged in a form of evaporating graffiti, writing new words, "bloody" or "shit", or drawing faces in the delicate granulated rime of icy white surfaces, making sure I was not late for school, taking time to hide my gloves and biscuit-tin lunch box, wrapping its contents in a stolen piece of newspaper so as not to be considered different from the other Australian children in the playground.

Leather straps were wielded with vigour and at random on blue hands or around chafed legs for not sitting still, or an incorrect answer to some simple question asked by the teacher. The hell of the hurt is still in my mind even now, as the "cuts" were administered in front of thirty-five boys and girls who watched hawk-eyed, without compassion, for a cry of pain or the sign of a tear.

But what compensations! Finishing homework on the kitchen table in front of a wood stove smelling of either roast beef or lamb, rabbits, shepherd's pie, scones and spices, and, of course, pudding. An evening meal in the dining room as a family by the gentle yellowness of two tall glass-chimneyed kerosene lamps, before a hot open fire of mallee roots.

The meal ending, table cleared, Harry and myself arguing as to who would wash the dishes and who would dry them. This seemed to be a perpetual argument. The games played on the table in front of the fire, discussions, reminiscences. My mother back in Whitby or Edinburgh, and my father answering questions at length on Mesopotamia or the Khyber Pass where he had spent a great deal of time during the war. The coloured pastels and pencils with which I drew many pictures, with the conversations of family and uncles and friends a background, triggering off flights of fancy on paper from anecdotes I had probably heard many times before.

A candle lit and so to bed!

During one summer we moved to yet another weatherboard house, with the usual lath and plaster ceiling and interior wallpapered hessian walls, in the suburb of Iron Bark, between Long Gully and Garden Gully, near sand dumps and mine-scarred, mullock-heaped heights high above Bendigo itself.

Bendigo lies along a low-lying gully parallel to the Bendigo Creek with its main street Pall Mall, a fountain, post office, the Shamrock Hotel and emporiums straight-lined on one side, and on the other, reached by a series of bridges, Rosalind Park and the maze in the fernery. A world of bushes, tall trees, flower beds, lawns and a cast-iron band rotunda, with an altogether sense of green peace, rising on grassy slopes to the spire of a pine and eucalypt-hidden two or three-storeyed bluestone and sandstone building, Central School, in incongruous treeless black asphalt on top of a cleanly shaved area of Camp Hill, railed and mesh-gated.

Iron Bark was a world apart. Its gum-tree-lined, switch-backed streets, pitched fretful and contrary, terminated in a deadend of hilly bluffs and high peaks of red earth, white clay and towering mullock heaps of grey-black slate torn from the earth hundreds of metres below.

There were huge areas of grey-white crushed quartz sand, high enough on their sloping sides for tobogganing rides on rusty bits of tin to the peppercorn trees below — with long, flat, soft, sandy tops for foot races, ball games and glorious imagined French Legionnaires battling the Bedouins or dying of thirst in the Sahara Desert.

Its hidden gullies, three-metre-deep man-made trenches, long dark tunnels, unexpected mine shafts, hidden tracks and grotesquely wind-sculptured rocky extrusions became my land. I peopled it with cowboys and Indians, soldiers, bushrangers and exciting sagas of daring that put Edgar Rice Burroughs and his Tarzan or Martian books to shame, wherein I always won, to return home sunbrowned, hard-soled barefooted, dirty and begrimed, and a hero. Always hungrier than ever I imagined I could have been, and always ready with an excuse for the state I was in.

We learnt to tell the time by the underground explosions of gelignite that shook the house as one shift of miners came up and another shift waited to go down after the tunnel or "drive dust" cleared.

Steam whistles from the winch room, housing gigantic drums of wire cable as thick as my wrists, which were the only connection between us above and those hundreds of metres below, announced midday, and the change of shifts for good measure.

The Lily Street gold battery shook the earth hour in and hour out, ceasing only at midnight on Saturdays for the following Sabbath. Lights went on in every window as the residents around the battery woke and as a family, pyjama-clad, proceeded to the kitchen for a cup of tea and a cold meat sandwich. It was like some mysterious archaic act of devotion which left families tossing and turning in bed afterwards, waiting impatiently for Sunday midnight when the stampers recommenced their ritual, shaking the ground, rattling the cups and saucers on the kitchen dresser and guaranteeing all within the area another week of restful sleep.

The capriciousness of our lifestyle in those days was in part due to the onset of the Great Depression and the break-up of the family.

Father returned to Scotland, and my brothers and uncles scattered throughout the state in search of work — any work. Brother John eventually sharefarmed with a cow cocky, ekeing out a living when butter fat brought starvation prices. Harry packed up one night and left to try his luck out back or overseas, humping his bluey. My uncles worked on the land for only their keep, or at fruit picking for a little more, up and down the irrigation area of the Murray River. Leaving my mother saddled with me to do the best she could.

Occasionally when blistering north winds blew the grey, off-white sand from the dumps, gale-forced through their unprepared crosshatched custodian peppercorn trees, Bendigo became a place of miasmic milkiness, a world seen through the opacity of cataracted eyes.

Doors, keyholes, windows and chimneys were hurriedly blocked with papers, rags, rolled carpet pieces and blankets were thumb-tacked over chinks in the armour of the weatherboard houses, denying entry to the stealthy gritty intruder, mostly to no avail.

The waxed linoleum strip of the passage became grey-patina-ed with the first wind gust, making it an instant drawing board, or a place to plant a bare footprint and relive the joys of Robinson Crusoe's finding of Man Friday.

Slices of bread and beef dripping were eaten with relish as always, accompanied by cracking, rasping head sounds as air-borne grit in bread and spreads was ground smaller by strong teeth, and washed into an acclimatised digestive tract with tea filmed over with a lighter dust.

When it was over, the next day or the day after that, we cleaned up, shaking blankets, beating cushions and rugs, washing all the dishes, dusting pink silk lampshades with scalloped and tasselled edges, and polishing everything from passage linoleum to windows. I washed dusty grey-leafed tomato plants, silverbeet, rhubarb and pumpkins in the backyard until they shone, sun-drenched and green, after which I was allowed to go out to play.

It was about this time that a deserted two-storeyed decaying mansion built in the golden era of Bendigo was bought by a retired country farmer and was being rehabilitated by brickies, joiners and glaziers.

For many years it had been a house of ghosts and broken window panes, a place where I used to experience self-induced, hair-raising fear by sneaking into its gloomy downstairs rooms to listen to the apparitions, werewolves and changelings in the rooms above.

I would stay just long enough to savour the delicious feeling of panic, until I couldn't stand it any longer, and I would run stricken through the tangled garden paths, chased by imaginary vampires and banshee wails which I knew were only rats, pigeons and the wind from the topmost chimneypots; it was a game played and ended as I streaked through the broken fence and decelerated into a contrived nonchalant saunter along the adjacent road so that none of my friends would catch sight of my frenzied exit.

When the new residents of the "Haunted House" were just settling, I hid about its very familiar garden which was still abandoned and overgrown, in barefooted silence, secret and inquisitive, watching furniture, household goods and mysterious boxes being transferred from horse-drawn carts to porch, or disappearing inside with much manoeuvring by sweating, grunting carriers.

When I finally walked through the hedge and over the weed-infested undulating patch that might have been a former kitchen garden, to the back door, neither the ex-farmer nor his wife seemed very surprised, even when I asked if there was anything I could do to help, sort of . . .? "Mrs Farmer" gave me a drink of milk and a biscuit while he hired me on the spot to help him unload a few crates on the front verandah. He'd talk about how much he'd pay later when the job was done, he said.

There were crates and more crates piled up on that front verandah. Crates whose rough splinter-ridden wood and weight defied all my efforts to move even the smallest of them, let alone help him carry them inside. I despaired.

However, with good humour and a pinch bar he unnailed the lids and exposed the backs of tightly-packed books. There were more books than I had ever seen in my life outside of the Bendigo Mechanics Institute, where, because it was free, I spent many Saturday afternoons poring over maps, reproductions of paintings, brown photographs of the wonders of the world in books entitled "My Ramblings Through South America, Africa and other Unlikely Places".

But these books were different. Some crates contained books all with red backs, others were blue, others were green and others were black. They were all uniform and unnumbered, with the title printed in white ink, small and tight, at the top of the spine. The farmer was at pains to explain to me that though he and his wife did not read very much, they had bought out an entire privately-owned country lending library which was going broke. He said a house like this needed a library and the colours would go well with the furniture.

We worked all afternoon, stacking them on shelves from floor to ceiling in rows of reds, greens, blues and blacks, in a front room that was going to house his desk near the window — which would give him a great view when he got the garden into shape, he said. Anyway, the kids would probably enjoy them when they came home from school for the holidays.

It took a few days to get the books unpacked, colour-regimented, and shelf-shifted, because the blues would be better nearer the floral carpet, or the blacks would be better one above the other straight up and down near the fireplace and not like a line of black in the middle of the bookcased wall.

He asked me if I read much and if my mother read. He was told about the Mechanics Institute. That was good, he'd pay me for helping him by allowing me to come over from time to time and borrow as many books as I wanted; no need to sign for them or anything like that, he'd be able to tell by the holes left in the rows, he said.

This was tremendous. As far as my imagination was concerned, I entered a place of grown-up fantasy that had far reaching consequences. My mother and I, given time, were determined to read his library from red to black and back again, as such opportunities were rarely presented during Depression days.

It was evident that the erstwhile country librarian's literary critical faculties had not been honed by the disciplines of the classics, but at that time — especially during the long winter nights — we blessed her for her choice of Rider Haggard, Marie Corelli, Sax Rohmer, Conan Doyle, anthologies of poetry, memoirs of colonial Australians, Rolf Boldrewood — and Zane Grey, who, alighting from a car in front of a Bendigo sports shop, must have been amused by a small boy trying to impress him with the fact that "*The Riders of the Purple Sage* is the greatest book I've ever read", and, "Let me help you carry your rods, Mr Zane". Which he did with a pat on my head, making me swear by all that was holy I'd be a big game fisherman, a gun-toting cowboy and an artist, in that order, after the Depression.

As the Depression peaked, my mother and I lived from day to day. After school I would run home and change my school clothes and only pair of shoes for my work or play clothes and bare feet, and run back to school to clean out the school lavatories for sixpence and two pounds of butter a week.

This was something I could only get over by imagining that I was fighting a raging inferno of some important building, risking life and limb to rescue other heroes, explorers or royal dignitaries from incineration. Reeling back with arm-covered face from the intensity of the holocaust, plying my hose to urinals, doors and lavatory pans with such brave intensity that the outcome was a foregone conclusion.

Having rolled up the hose, replaced the can of Phenyl and the brushes in the school's toolshed, I would stand under the flagpole where we saluted the Union Jack with religious fervour every Monday morning, and be decorated by the King of England with a Victoria Cross, or even knighted by the Queen herself, keeping a wary eye out for any late school friends who might have seen me bowing and mumbling, "I thank you Sire."

My mother sewed and scrubbed for other people and cut down old tweed sports jackets to make an extra pair of pants or a blazer for me, while she embraced a multiplicity of religions.

I would like to say that during this time life was hell, but I cannot. I drew, carved soft claystone, spent three hours a week with Miss Jackson, the piano and drawing teacher, and carried the free art of the Bendigo Art Gallery into my dream world.

The reality of living was a heady business. There was an ever-present sense of material and spiritual feasts and famines, with periods of eruptive frustration or periods of quiescence which allowed me to live imaginatively and free in my own private world, or, if need be, to savour the gradual processes of growing up in a world where survival of spirit and mind was indeed a privilege.

Perhaps it was more like the surprising taste of an exquisite wine that vanishes in the early hours of the morning after rougher red, or remains with one always as a part of the fabric of a mature palate.

The ambivalence of my mother's religious zealousness during that period fascinated me for years. It sometimes appeared as an extension of my own fantasy world which I shared with her, uninhibitedly and with much enthusiasm.

From sacraments to seances, all in the name of Christianity and the cleansing of both our souls; not that it ever stopped her making plum jam, apricot conserve or quince jelly knowing I had filled my shirt with fruit from the neighbouring gardens whose high fences and barking dogs added to the excitement of not getting caught.

I remember once she even presented a plundered neighbour with a couple of jars of her special jelly, straight-faced and neighbourly, saying something about her brother sending her down too many apples for the two of us to get through.

I experienced the laying on of hands, the blessings, the total immersion in the waters of Jordan, that is, a full-sized baptismal tank under the stage of a dusty, echoing hall. There were fervent appeals and evocations from half-filled halls, blistering diatribes from pulpits, prayers and hymns.

One week I would be singing in the Methodist Church choir, practising for the annual anniversary singing event, and the next week winding up an old Decca gramophone to play "Nearer My God to Thee" before the medium could receive the proper musical and mystical vibrations which would enable her to commence a flower reading seance, and perhaps a couple of weeks later I would be handing around plates of sandwiches to Brother this or Sister that.

It was a kaleidoscope of people, priests, preachers, pastors and elders. It was churches, tabernacles, halls and other people's homes, whose philosophical and religious colours changed with such unexpected transience it made browsing through Frazer's *Golden Bough*, in later years, boring in the extreme — a condition I never suffered from during that period.

Later, when my father returned and we were reunited as a family, my mother's search for the Holy Grail appeared to be forgotten without a regret in the face of Sunday night sing-songs around the piano. Songs that were gusty, sentimental and at times nostalgically Irish and Scottish; and for good measure, brother Harry and herself did the Charleston or the Black Bottom up and down the passage to flapper era music from scratched records on the same old "Nearer My God to Thee" Decca gramophone.

At fourteen, formal school came to an end, and with it much of my world of make believe. The long days became periods of physical restriction and mental boredom, as I cleaned the windows and polished the brass surrounds, swept the footpath and sweated or froze cold and wet as I cycled up hills and more hills to deliver a thirteen and sixpenny pair of shoes to houses kilometres away from Ezywalkin Pty Ltd.

When I was not out in all weathers, peddling in haste to get back to the shop in some arbitrary allocated time — "It should take you ten minutes there and back" — I spent hours in the narrow basement, relabelling empty boxes using dirty white paste smelling rancidly of over-ripe pumpkins. I would straighten and sort piles of tissue paper; stack, in appropriate sizes or lasts, footwear from hobnailed boots to patent leather dancing pumps in racks downstairs or in neat boxed rows in the shelves in the shop above.

With a steady weekly wage of seven and sixpence, we paid for good business suits at sixpence per week and a Malvern Star bicycle for a shilling a week, which allowed me to contribute five shillings and sixpence to the household and have a whole sixpence per week for myself. My mother paid a nominal sum for me to continue drawing and ticket-writing lessons two nights a week at the School of Mines.

The years of the early thirties passed with the speed of an impatient crowd of bargain hunters entering and leaving a store through a revolving door.

I realise now, with some misgivings, that I graduated to junior salesman after a service of four years with Ezywalkin Pty Ltd on a wage of twenty-seven and sixpence per week — serving customers, wrapping shoes, writing dockets and handing out parcelled boxes to another young fourteen-year-old message boy to be delivered in all weathers.

The years of the living times, outside working hours, were spent finding new experiences, in transient poetic romantic relationships with adolescent girls.

Weekends were solitary bike rides to the Campaspe and Loddon Rivers or Piccaninny Creek, to camp out and fish with a passionate obsession, free from the shop and the shame of a disruptive home situation. To examine the bush with its surprising beauty and subtle seasonal changes.

Hot, parched earth, flaccid trees whose leaves drooped defencelessly, throwing stifling windless shade on silver spear grass and aggressive thorns and three-cornered prickles and stink-wort under foot. Creeks dying in pools of muddy black putrescence from the dead gum leaves of a summer drought.

Autumn and winter fused, identified only by the high wet wind of one, and the other's frost-burnt trees, white crystal-laced bushes hidden where the sun had not yet reached, with creeks and rivers that flushed away mud and blackness, brownly disturbed in stuttering gushes until spring.

Spring and the promise of summer again, bird-called, filled with multi-coloured wax flowers, brown and yellow egg and bacon plants, flashes of dripping gold from early wattles, eucalypts clean as parade ground soldiers, and pale yellow feathered scrubs along creeks clear now, sweet, flashing between boulders and under tree bridges.

All this without the need to resort to fantasy — I was growing up.

In the late thirties, I joined the 17th Light Horse Regiment as a part-time/weekend soldier, partly because of its feather-plumed slouch hats, mirror polished leather bandoliers worn across the chest, riding breeches and leggings, and the broad shouldered manly cut of the tunic — a costume to keep alive much of my make believe — and partly because I had admired my father's fairly modest and patient expositions of the north-west of India and his role in it during the First World War. Further to this, he at least approved of such a step.

Having been in the regiment, polishing, pressing, drilling and parading for some time, I was selected for a special force being recruited for Darwin of 250 men from all states of the Commonwealth, to form a special cadre — the Darwin Mobile Force — on a contract for three years with an officers' training course at the end of it.

The decision to leave Bendigo was not all that hard. It was Ezywalkin's for another four years and perhaps a rise in salary to the dizzy heights of three pounds ten a week, or the realisation of my childhood imaginings — a chance to explore Australia, new places, and to follow in the steps of Cook, Flinders, Kennedy, Leichhardt and McDouall Stuart. There would be travel and escape, and as the family put it, security(?). But most of all, there was my love of the Australian bush I knew, and the Australia I wanted to find out about.

I feel I should hurry through this next period of my life — the impact Sydney had on me for the first time, the sea voyage on the Burns Philp *Montoro*, through Whitsunday Passage to Thursday Island and on to Darwin.

But I would like to touch on a small segment of life as it was in Darwin, and its lasting effects on my approach to art in theory and practice — the life in what was then a tropical outpost of Australia, the war years and living through the subsequent post-war years with my training, teaching, helping to bring up a family of boys, years of work in the outback and the Northern Territory with the Aboriginal Welfare Branch of the Northern Territory Administration.

Life was fairly rugged for a while in the early days of Darwin. We were barked at, bullied, punished and praised. We were parade-ground drilled, route marched and bivouacked, and we mastered the intricacies of a diverse selection of destructive weapons from small arms to Vickers machine guns and ear-blasting eighteen pounders, during an enervating "Wet" of prickly heat, dengue fever, hook worm and other ills, in stifling dampness and rigid discipline.

We repeated it all over and over again during the "Dry", on hard sun-cracked earth under a blazing sky, until we became work and word perfect, a team of 250 men moving and working in unison with Bolshoi precision, from a dilapidated tin and concrete building overlooking the sea which had been Vesty's Meat Works during the First World War.

It became a time of physical toughness — bursting with life and energy — a special commune on the edge of a town housing about 700 itinerant civilians, expatriates, buffalo shooters, prospectors, seamen and pearl divers, bushmen and quiet law-abiding merchant Chinese, as well as gentle, eager, fun-loving, curious Aborigines from the town and proudly tall, dignified tribal people from the bush and surrounding islands, who came and went without leaving a footprint.

The two seasons, the "Wet" and the "Dry" were as uniquely disparate as their local titles suggest. One was of approximately three months' duration when each day, regularly on time, towering grey-blacked green mountains of lightning-incised clouds rolled in slowly from the Timor or Arafura Seas. They were heralded by an almost cold wind, timid at first, feeling its way through palm tops, along golden beaches and the evergreen foreshores, to strengthen its grip as it gained confidence in an air-pressured, fumbling muscular contraction, which increased to a battery of giant-like fist blows, bending along palm trunks, pandanas, poinsettia, frangipanni and vine-topped, roped tied and tangled ficus and eucalypts. A softening up process for the blind fury of the sheeted rain blotting out a landscape dominated by a dome-shaped resonance of earth-shaking thunder, with dazzling carbon arc-lit blue-black clouds, low and convulsed.

It abated as quickly as it had arrived, leaving the land and its creatures beneath cowered and breathlessly waiting in the silence for the next onslaught, disturbed only by the sawing of a thousand cicadas and the croaking of frogs.

This was a time for indoor study, sketching and reading until lights out, with the one leave night per week to go to town and listen, bar-propped in the original Don Hotel (the "Blood House") or the Victoria (locally called the "Shady Tree") in the same street as Jolly's store, or perhaps the weatherboard prestigious hotel, the "Club". To listen to the tales of the history of the Territory by old Territorians who had had a hand in shaping it.

Tales of hardship and ease, of former blackbirders whose knowledge of Papua, the Fly River and Queensland cane fields was disconcertingly frank and brutal. Of lost and found pearls the size of pigeons' eggs, crocodiles and buffalo hides, El Dorado mines and penal establishments from Boggo Road to Long Bay.

There were songs, stories and poems from men in a world of men calloused by work and their exploits, academic dropouts, confidence men and wife-dodging runaways, beer swilling, happy, bitter and at times tearful, each and all trapped by the easy-going, no-questions-asked lifestyle of pre-war Darwin.

The eight or so months that were the "Dry" were halcyon days — spiced warm breezes from Timor and distant Surabaya, or iridescent seas, bland nights, silver moonlit sands, enscribed by hermit crab shell-house drag marks or paddle-printed in the slow urgency of female turtles seeking soft burrowing sandhills above high water mark.

Hot, clear and blue kingfisher presented days, to shark fish from a hired ketch-rigged lugger off Melville Island, or to watch with adolescent bawdiness the bare-skinned Japanese women pearl divers in the transparent blue-green waters off the nearest shore edge of the Continental Shelf.

There were tribal Aborigines lined up on the long wharf, collared and neck-chained one to the other, waiting for transportation to Channel or Mud Islands in the bay towards Beagle Gulf, for a life of isolation in those leper colonies where days were long and the treatment of leprosy was in its infancy.

Shortages of fresh meat and flour. The waiting with unconcealed anticipation for the arrival of a Burns Philp coastal trader bringing provisions, beer and letters from down south. Or the arrival of the Sunderland flying boat to be moored and guarded in the harbour. The preoccupation with survival in an everchanging bushland, rugged, mountainous, river scarred, in places impenetrable, or the prairie cattle stations terminating abruptly on the edge of the endless wasteland's sand ridges of the Tanami and the Great Central Deserts.

The outbreak of war in 1939 ended all that.

Leaving it all for foreign countries and new experiences temporarily over-shadowed the spell of outback Australia, tropical coastline and the subtle consolidation of one's ties to its beauty and mystery.

During the war I did not really "worry" about Judas Iscariot. His unseemly end, for whatever reason, was just part of my questioning — my refusal to attend church parades, armed with a rifle, gas mask and tin hat, singing the praises of the Lord and damning our enemies to Iscariot ends.

Somehow I felt it was pertinent that I should think twice about religion and liturgical worship in the face of fear, stupidity, wastage and courage, which, from this distance in time, still appears to me to have been "a tale told by an idiot ...".

In truth, it was probably a time for me spent re-examining much of that which I had taken for granted.

On pre-embarkation leave I returned to Bendigo to marry, leaving for England, retracing my eleven-year-old tracks to Cape Town, Freetown, Scotland and England, and finally ending up in the Western Desert of the Middle East. I served in Israel, Lebanon, Syria and Ceylon, making a dream come true on a magic carpet stained and tattered with fear and transience.

Through those homesick years, I gradually realised that I wanted to be shot of the whole bloody fiasco and left alone to unravel the brain-tangling cacophony of new countries, their people and customs and unprecedented situations. I needed time to evaluate, digest and act upon a wholly unique set of facts and circumstances and the effects they were having on my preconditioned juvenile attitudes, spurious moral judgments, expectations and ambitions.

After the war I was gratuitously given a second bite at the educational cherry through the Commonwealth Rehabilitation Scheme, making art and education an all-consuming lifestyle of painting, printmaking, sculpture, teaching and lecturing, obsessed with visual imagery and educational ideas.

I watched a family of four sons growing up in an environment I hoped would give them a liberal approach to life and the arts, as well as a humane understanding of themselves and political awareness of their own era.

Years later I remarried, returning to Darwin to pioneer art education activities and resources for the Aboriginal Welfare Branch.

It was an exhilarating time of travel, teaching and demonstration, living with scattered Aboriginal communities on settlements, mission stations and pastoral properties and the rest, with the length and breadth of the Territory as a classroom. From the Wessel group of islands in the north, to Yuendumu, Papunya and Hermannsburg in the south; Daly River and Hooker Creek in the west to Santa Teresa Mission in the east.

The omniscience of the land and the Aboriginal people with whom I was in daily contact gave a new authority to my personal philosophy of living and art during this period of trial, practical experience and growing conviction.

Ideas became much-discussed plans, plans became urgent action, and Anne and I decided to leave Darwin for Sydney.

A sensation of joyous spontaneity saw us travelling down "The Track", just ahead of whispers of the "Wet".

Having waited for the sun to disappear behind distant mountains, plain pushed and abrupt, we would camp for the night and cook a meal in the peace of vastness in half-light. The sun seemed to vanish in a vortex of diminishing light, sucking with it, like some giant vacuum cleaner, the myriad bush flies that made eating outside during its dazzling hours unbearable and impossible.

Breakfast time reversed the process so our days began under a sun vacant sky in a cool world of grey half-seen things, filled with the early-warning alarms and fluttering calls of a stirring hidden population.

Hopes and a sense of adventure accompanied us heading south, occasionally laced with trepidation which we dispelled by endlessly planning or becoming completely immersed in the ever-changing landscape, the one pub and general store and post office "townships" and visits to outback friends I had made during the time I worked out of Darwin.

Though we thought we were making good time as the kilometres ticked by, now and then we were not fast enough to escape the single-mindedness of massed, sun-thickened cloud sentinels, pursuing us in a lachrymose tropical farewell.

It was Annie's first visit to Sydney, and its charm worked on her in those early days of the sixties as it had for me back in the thirties, when I remembered my youthful romantic reaction to the energy of the unexpected twisted streets of flats and gradients, narrowed by half in places where trams clanged and bucked up and down Pitt Street to Circular Quay. Cabs, Oldsmobiles, Baby Austins, open-topped ... Chevrolets (?), some with wooden-spoked spare wheels racked to the side of the front mudguard, or the four-abreast, draught-horsed, flat top lorries of barrels and bales.

Though there had been three decades of change with suburbia sprawling out towards the very foothills of the Blue Mountains, skyscrapers, modern shops, plazas, and buses where the trams used to run, we shared an immediate excitement of exploration and challenge.

Sydney, after the tropics, was overcoat and scarf cold, but we found warmth still encased in its fretted sandstone wallings, in the concavities of its foot-worn sculptured steps in living rock, and its mellow high and low asquint streets and lanes.

When we finally settled in a house in Paddington with its own studio, I lectured and taught and prepared exhibitions of paintings from the Territory for Canberra, Adelaide, Sydney and Brisbane, with just the germ of an idea for a print studio.

The small beginnings of the studio solved two problems simultaneously. I had the urge to produce some print editions for the exhibitions I had planned for the different states, and a pupil from the Mary White School of Design asked me to help her with the techniques involved in printing as she intended to concentrate full-time as a printmaker.

With a few handscreens, pegs on string which bisected the narrow single-roomed shop with its balcony of cast-iron lace in a row of terrace houses, bric-à-brac shops, butchers, green grocers and pastry makers, we began. We produced a few posters for the Old Tote Theatre, as well as some large Aubrey Beardsley reproductions and wrapping paper to pay the rent — and our first print edition, "Human Image", in collaboration with Rodney Milgate.

Small as it was, it was the beginning of many exciting art experiences, years of long concentrated work, lasting friendships and many fine prints, overlaid with the insecurity of tenure of premises and the anxiety of always being just a few steps ahead of liquidation.

When I started writing this afterword, I thought I would be able to recount the development of the embryonic venture of the early sixties to its adolescent demise in the seventies with impartial ease.

I find now that I overestimated my objectivity.

I can tell of the moving from one place to another. Of the premises which were our first adequate studio, in Little Oxford Street, in a lane behind a funeral parlour in Taylor Square, and the back doors that opened on to it of restaurants, green grocers and a multiplicity of shops serving thronged Oxford Street; bins of garbage spilling pungently into its narrowness, at times littered with empty wine bottles, papers and pieces of coloured cloth and cotton threads from the sweat shops in the lane.

I can recall tired, tightfaced, black-haired women, black shawl-dressed, clutching large message bags, and how each morning the women of all ages, shapes and sizes hurried into featureless grime-ridden buildings to three flights up and a narrow room, to sit working nonstop at sewing machines until released once more into the lane at five.

There were doorways which were bolt-holes of forgetfulness for human derelicts, and passages that rattled and purred hour after hour with the sound of machines sewing bolts of cloth into garments in a part of the city which was but a fraction of the thriving Sydney rag trade.

It was here that we occupied an identical room to those above and below us, at the end of a long passage.

Paddington Print Studio began in earnest, and we filled it with prints, artists, friends, visitors and plans for the future. It was an atmosphere of goodwill, slow exacting work and endless hours of satisfying creative activity, with moral and practical support from staff, artist friends, colleagues and family.

Perhaps it is here that I should detail the short life of the Little Oxford Street studio, and at the same time include the folding up of the studio in Brisbane Street, where, on legal advice, we had formed a limited company, moving slowly to wider horizons, expanded visions and a greater feeling of successful achievement.

To do this, however, would produce a litany of acrimony I wish to avoid, as I discover with startling surprise that the disappointments, frustrations and painful memories accompanying the gradational exit of Paddington Print Studio from the Sydney art world are not yet time-calloused enough to be rubbed for reasoned words or logical explanations.

Anne and I returned to South Australia where I started to paint an exhibition of unfamiliar imagery, probably for therapeutic reasons.

It meant many weeks of being alone along the Murray River, with silent reed tunnels, overhanging willows and acacias in hidden unexpected re-entrants of deathly still water, straddled by the massive torsos of fallen sugar gum-tree warriors. It was days and nights sound-filled with water hens, shrikes and more melodious callers.

Days of drifting or being moored to overhanging branches, without human interference, sketching, drawing and licking old wounds. Side-stepping reality in a pavan to a day that had died.

After the exhibition, eight months later, I was back in a familiar landscape in the outback. A landscape that cut one down to size, making the petty trivialities of past hurts and hopes secondary to its overwhelming mystique. A landscape vast, timeless and in places ruggedly harsh, where the privilege to survive rested wholly on one's ability to accept and be accepted by its inherent mysteries and inconsistent moodiness.

The South Australian Aboriginal Resources Branch sent me back to the bush and the outback, to places I'd camped in and painted for over twenty years.

It was a life of travel. Thousands of kilometres, from one end of the state to the other, with a long wheelbase, four-wheel-drive vehicle, complete with camping gear, long distance petrol and water tanks, and a two-way radio for company. On other occasions, a smart conventional sedan to Port Augusta or Port Lincoln, alone but never lonely. A life abundant with unique experiences, a prevailing sense of wellbeing, achievement and communion.

Between solitary trips across the great stretches of gibber plains, passing the white glare of Lake Eyre to Oodnadatta and the edges of the Musgrave, Mann, and the enigmatic Petermann Ranges in the north-west corner of the state, we watched my studio slowly take shape in a backyard native tree-planted and eucalypt-filled.

One week I would be in Coober Pedy, handling translucent opals sparkling with inner fire, the next, south near the open sea, talking about pens for the breeding of yabbies. There were months spent in the lower and upper Flinders Ranges in consultation with elders of a whole settlement, Aboriginal drovers and station hands, and fringe dwellers of country townships.

When I decided to call it a day and accept a position as a lecturer in Adelaide, with a studio to regurgitate, in an Expressionistic sense, the haunting visions of the land and the people I felt I was beginning to understand, I made contact with Charles Blackman, loyal and sympathetic as ever.

With enthusiasm, sketches and drawings, he backed his arguments that my retirement from the print scene had left a gap in the Australian printmaking scene, so we collaborated yet again.

The Blackman prints were the harbingers of many local print editions, Robert Juniper from the West, and Frank Hodgkinson, whose sojourn in New Guinea during the time of proofing up "Genesis" gave us a great deal of worry with custom authorities of Papua, and took nearly three months to complete.

I suppose what I like about the present print studio is that it does fill many of the specifications of the ideas of the past. Experimentation in combinations of print media is possible, and there is no urgency.

The trees have topped the house and created a mellow greenness near the studio windows, overgrown in places, making me feel that I am making some ecological contribution to the lungs of Prospect. Here I can pot, or sculpt, but most importantly, it is a secluded place without business hassles, removed in spirit at least from suburbia and neighbours on three sides.

It is a place where creative processes can take place, to be written up, sculptured, painted or wheel thrown, in an atmosphere of a quiet, but very small piece of Australian bushland.

Notes on the Artists

JOHN ALAND was born in Brisbane in 1937 and has lived and worked in Queensland, Melbourne and Sydney. He is best known as a painter and teacher of art. He has had one-man shows in Brisbane, Sydney and Canberra and among the major awards he has won is the Australian-TAA Invitation Prize in Victoria in 1971. He received a Visual Arts Board grant in 1974. He is represented in the collections of the Australian National Gallery, Canberra, the art galleries of New South Wales and Queensland, the Australian National University and the Mornington Arts Centre, and numerous institutional and private collections.

ROSS BATEUP, born in 1942, is best known as a political cartoonist in the press, particularly in South Australia where his work has appeared in the *Advertiser* and the *Sunday Mail*; and he has contributed to the *Bulletin*, the *Australian* and *Australian Playboy*. He is an architect-planner by training, having studied at the University of Adelaide and the University of Pennsylvania, and he paints urban scenes. He lived in the USA from 1968 to 1973 and his cartoons appeared in the *New Yorker*, the *New York Times* and the *London Daily Telegraph*.

CHARLES BLACKMAN was born in Sydney in 1928, studied at East Sydney Technical College and worked as an artist on the *Sun* newspaper before taking up painting full-time in Melbourne in 1950. He has had many one-man exhibitions in all Australian capitals and London and his work has been included in international exhibitions in Europe and Asia. In addition to various major prizes, including the 1960 Crouch Prize, he was awarded the OBE and Queen's Silver Jubilee Medal for services to art in 1977. He is represented in all Australian state galleries and numerous institutional and private collections.

His art has been the subject of three books and innumerable articles.

DAVID BOYD, born in Melbourne in 1924, studied music before he took up pottery and painting. He has spent much of his life in Europe, living in Rome, London and the south of France. He has exhibited continuously in all Australian states and in England and is represented in all Australian public collections.

KEVIN CONNOR is a graphic artist, teacher, designer and painter. He was born in Sydney in 1932 and has studied and worked in Australia, England and Canada. He has exhibited here and in Japan, England and New Zealand. In 1979 he travelled to Egypt. He has won major prizes and is represented in the art galleries of New South Wales, Tasmania, Western Australia, the National Gallery of Victoria, the Newcastle City Art Gallery and the Australian National Gallery, Canberra. He is a trustee of the Art Gallery of New South Wales.

KEITH COWLAM was born in England in 1946, and studied at Croydon College of Art in 1963-1964 and Ravensbourne College of Art 1964-1965. He came to Australia in 1977 and studied printmaking at the SA School of Art 1978-1980. He won the West Lakes Art Prize in 1980, and the Victor Harbour and Whyalla Prizes in 1981. In 1982 he had a one-man exhibition at the Bonython Gallery, Adelaide.

RAY CROOKE began painting in Borneo and the Pacific Islands during the Second World War. He was born in Melbourne in 1922 and studied at the Swinburne Technical College. He has exhibited all over Australia and overseas, including at the Tate Gallery, London. His work is represented in all state art galleries in Australia and in the Australian National Gallery, Canberra. In 1978 he won the Archibald Prize (Art Gallery of New South Wales) with a portrait of the author George Johnston.

WILLIAM DEGAN, born in New South Wales in 1932, studied at East Sydney Technical College but first exhibited in Melbourne in 1958. He returned to Sydney in the early sixties but later went to live in Europe.

PAUL DELPRAT is best known for his paintings of nudes, but he is also a printmaker. He was born in Sydney in 1942 and after studying at the Julian Ashton School he visited England and the USA before taking up a series of teaching appointments. He has shown in Sydney, Melbourne, Adelaide, Perth and Newcastle, and London. He is represented in the Australian National Gallery, Canberra.

ROBERT DICKERSON, born in New South Wales in 1924, had no formal art education and did not commence painting until the end of the Second World War. He has exhibited in all Australian states and in England, the USA and South America. He has won several major prizes and was a finalist for the Blake Prize in 1965. He visited Europe (including England) in 1972-1973 and the USA in 1978, and his latest series of paintings are based on experiences in New York. He is represented in numerous Australian public, institutional and private collections.

DAVID DRIDAN, born in Adelaide in 1932, has studied in South Australia, Sydney and also in England. He is a teacher, a former commercial gallery director, and was curator of paintings at the Art Gallery of South Australia from 1962-1964. In 1980 he was appointed to the Board of the Art Gallery of South Australia. He has exhibited in Adelaide, Melbourne, Sydney, Perth, London and Paris, and is represented in the collections of the art galleries of South Australia and Western Australia and the Australian National Gallery, Canberra. In the late seventies he established himself as a winemaker, while continuing to paint in the Southern Vales region of South Australia.

CEDRIC FLOWER is a commercial artist-designer as well as painter, printmaker, author and editor of a series of art books. He was born in Sydney in 1920 and has served as president of the National Trust of New South Wales. Between 1950 and 1955 he lived in England and Europe. He has exhibited widely in Australia and is represented in the art galleries of South Australia, New South Wales, Queensland and the Australian National Gallery, Canberra.

BASIL HADLEY was born in London in 1940 and after some travel settled in Australia in 1964. He has exhibited throughout Australia and has had exceptional success in print and painting competitions. He is represented in the Development Collection (Michell Endowment) of the National Gallery of Victoria and numerous institutional and private collections in Australia and Papua New Guinea. In 1979 he received a major commission from the South Australian branch of the Australian Labor Party — the painting now hangs in the Adelaide Festival Centre.

PRO HART, whose given name is Kevin, has worked all his life in Broken Hill, New South Wales, where he was born in 1928. He is a painter, sculptor, illustrator and gallery owner. He is represented in the Australian National Gallery, Canberra, and other major collections and has exhibited continuously throughout Australia and attracted considerable attention in London and the USA.

FRANK HODGKINSON was born in Sydney in 1919 and studied under Dattilo Rubbo from 1936-1938. He has lived, travelled and worked in Europe, the USA and Papua New Guinea (he was artist-in-residence at the National Arts School at Port Moresby in 1977). He has exhibited frequently in many countries and his work is represented in the National Gallery of Victoria, the art galleries of South Australia, New South Wales and Western Australia, and the Australian National Gallery, Canberra. A major series of his paintings was purchased for the Northern Territory Collection in 1979 and he is represented in various institutional collections.

ROBERT JUNIPER lives and works in Western Australia where he was born in 1929. He has exhibited in Australia and the USA since the mid fifties, and won the Wynn Prize (for landscape, at the Art Gallery of New South Wales), in 1976 and 1980. In addition to paintings in the art galleries of New South Wales, Western Australia, and the National Gallery of Victoria, he has reached a wide public with his book illustrations, particularly for *Mason Judy* and the cover of the Penguin edition of Randolph Stow's *To the Islands.* In 1982 he became the first Western Australian artist to be represented in the collection of the Australiana Fund.

FRANCIS LYMBURNER (1916-1972) was born in Brisbane. He lived in England for ten years from 1953 and his Australian reputation is based mainly on his draftsmanship.

RODNEY MILGATE, born in New South Wales in 1934, is a painter as well as a teacher and writer. He has studied in New South Wales and privately overseas, and exhibited in Sydney, Melbourne, Canberra and Brisbane. In London he shared an exhibition with Kevin Connor at the Commonwealth Institute Galleries, and he has shown in Japan and the USA. He won the Blake Prize in 1966 and is included in the collections of the Australian National Gallery, Canberra, the art galleries of New South Wales and Western Australia, and several regional galleries.

MICHAEL NICHOLSON was born in England in 1916 and came to Australia in 1960 after establishing himself as an artist and teacher. He is represented in the Art Gallery of New South Wales and is a sculptor as well as a painter and graphic artist, and has participated in the Sydney Biennale 1976, with a video sculpture; Venice Biennale 1980; Kobe Video International (Japan) 1980; and has won prizes at Mildura 1973, 1975.

DAVID SCHLUNKE was born in 1942 at Temora in New South Wales, the place which is the subject of many of his images. He has exhibited regularly in Sydney and Melbourne and occasionally in Perth and Adelaide. He is represented in private collections and the Australian National Gallery, Canberra.

ERIC SMITH was born in Melbourne in 1919 and studied at Brunswick and RMIT; both commercial art and painting. He has exhibited regularly in Sydney and Melbourne for the past three decades, specialising in abstracts, portraits and, more recently, animal studies. His work has been shown in the USA and in various competition exhibitions here, including the Blake and the Art Gallery of New South Wales prizes. He won the Blake Prize in 1956, 1958, 1959, 1962 and was equal winner in 1970 (with Roger Kemp). He is represented in the Australian National Gallery in Canberra, the National Gallery of Victoria, the art galleries of South Australia, New South Wales, Queensland and Western Australia, and other collections. He won the 1981 Archibald Prize.

MERVYN SMITH achieved recognition as one of Australia's greatest water-colourists in the sixties, but he was trained as an architect. He was born in Sydney in 1904, but has lived in South Australia most of his life. He has exhibited all over Australia and is represented in every state gallery. He has won the Maude Vizard-Wholohan Prize (Art Gallery of South Australia, 1966), and the Perth Prize four times.

RICHARD TIPPING, born in 1949, is primarily a poet. He studied at Flinders University in the late sixties and moved from Adelaide to Sydney in 1979. He exhibited "concrete poems", carved in stone, at the Adelaide Festival Centre Gallery in 1978, and created a special piece there for the 1982 Festival.

THE PRINTS

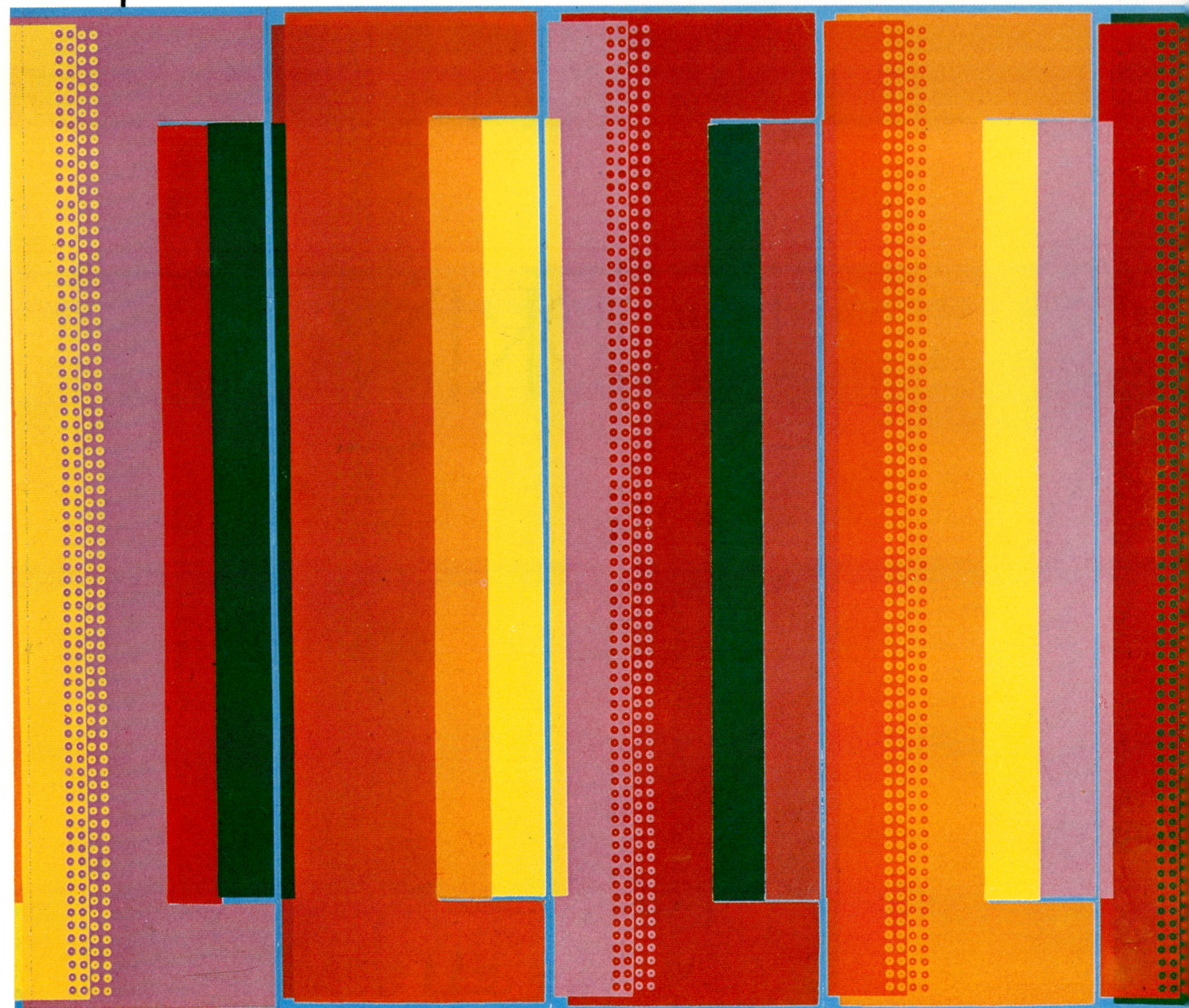

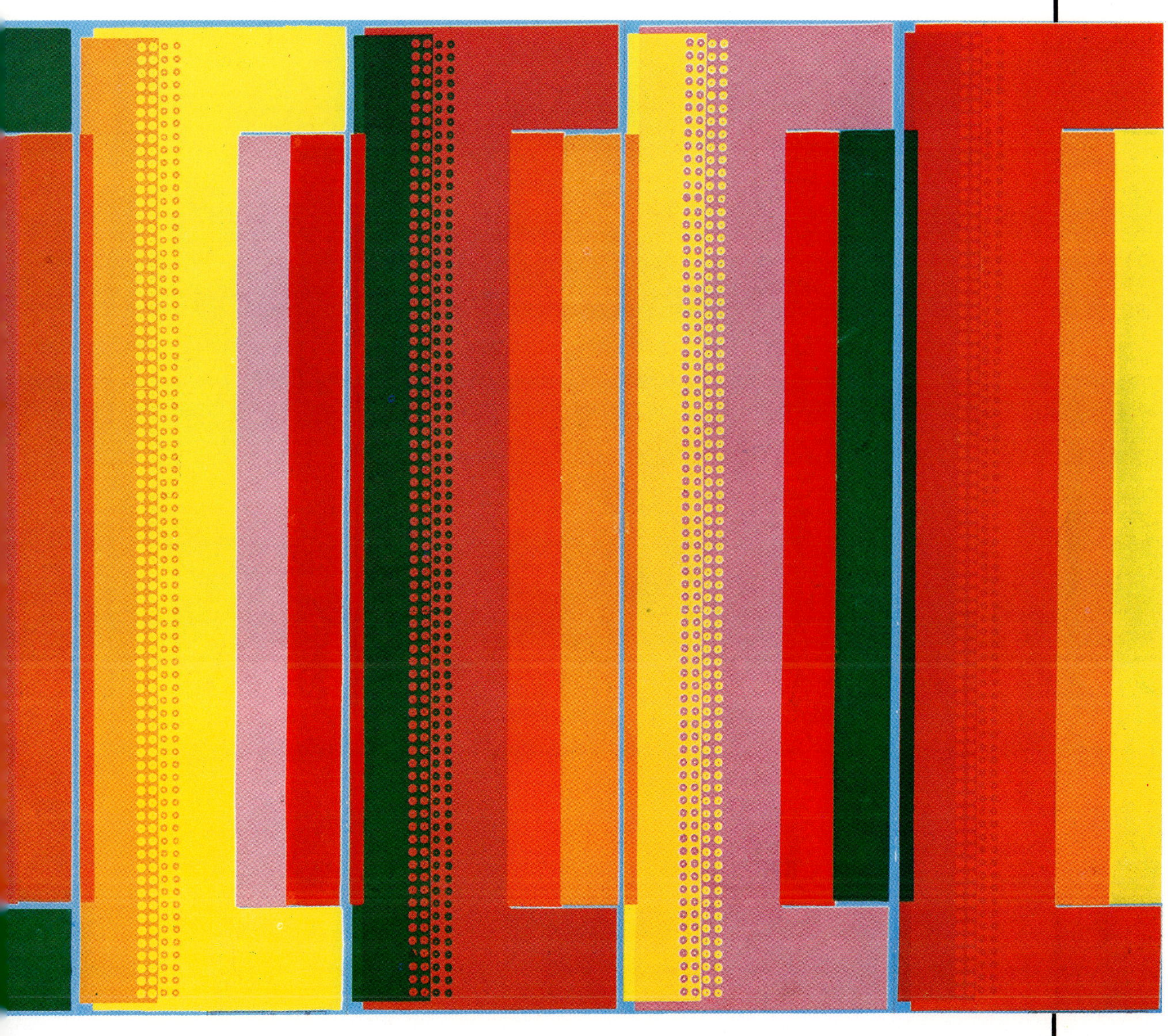

Michael Nicholson
"Modular Strip Art-oons" 1971

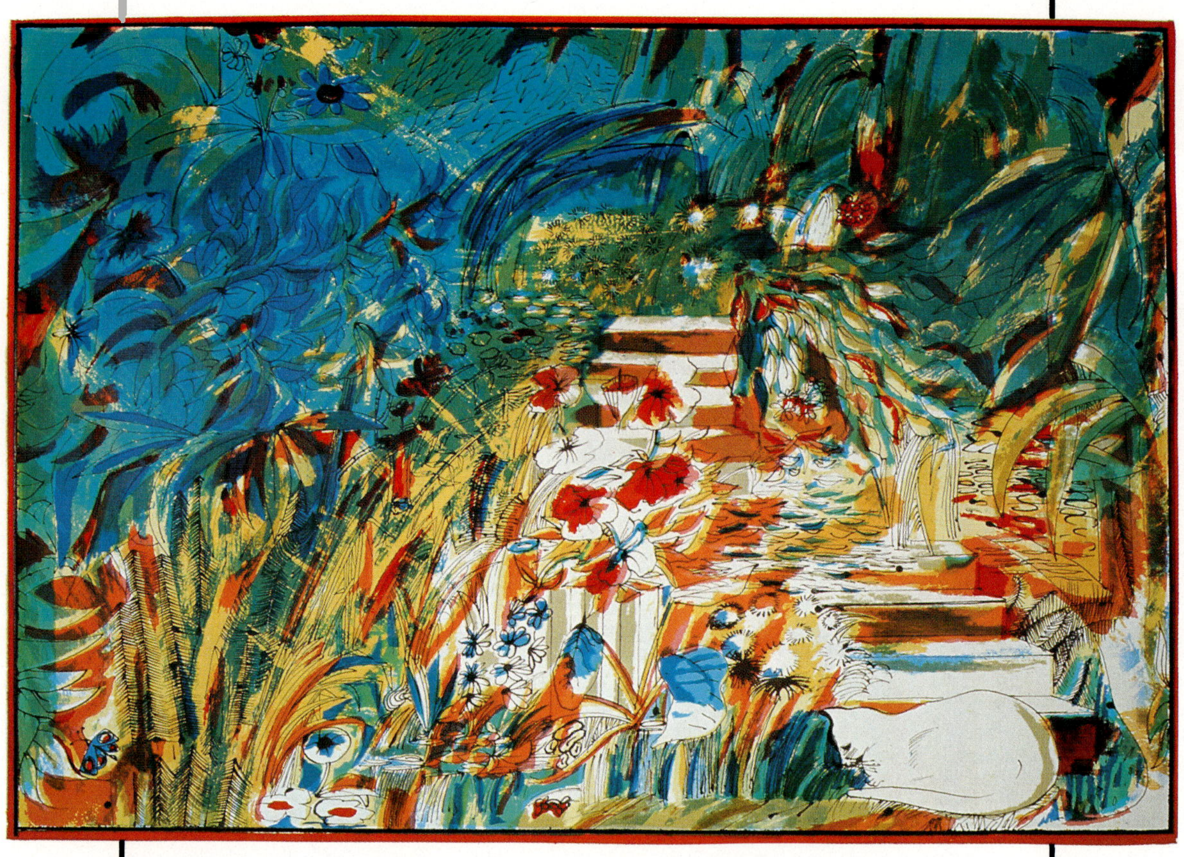

2
Charles Blackman
"Eclipse in the White Cat's Garden" 1976

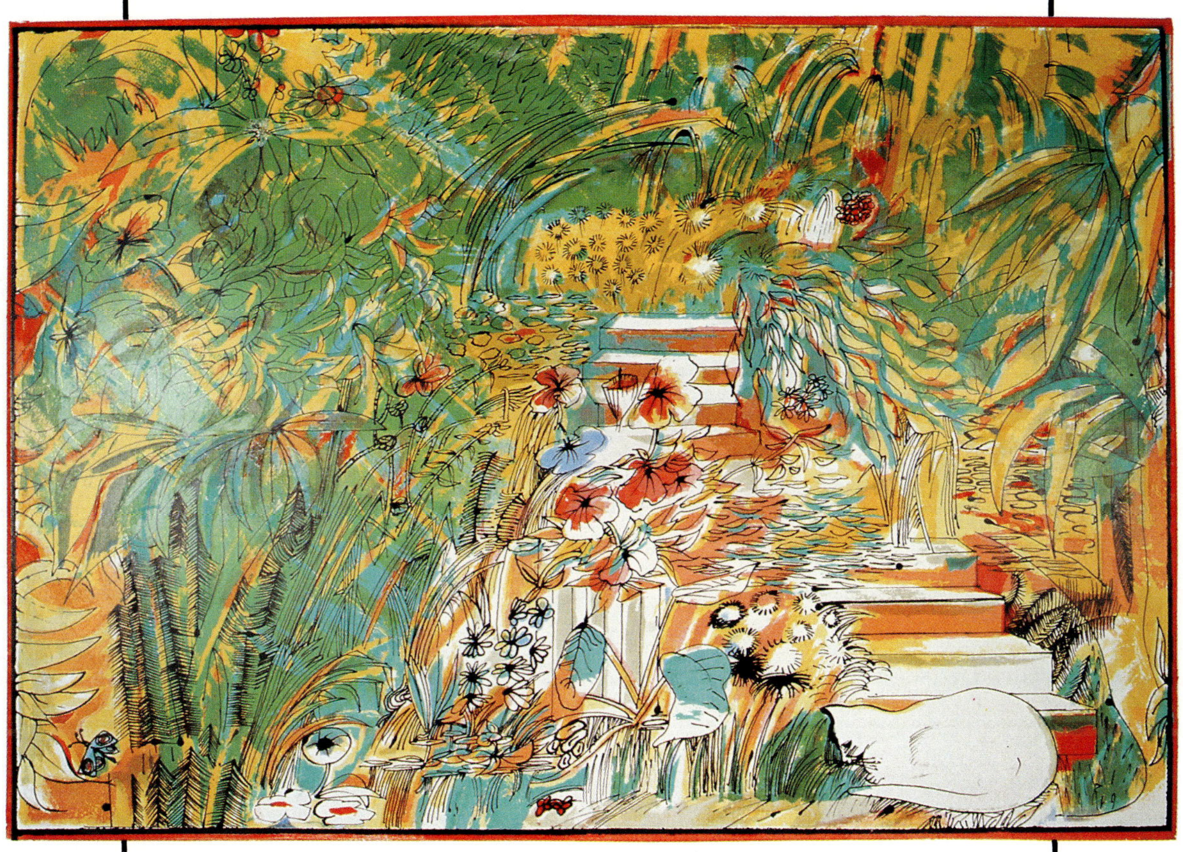

3
Charles Blackman
"Passing Clouds in the White Cat's Garden" 1976

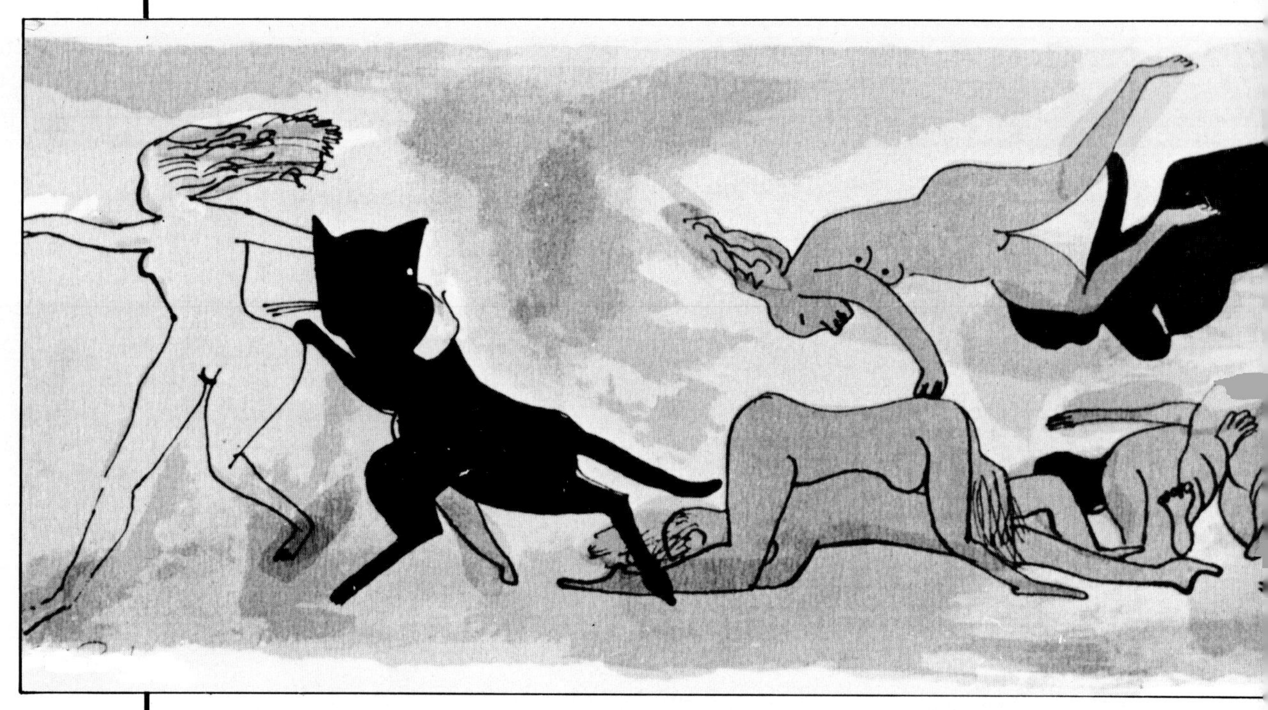

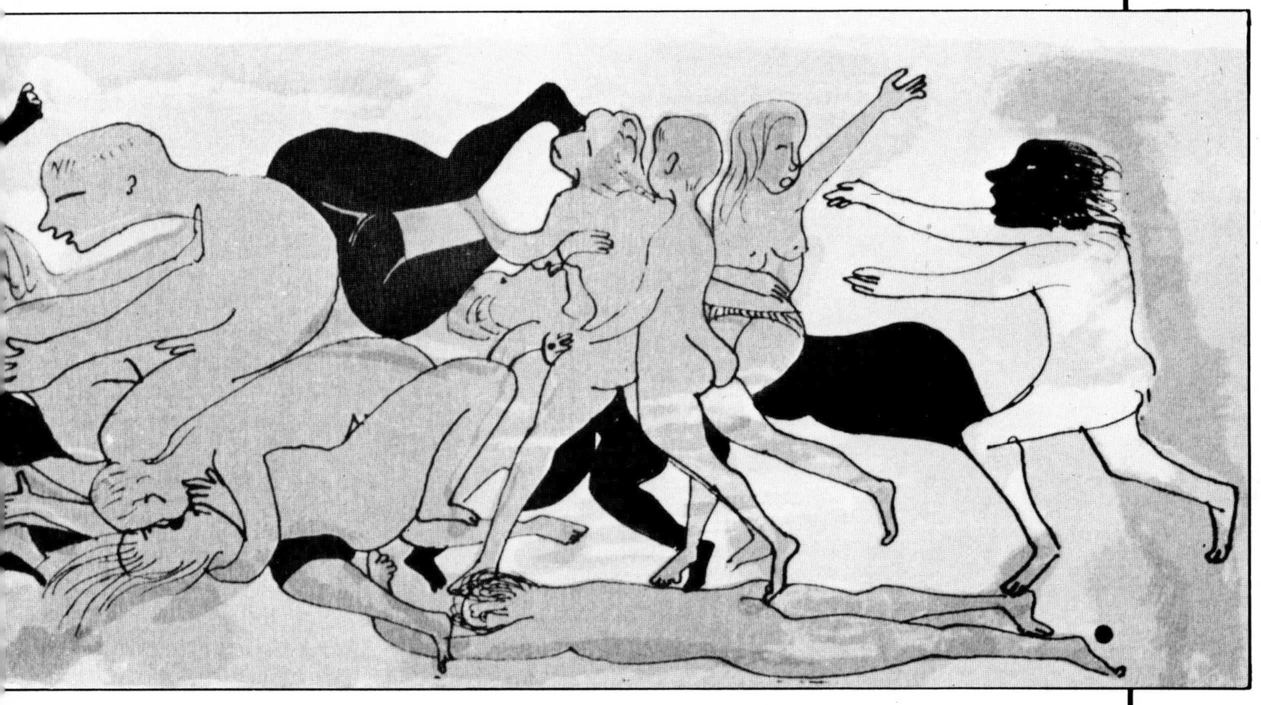

Charles Blackman
"Witches Sabbath" 1969

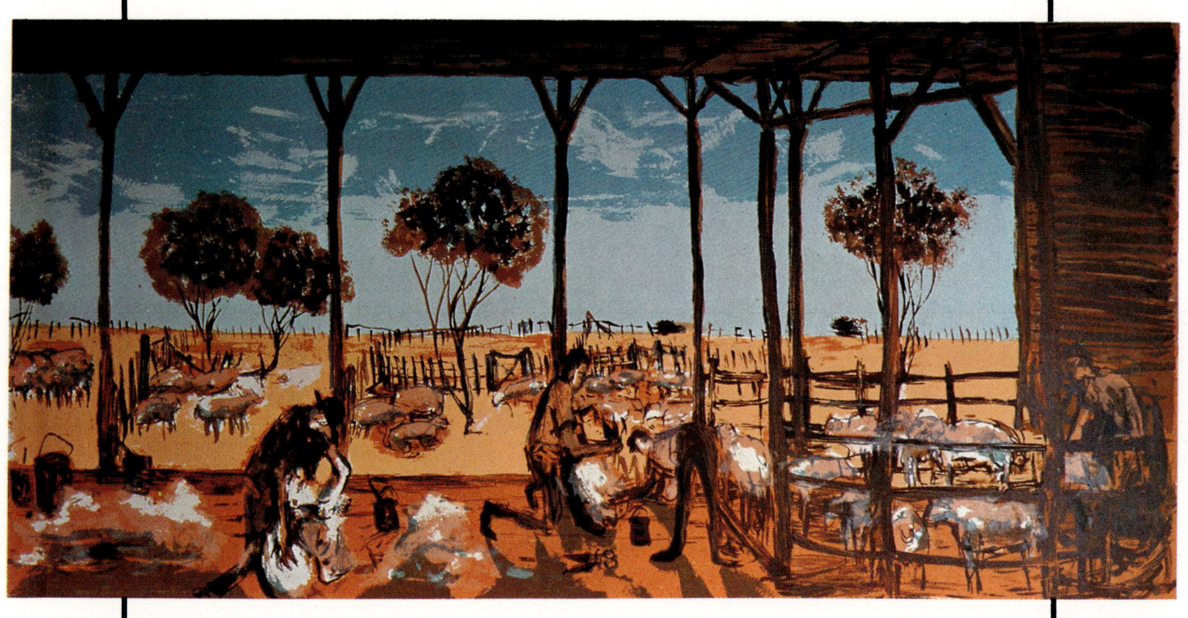

5

(Kevin) Pro Hart
"The Blade Shearers" 1969

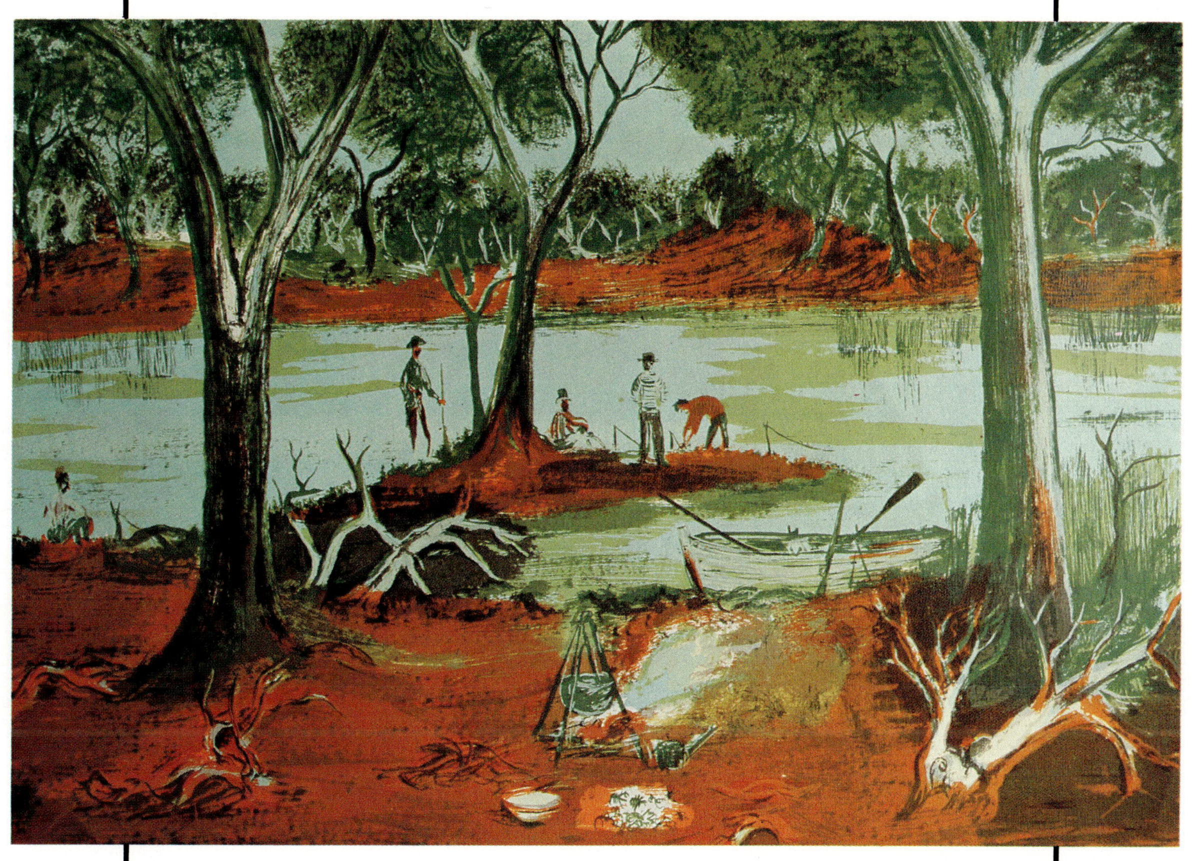

6
(Kevin) Pro Hart
"Cook Discovering Yabbies" 1969

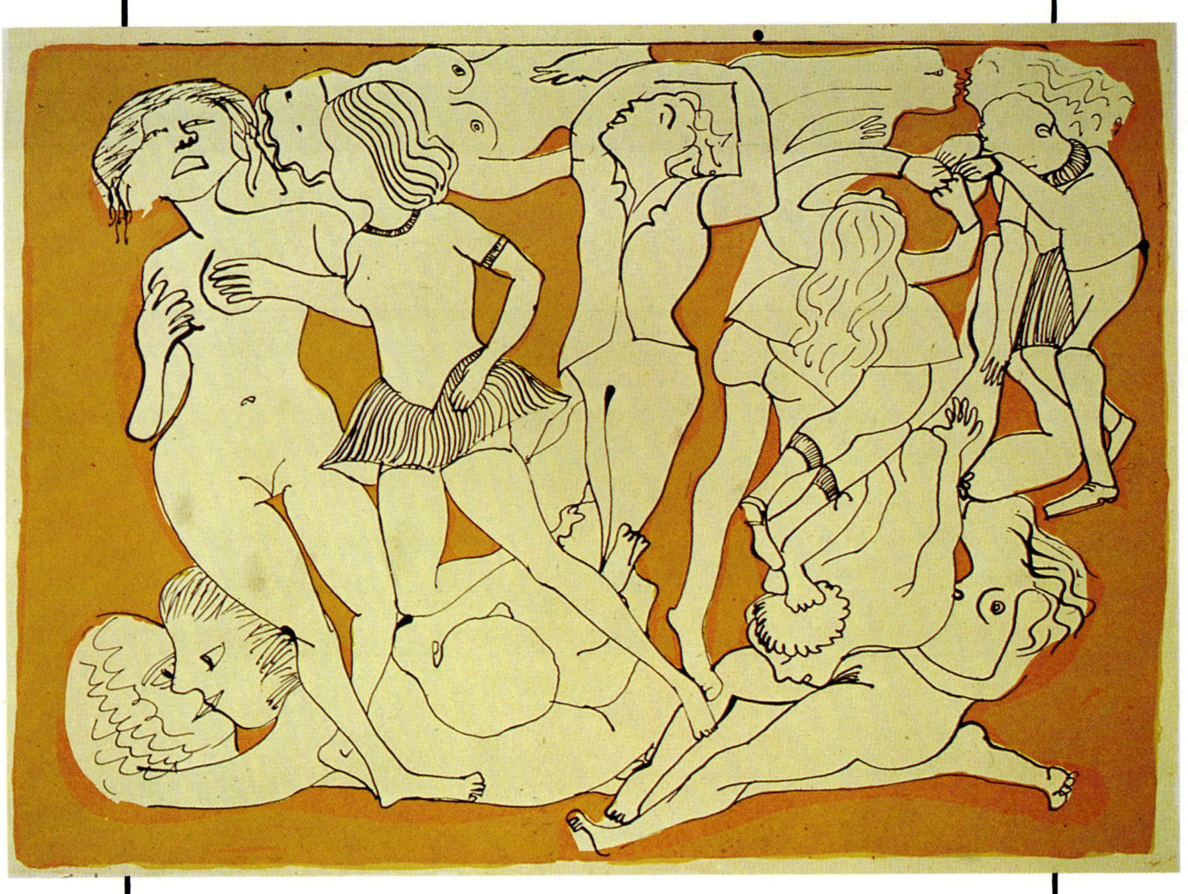

7

Charles Blackman
"I Love Tom Jones" 1969

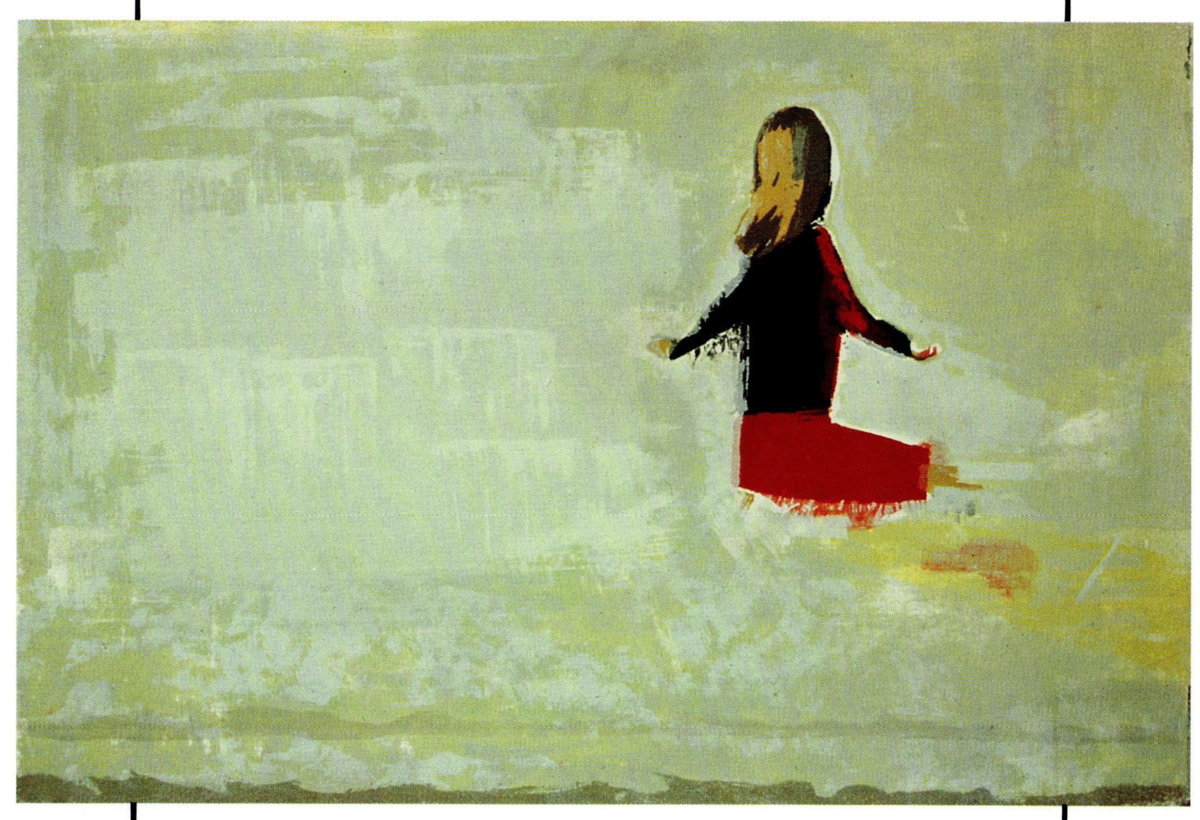

8
Charles Blackman
"Girl on a Beach" 1969

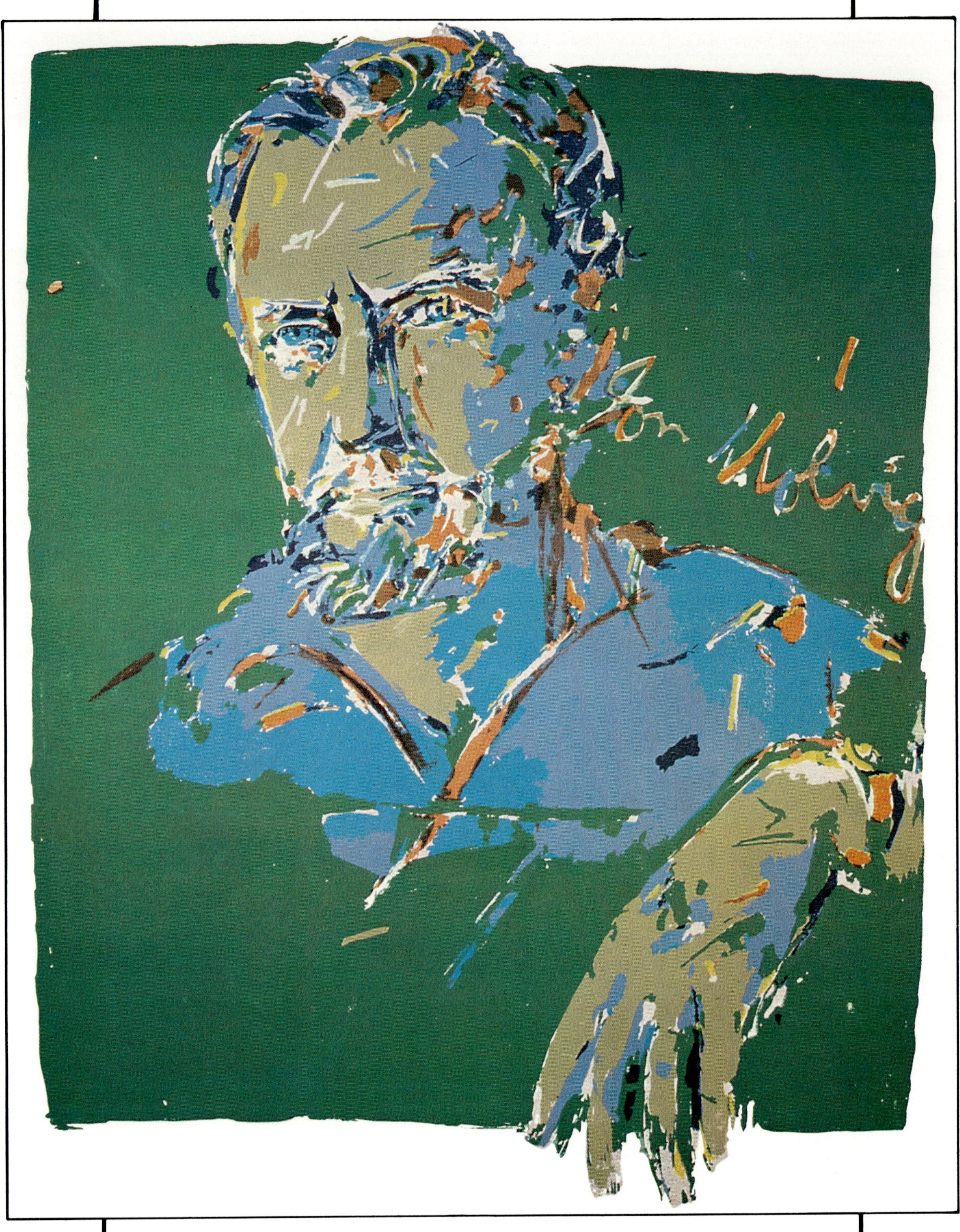

9
Eric Smith
"Portrait of Jon Molvig" 1969

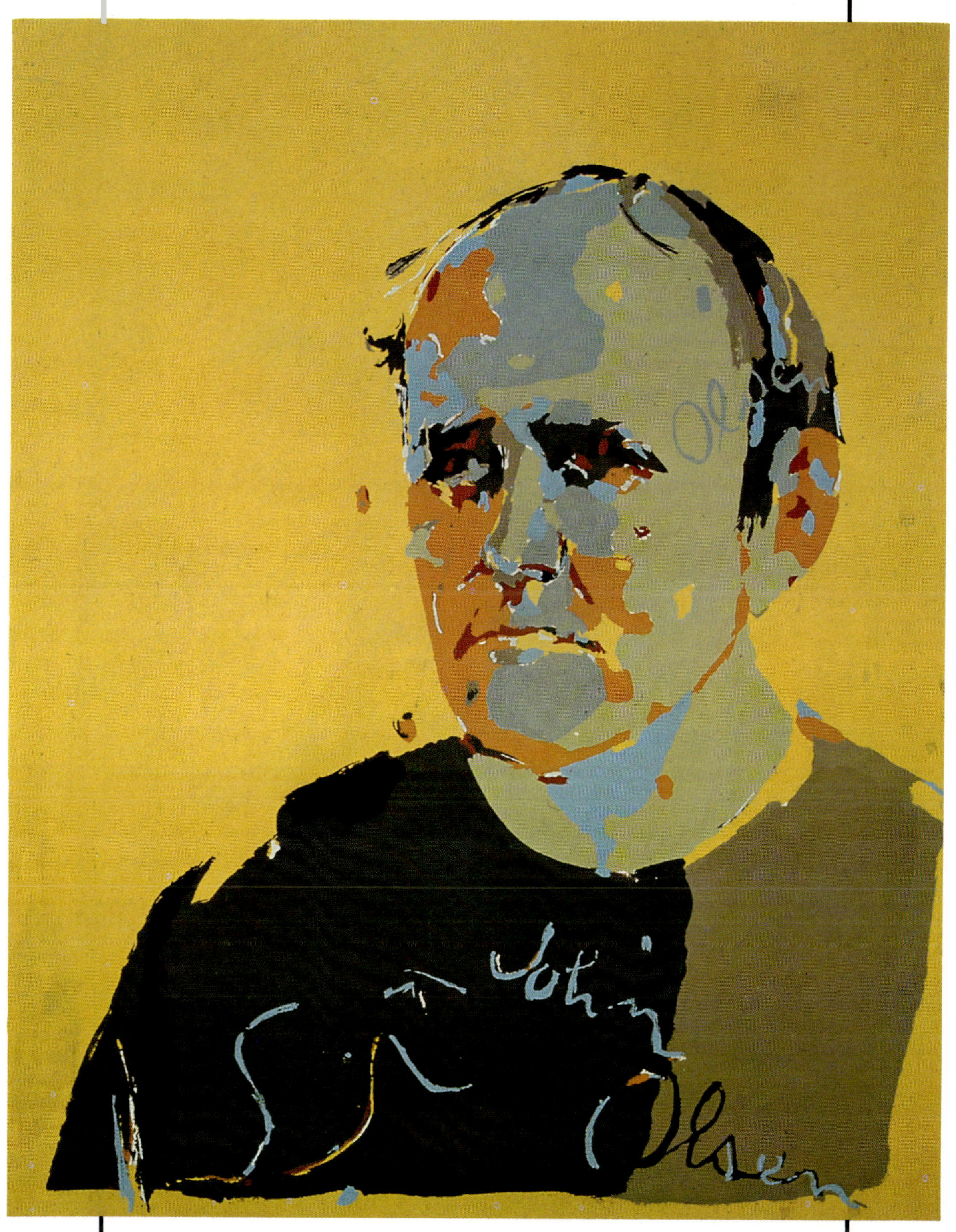

10
Eric Smith
"Portrait of John Olsen" 1969

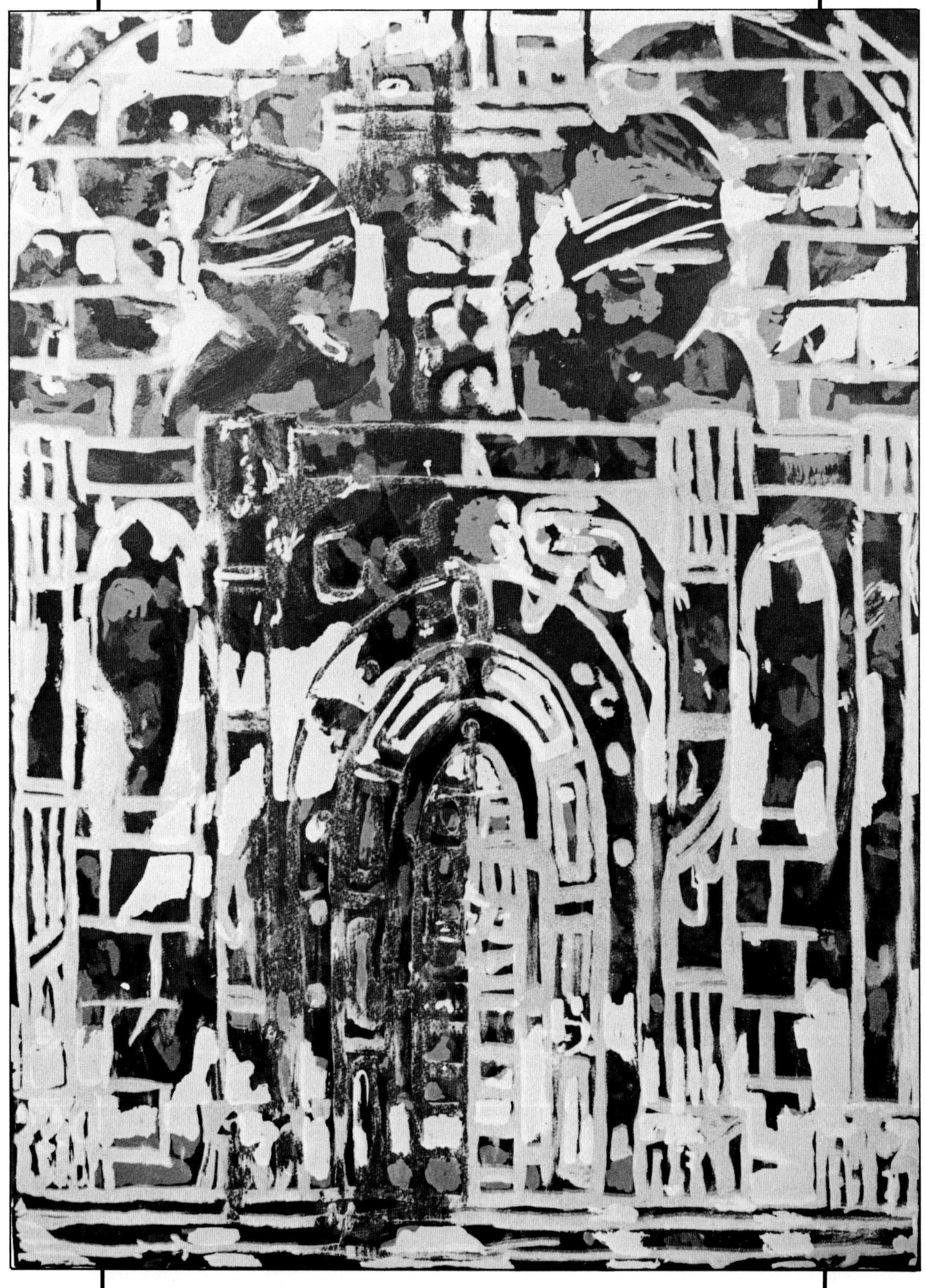

11
Rodney Milgate
"Dilemma" 1970

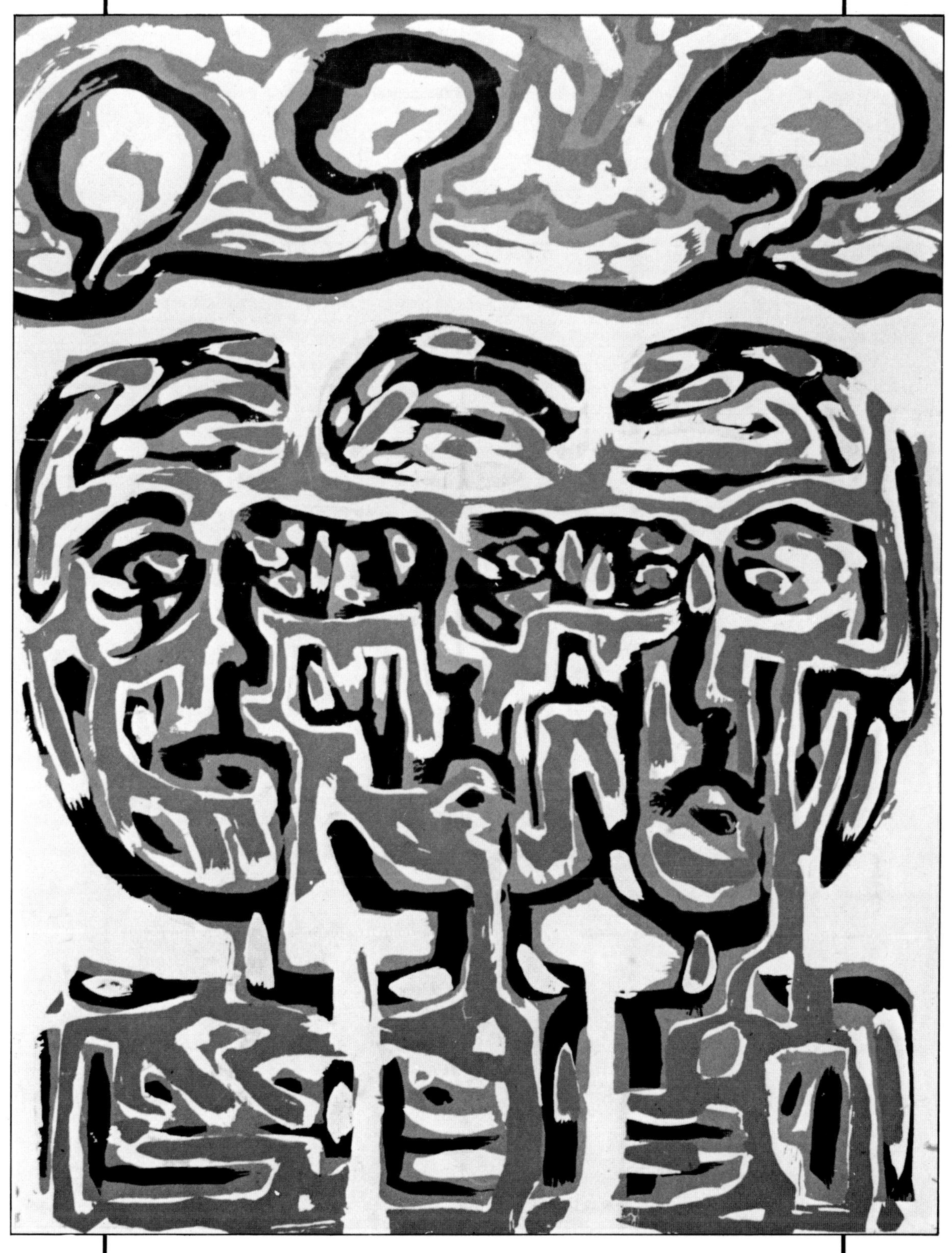

12
Rodney Milgate
"Human Image" 1967

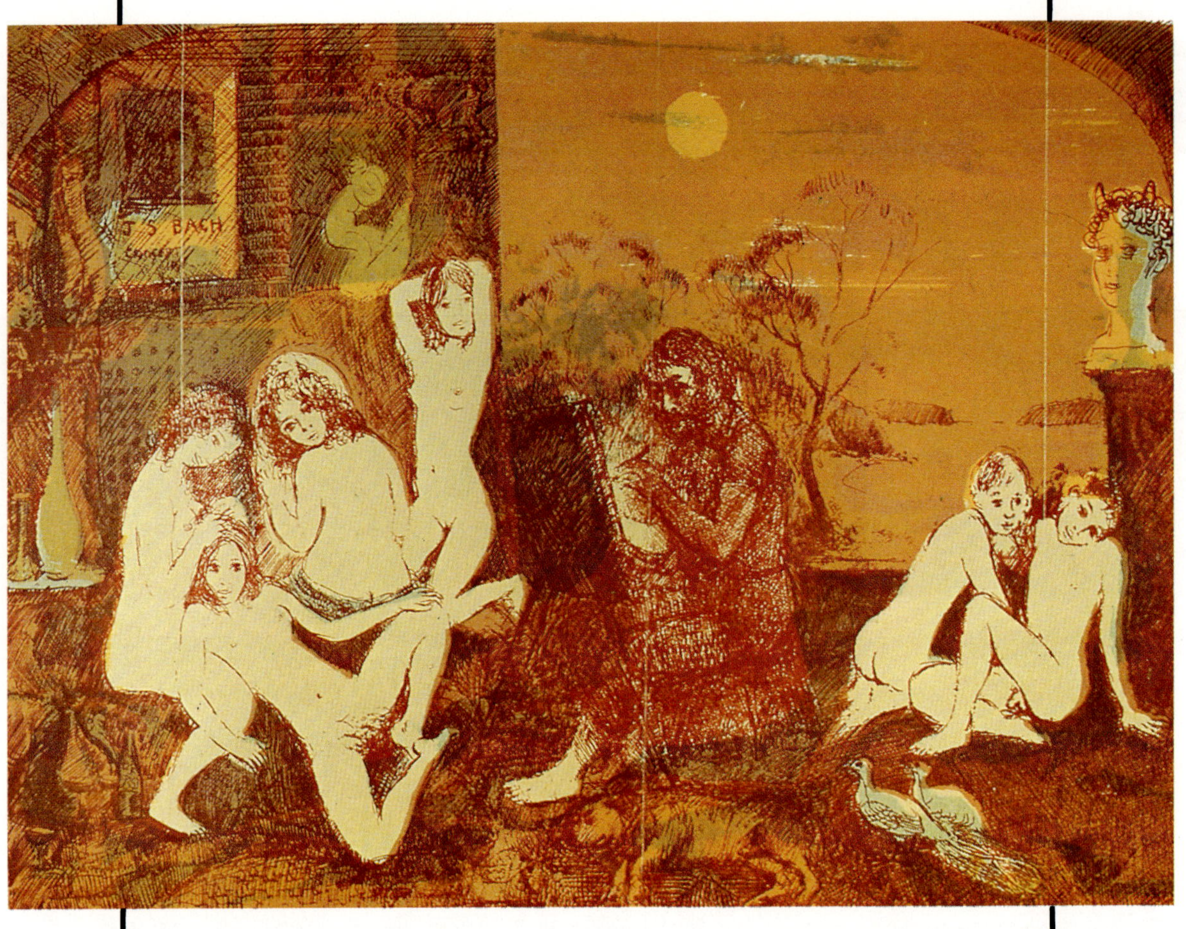

13

Paul Delprat
"Artist's Studio" (orange version) 1969

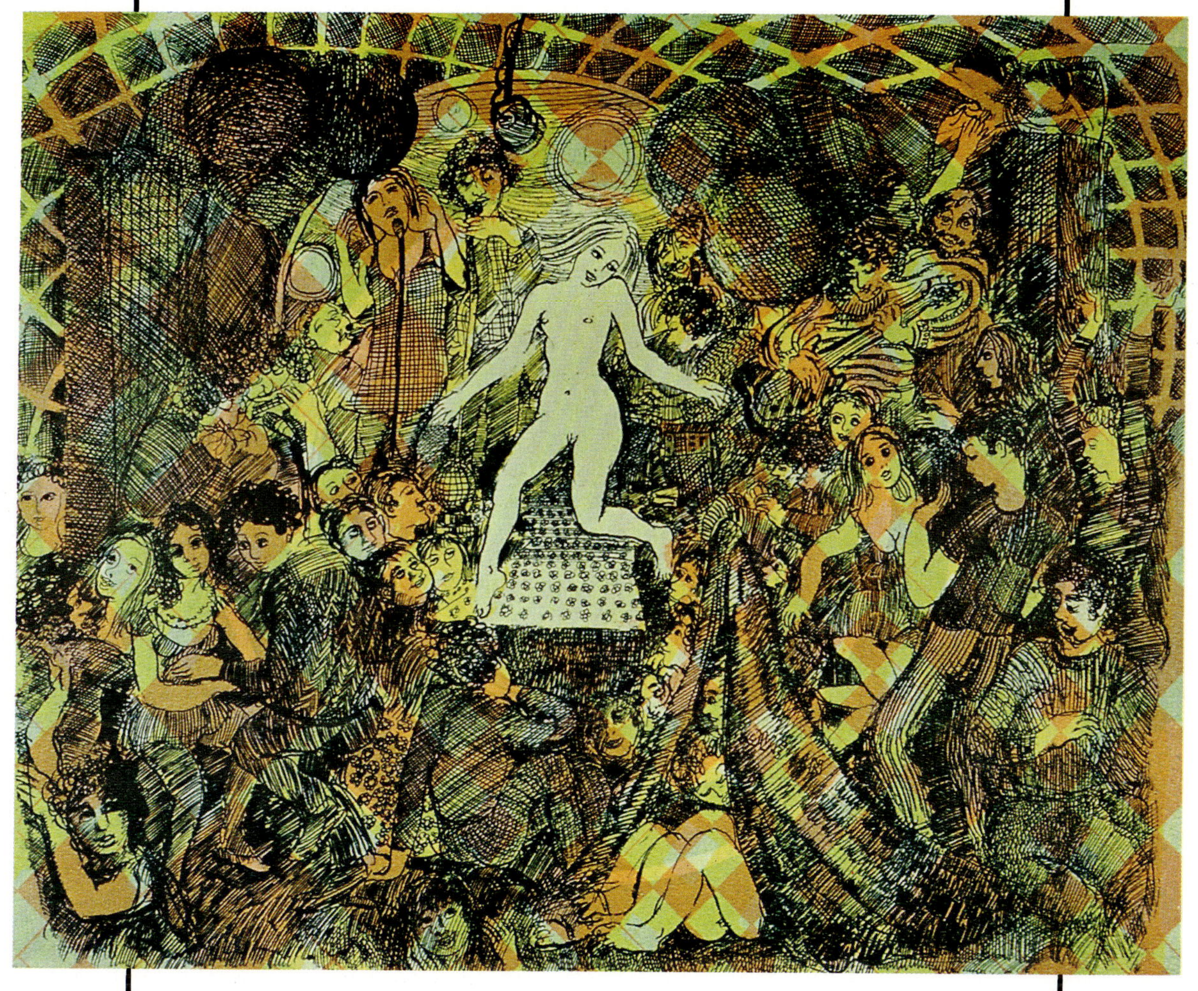

14
Paul Delprat
"Discotheque" 1969

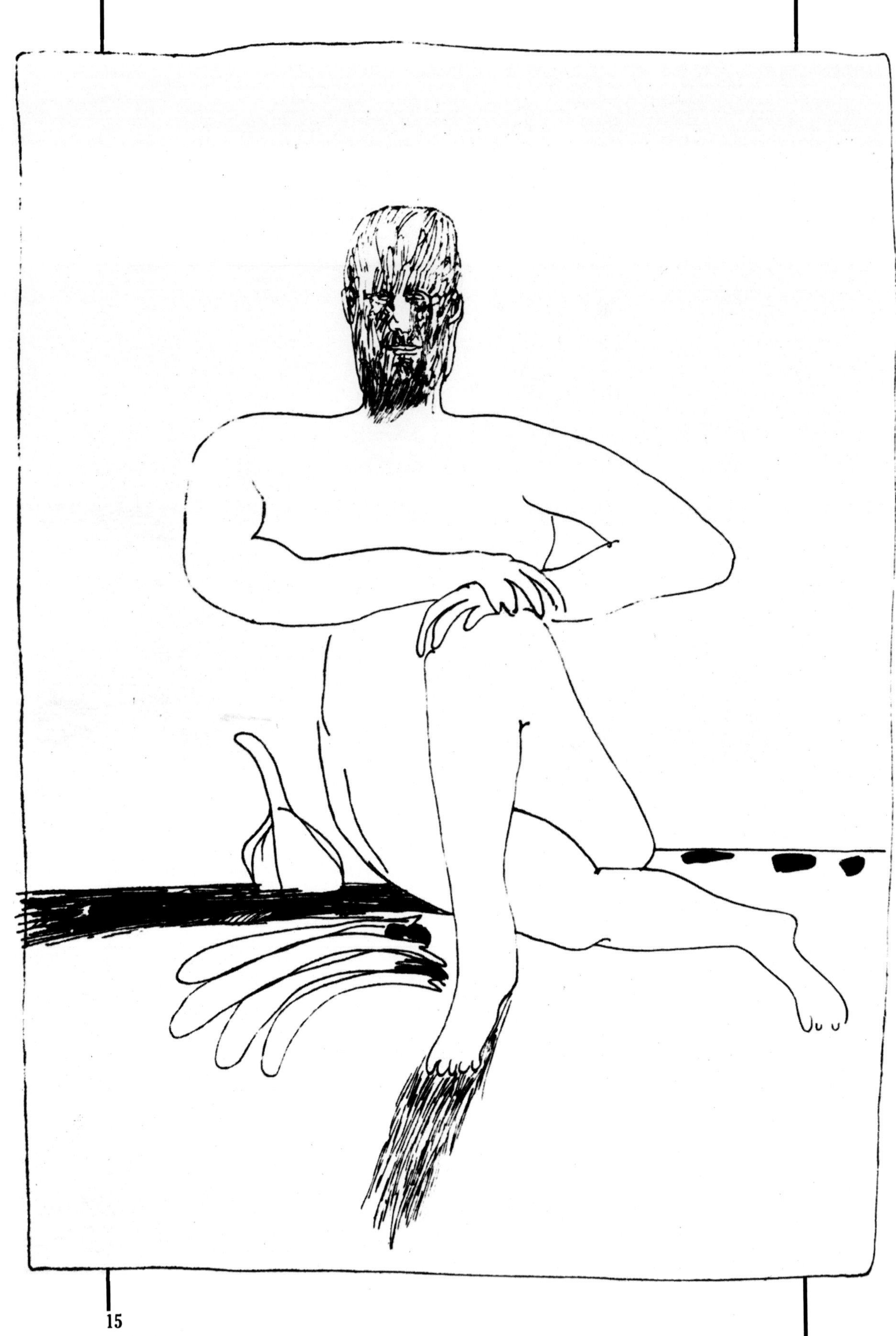

15
Kevin Connor
"Andalusian Portfolio" 1970

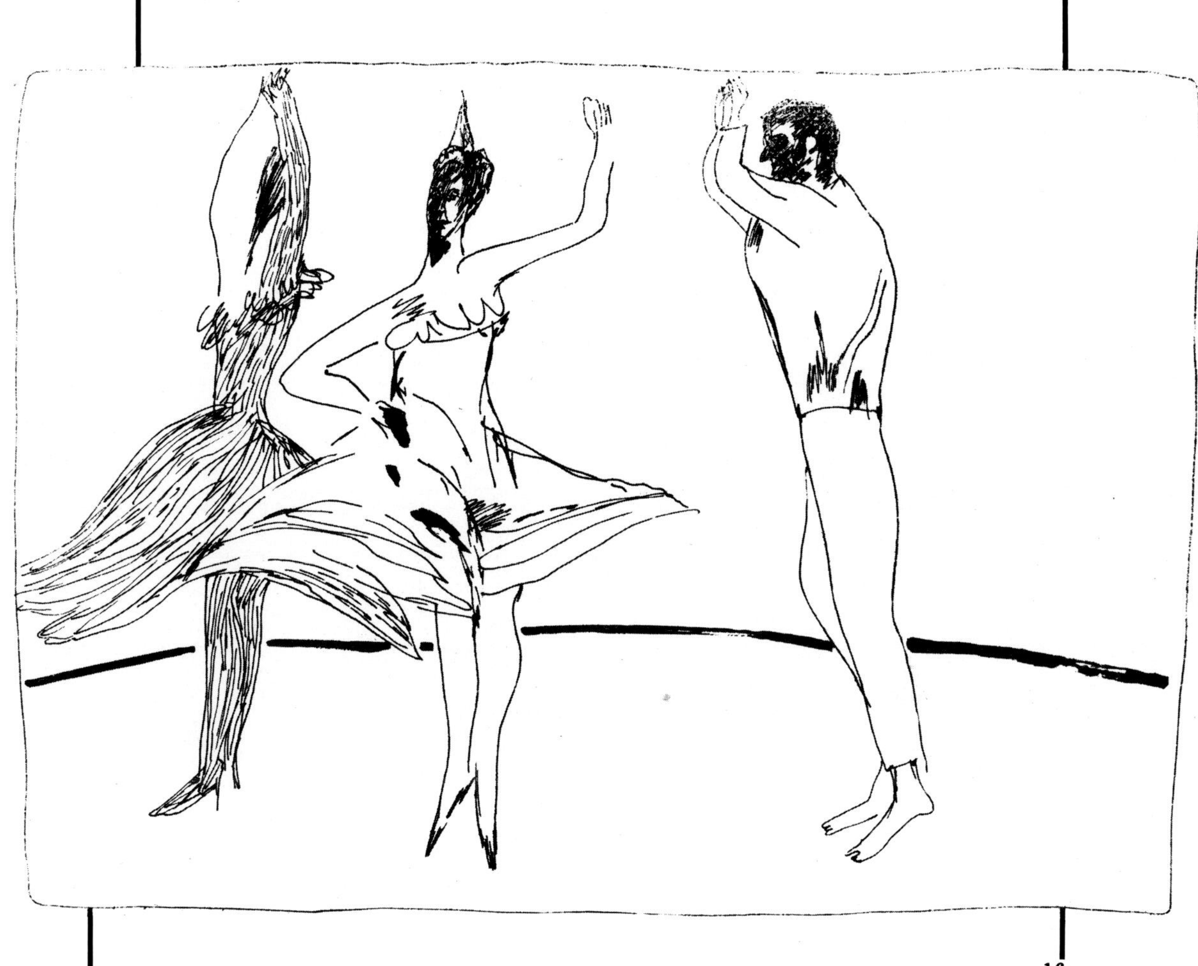

16
Kevin Connor
"Andalusian Portfolio" 1970

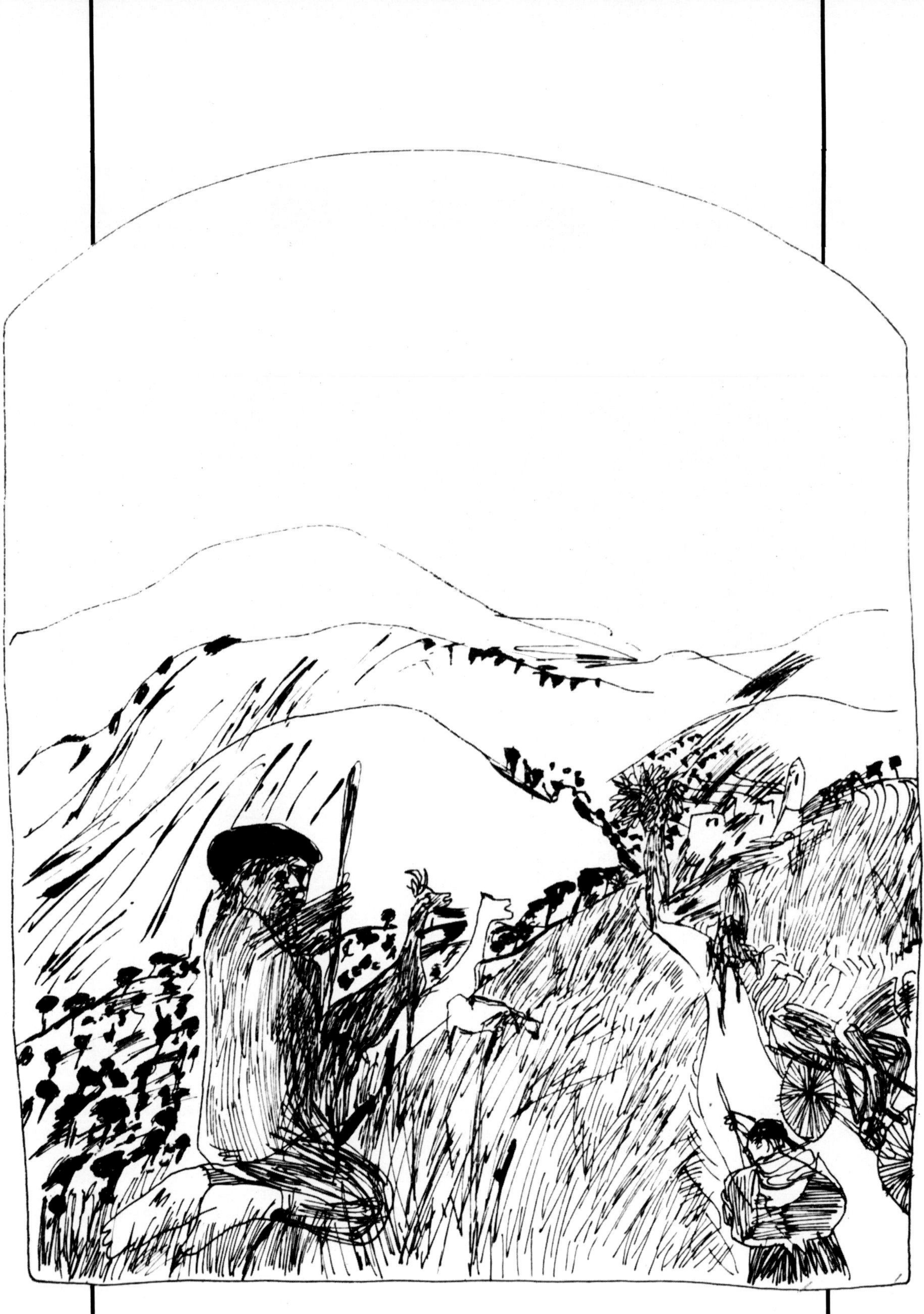

17
Kevin Connor
"Andalusian Portfolio" 1970

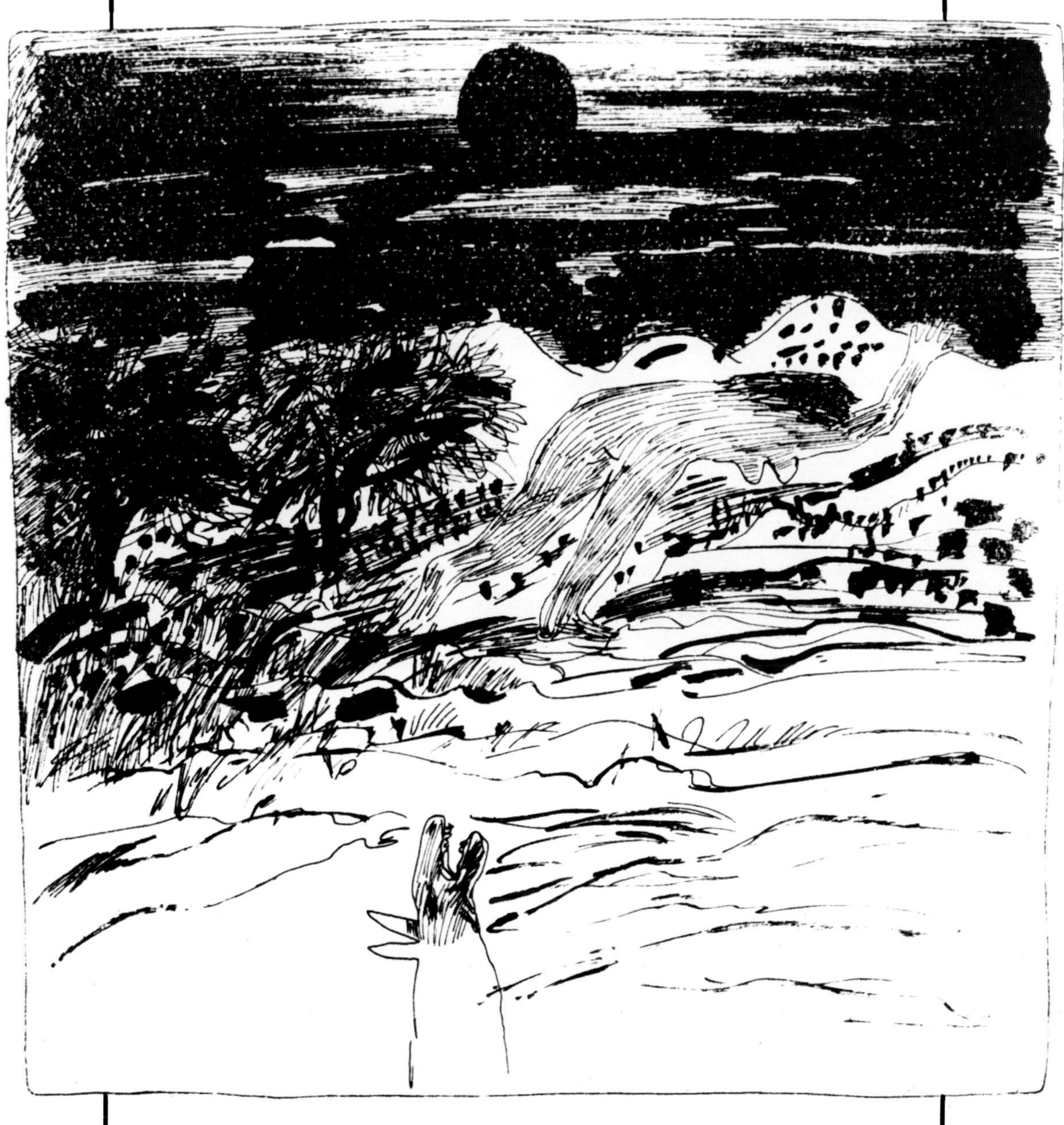

18
Kevin Connor
"Andalusian Portfolio" 1970

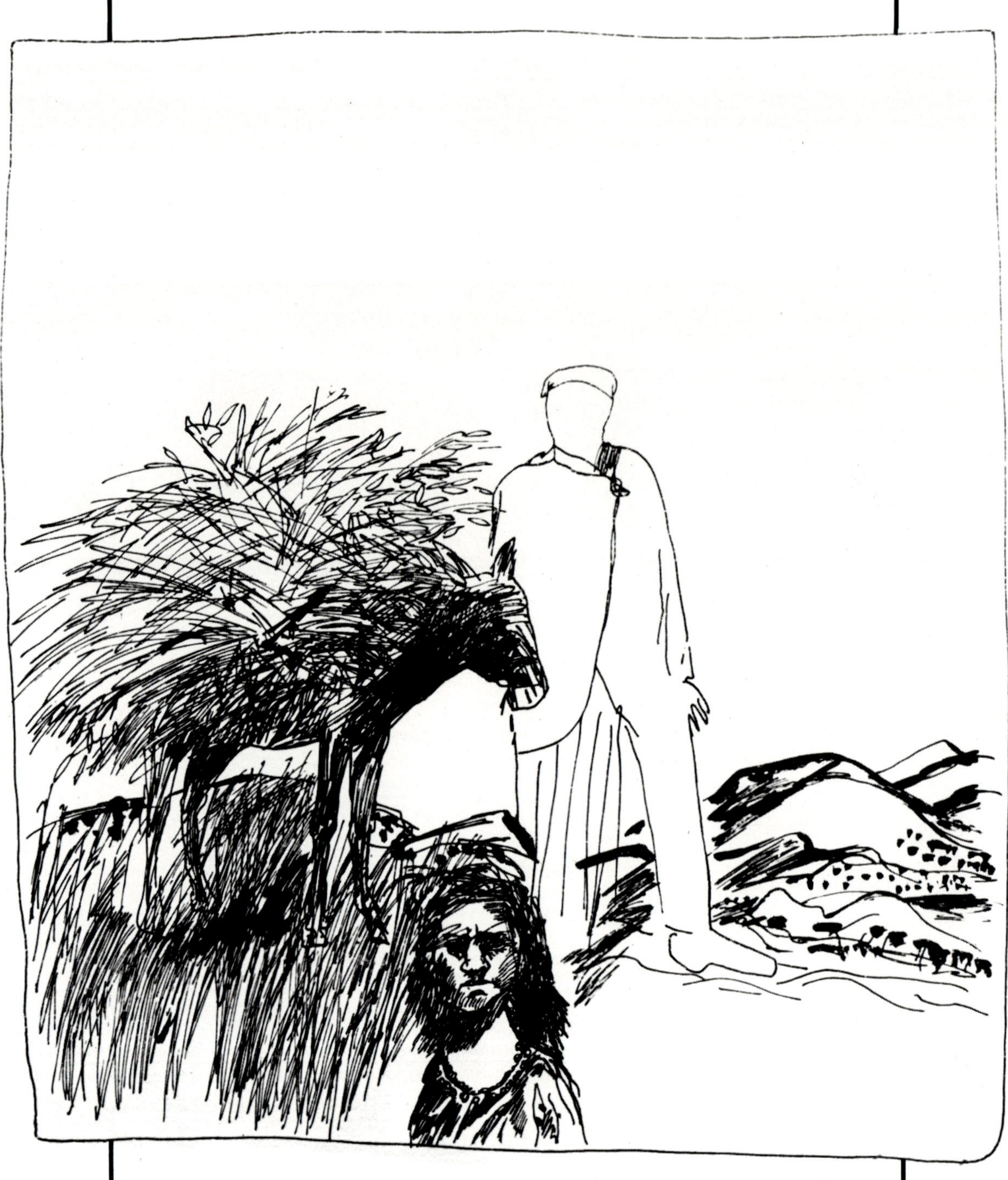

19
Kevin Connor
"Andalusian Portfolio" 1970

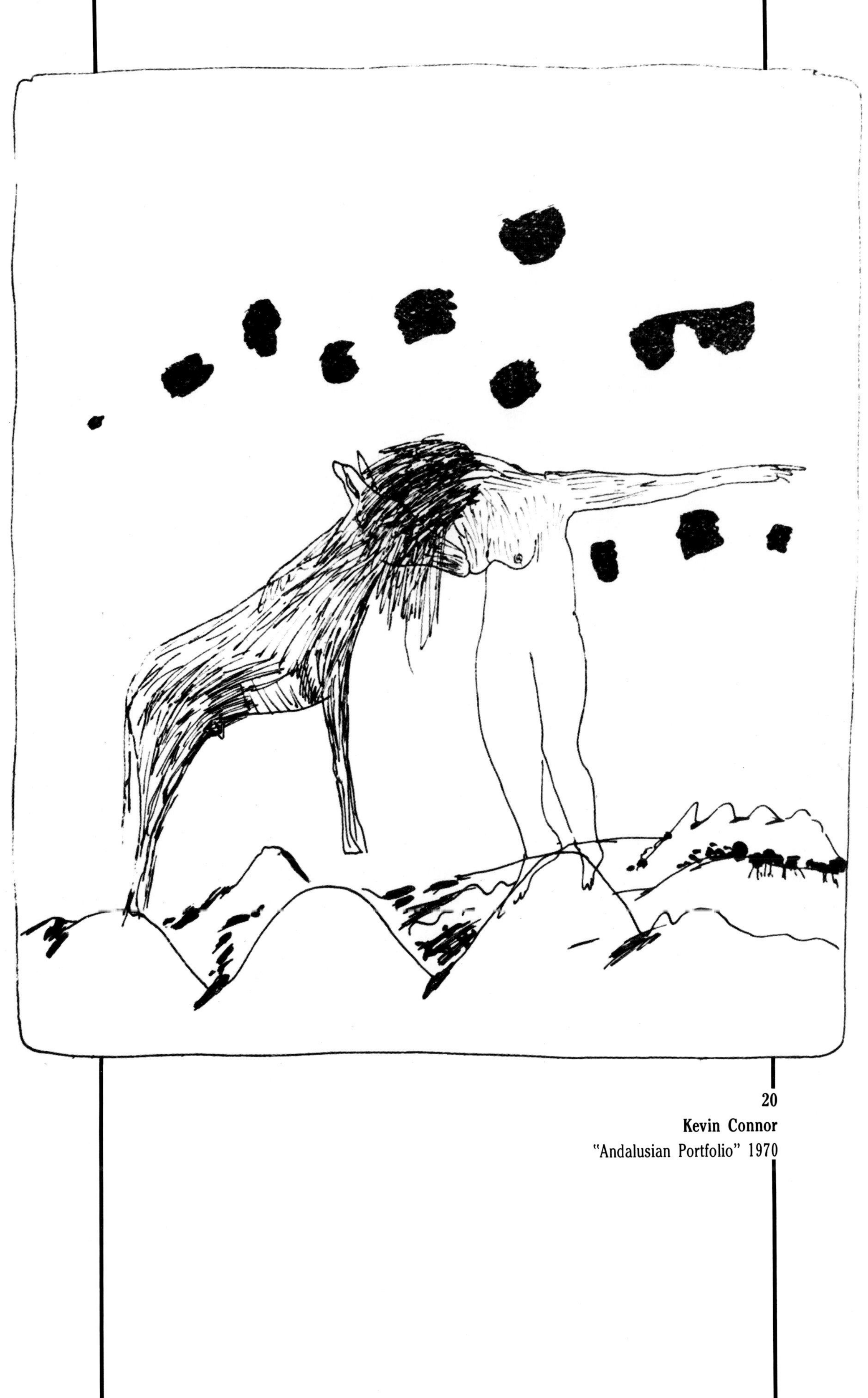

20
Kevin Connor
"Andalusian Portfolio" 1970

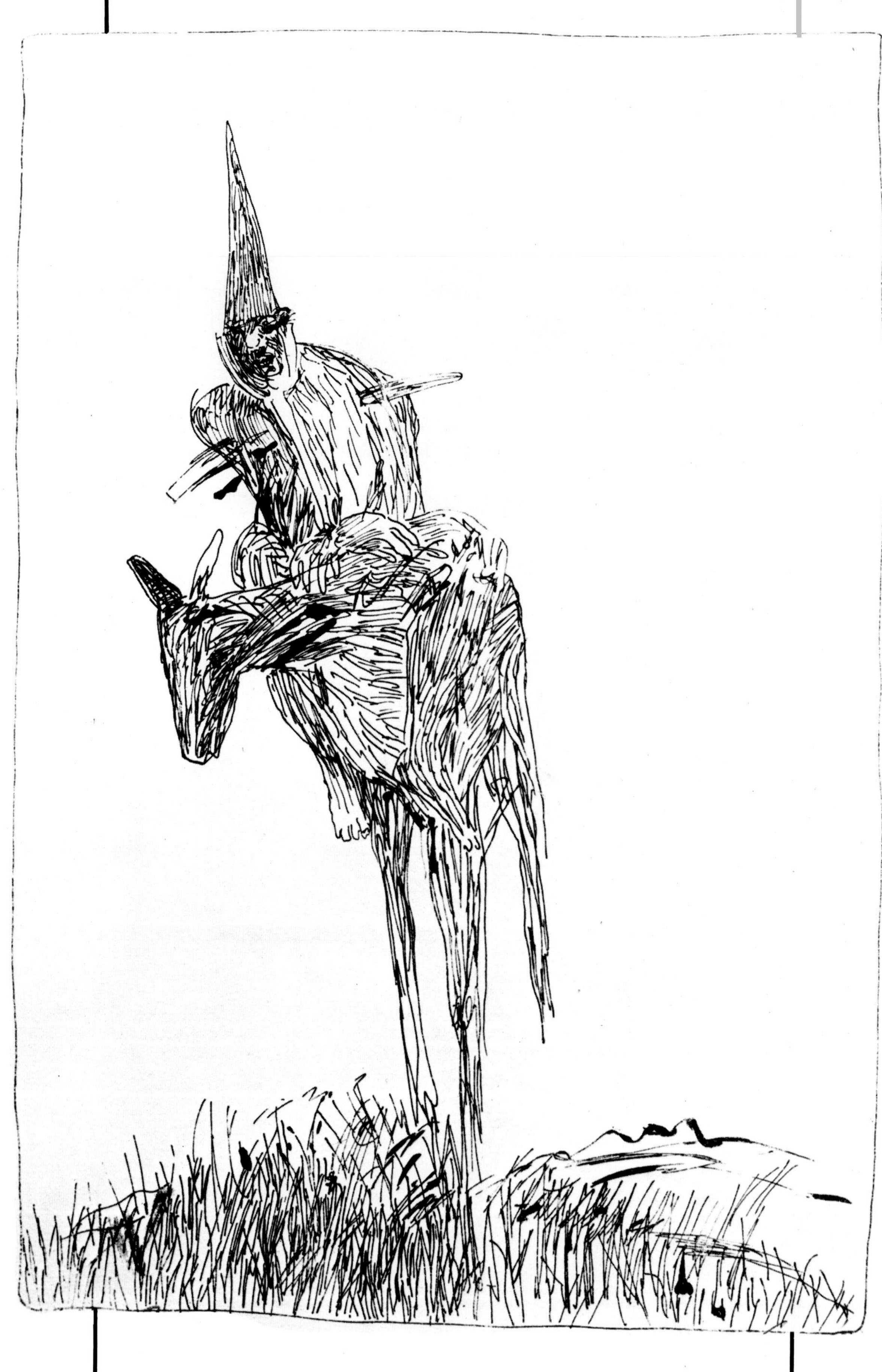

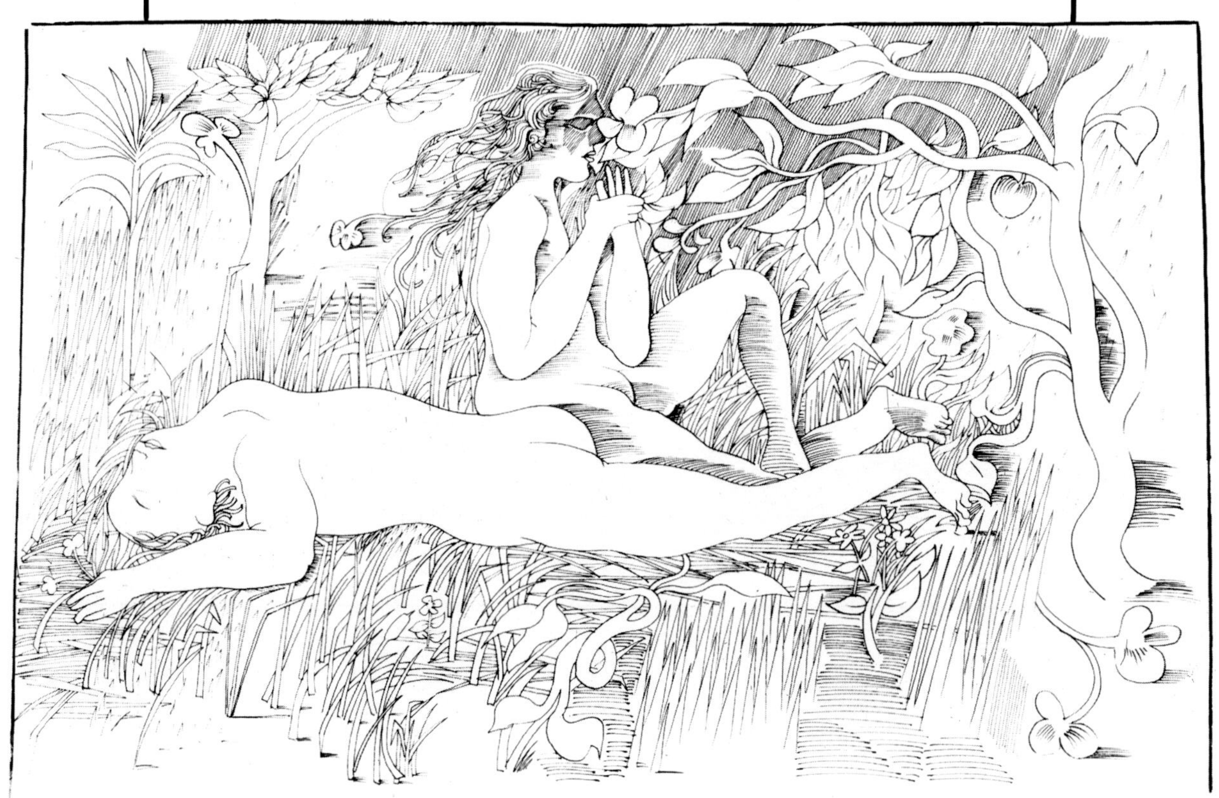

22
Charles Blackman
"Paradise Garden" 1976

21
Kevin Connor
"Andalusian Portfolio" 1970

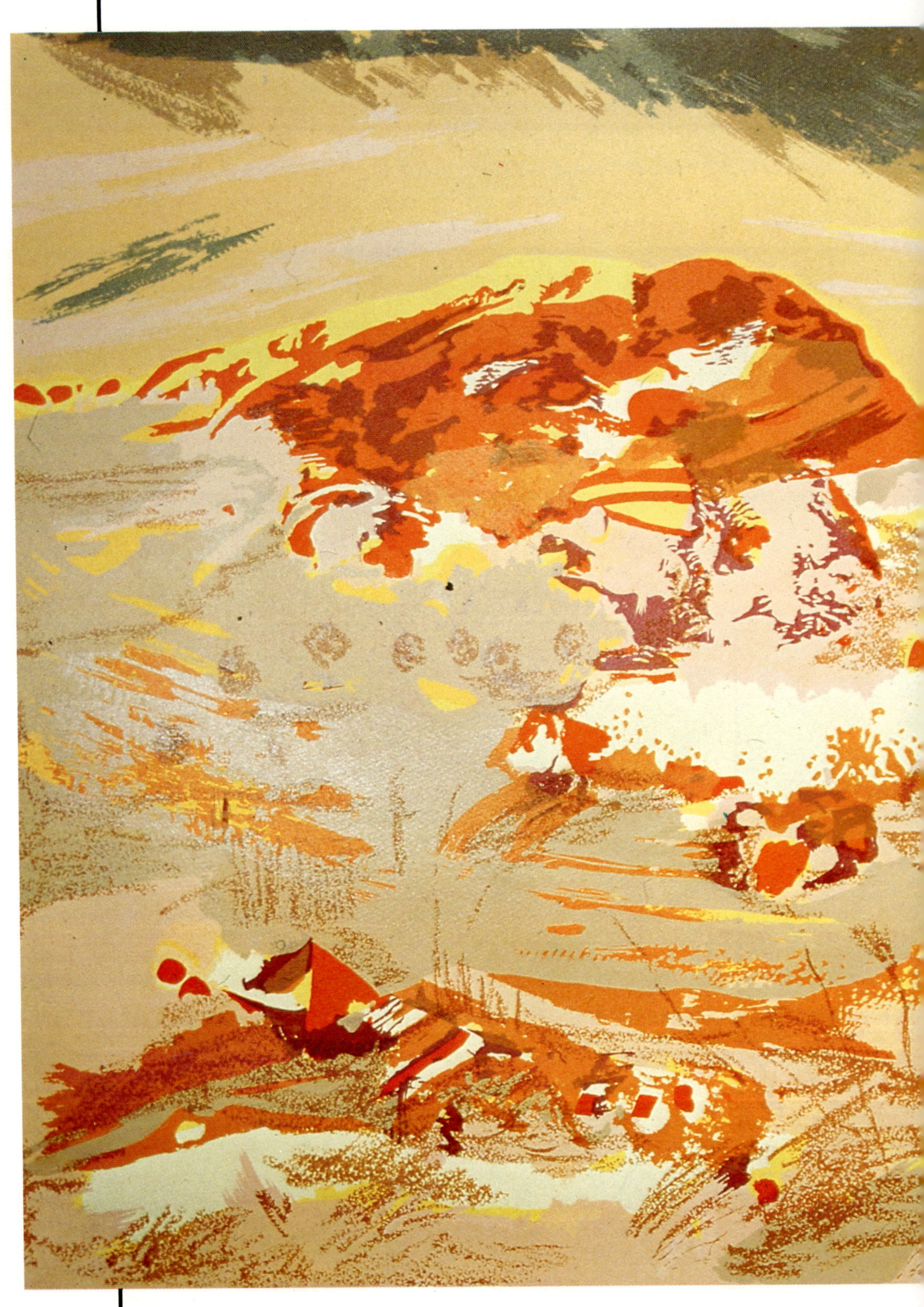

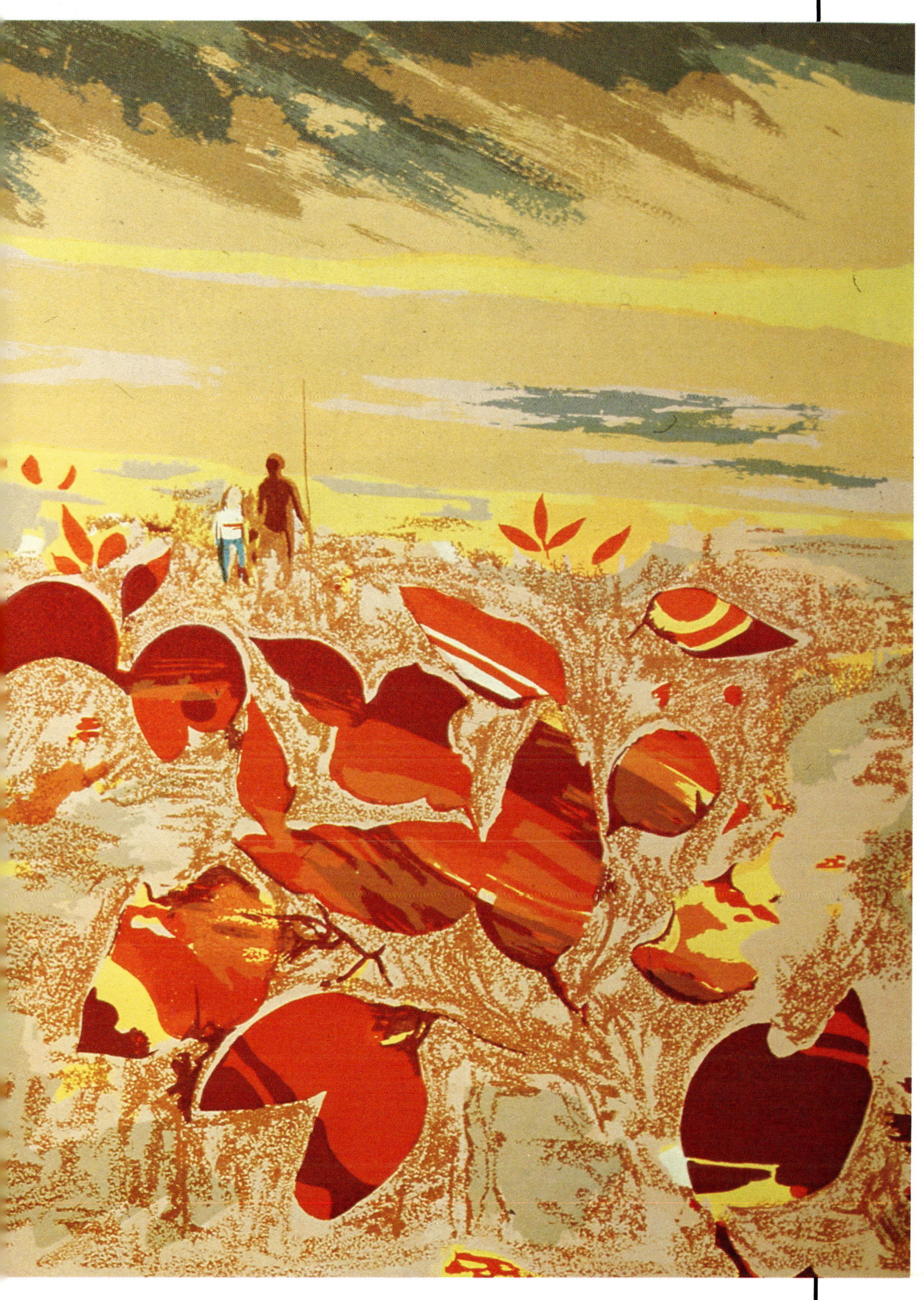

23
Robert Juniper
"Alcheringa" 1978

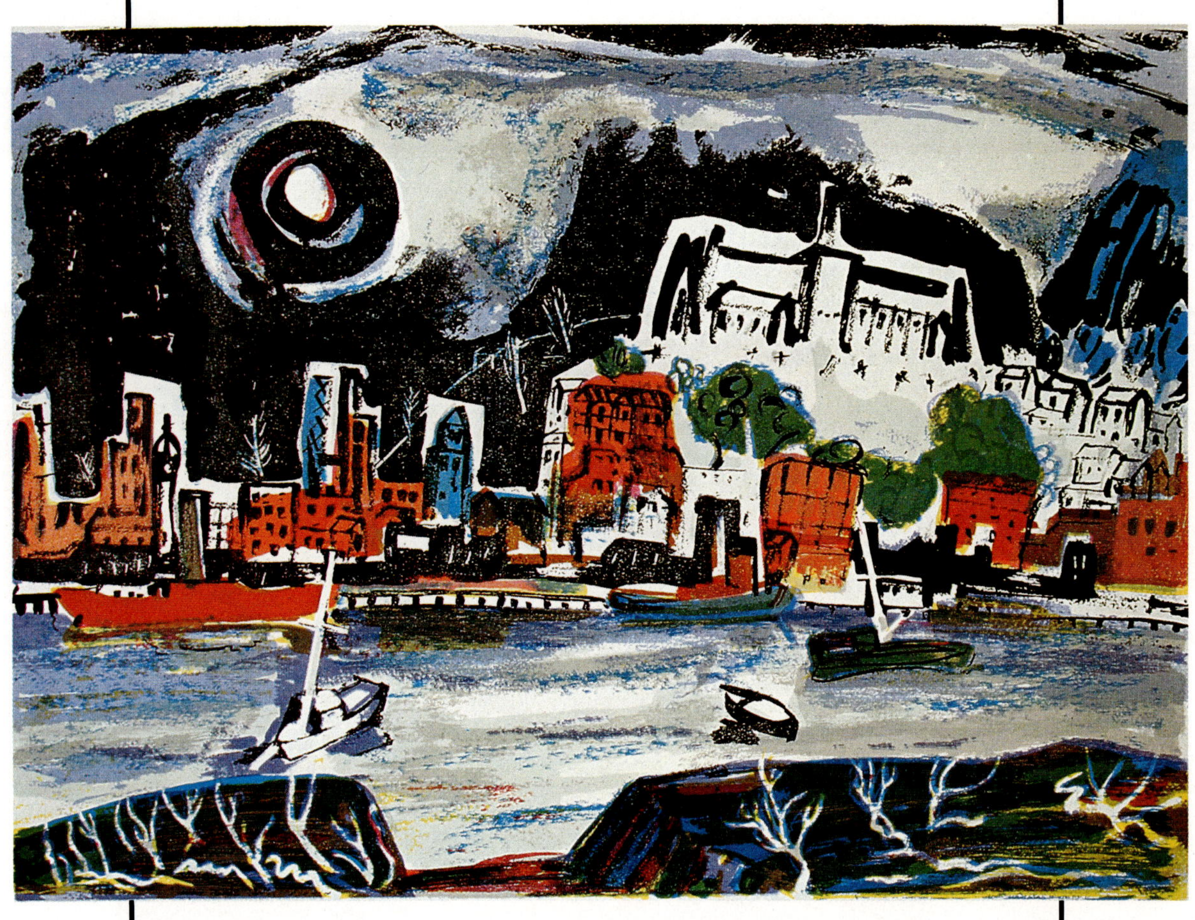

24
Mervyn Smith
"Newcastle" 1977

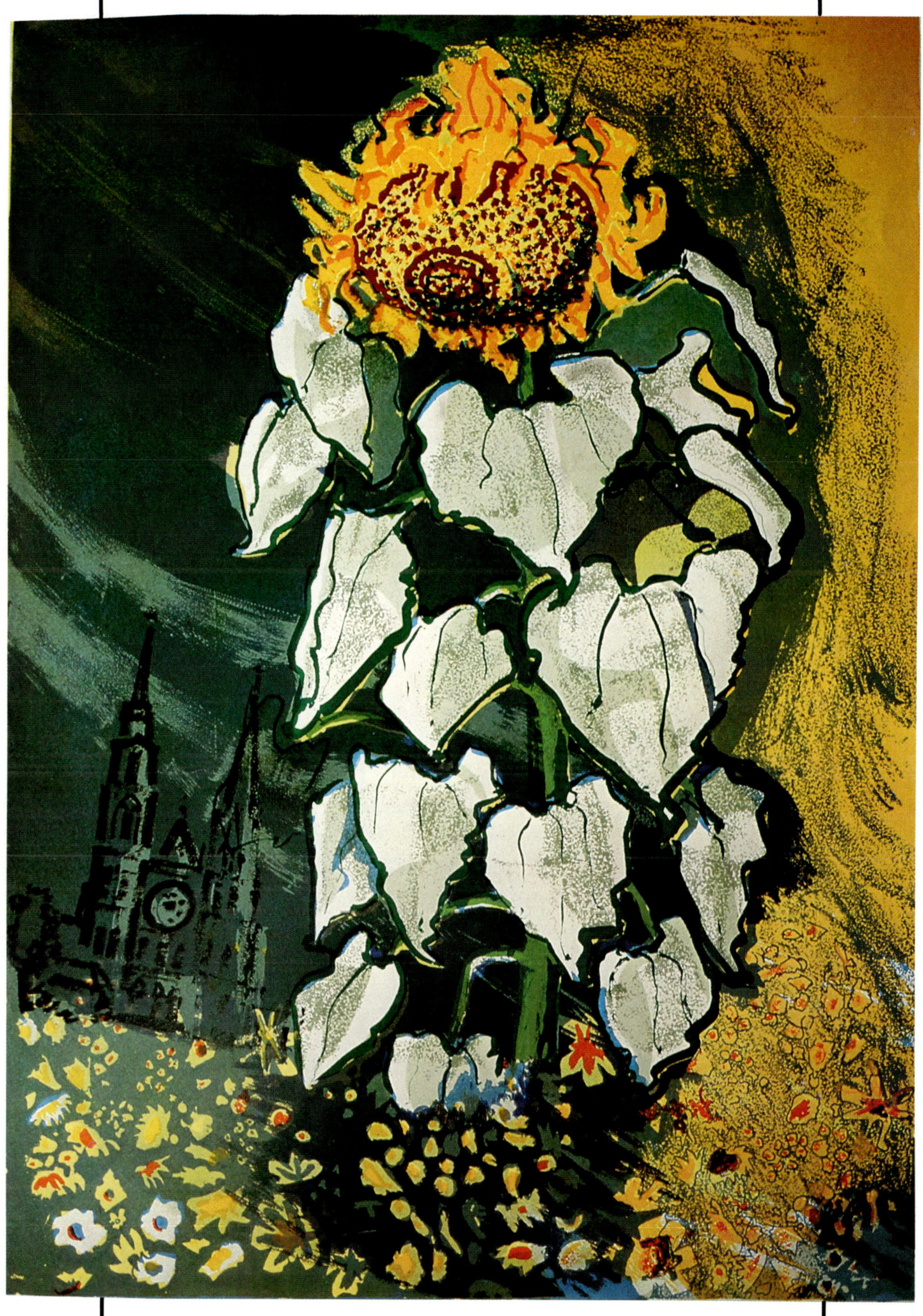

25
Mervyn Smith
"Sunflower with Cathedral" 1978

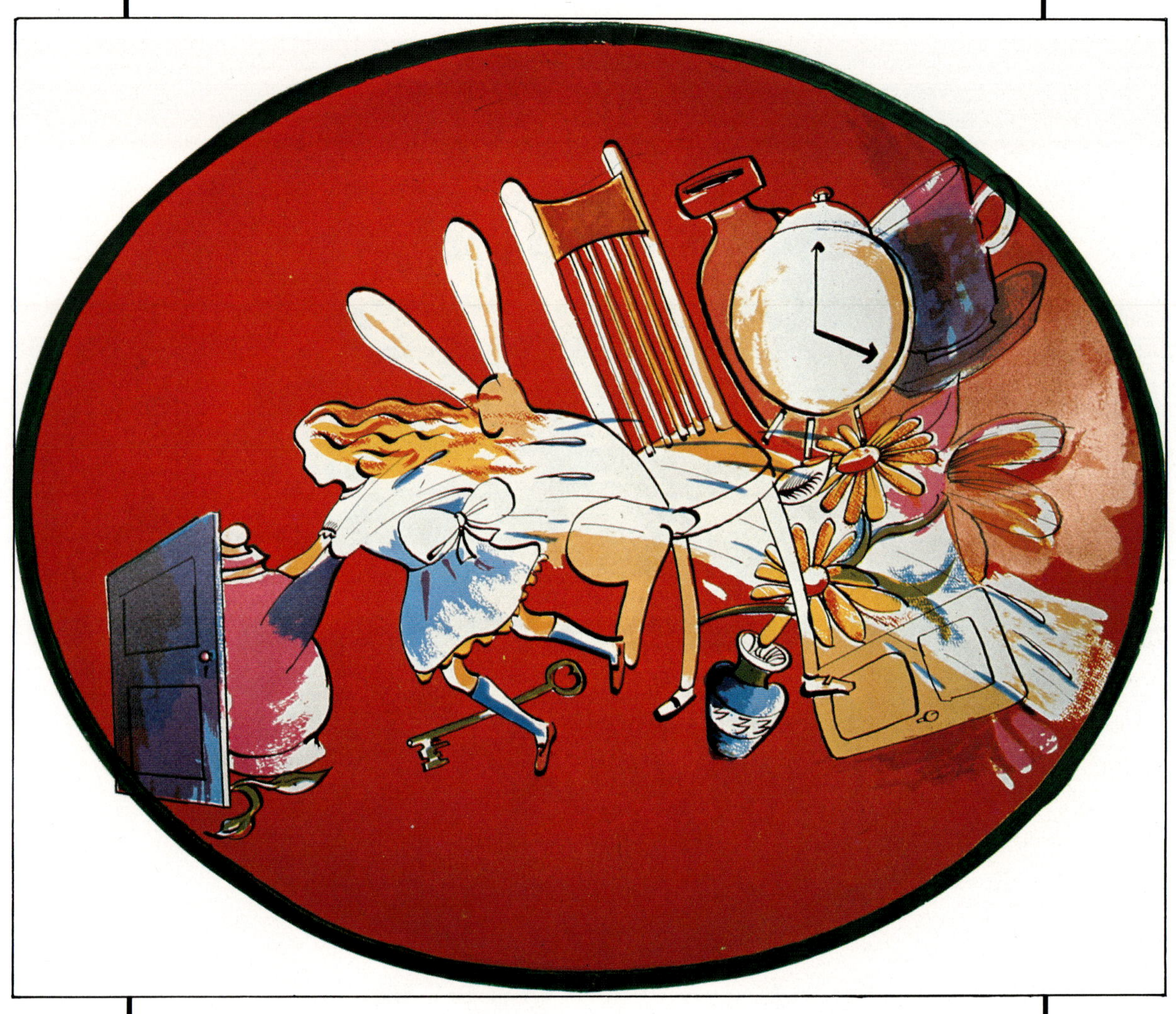

26
Charles Blackman
"Alice in Wonderland" 1977

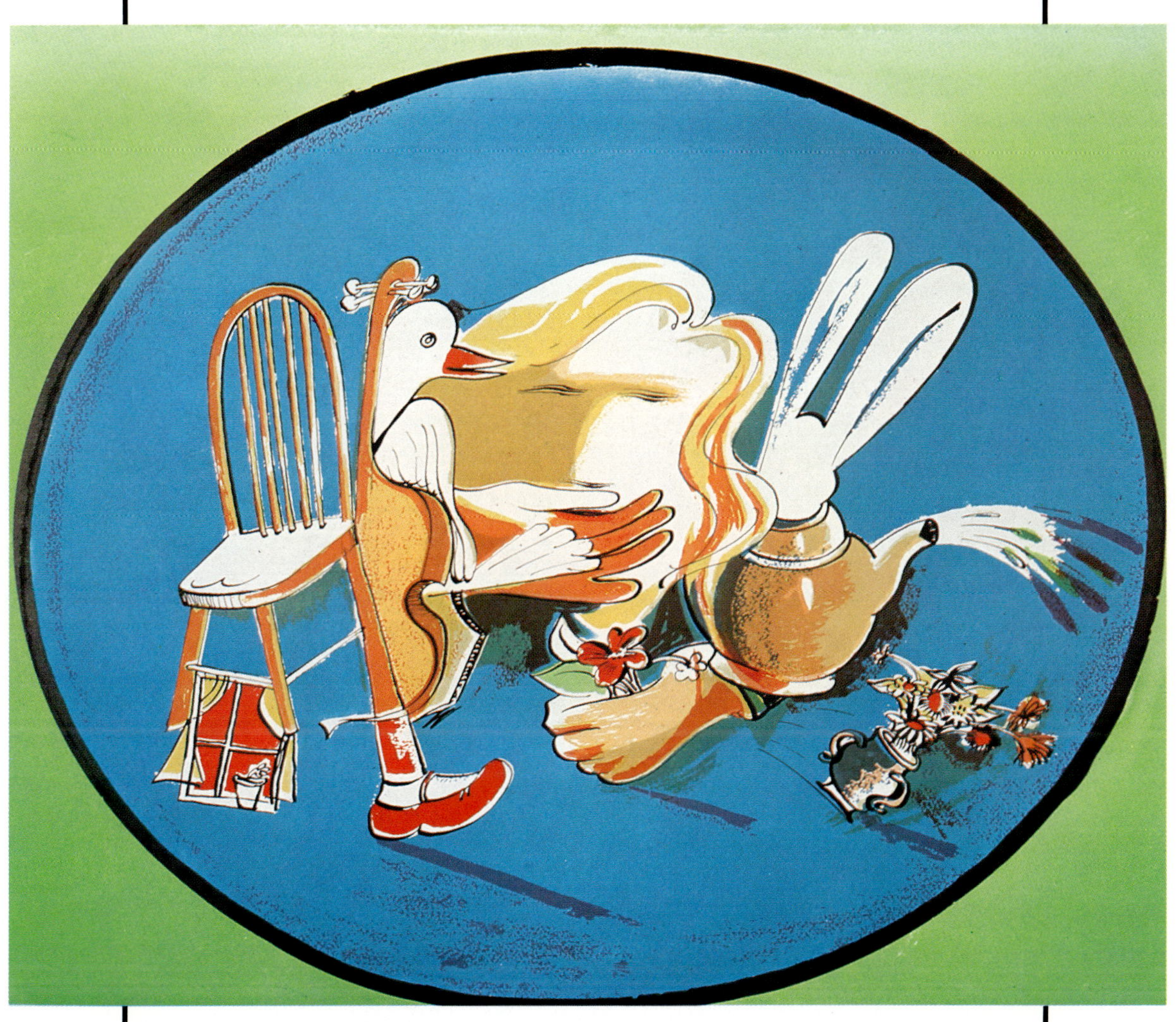

27
Charles Blackman
"Alice Through the Looking Glass" 1977

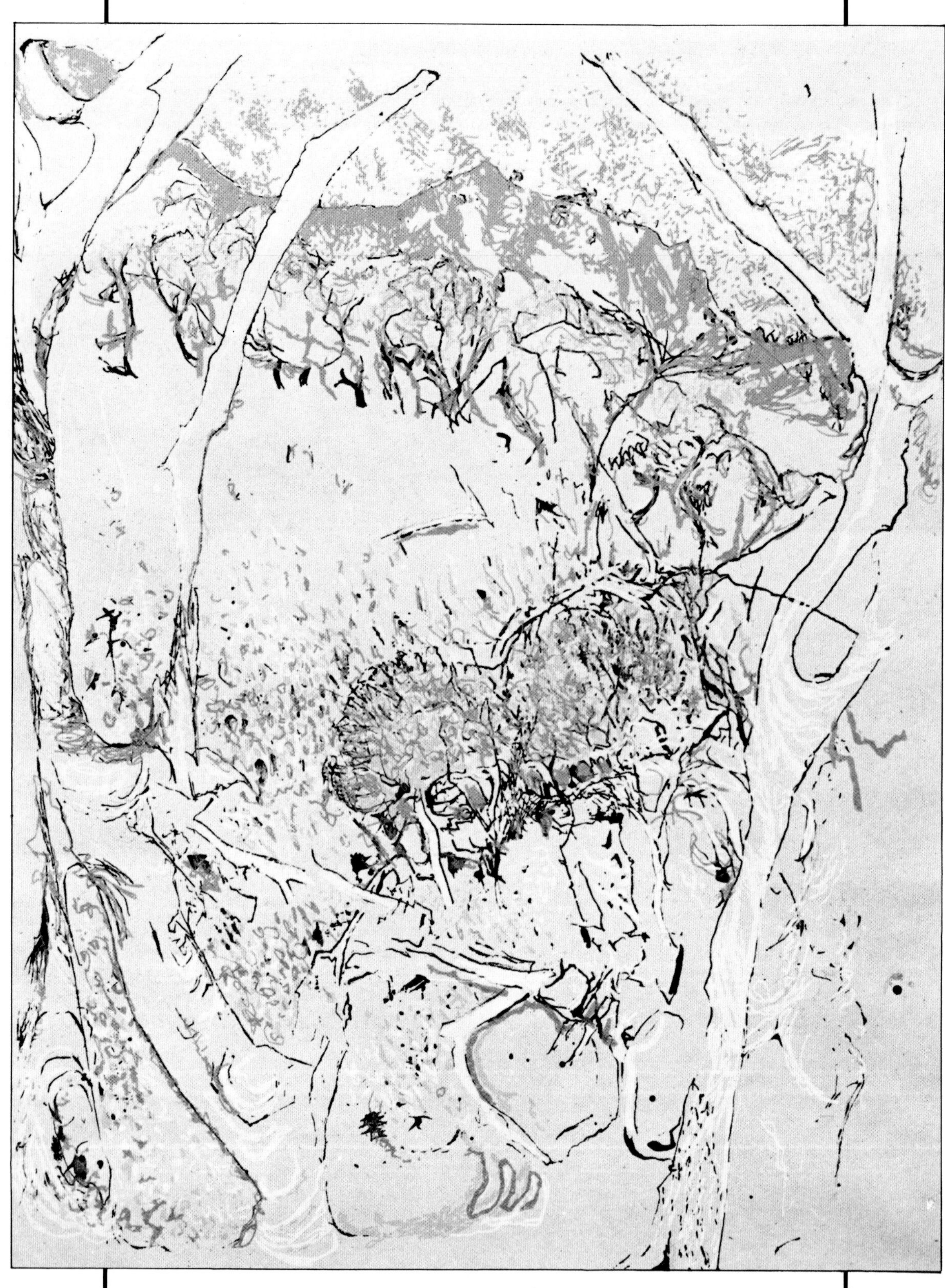

28
David Schlunke
"Temora" 1969

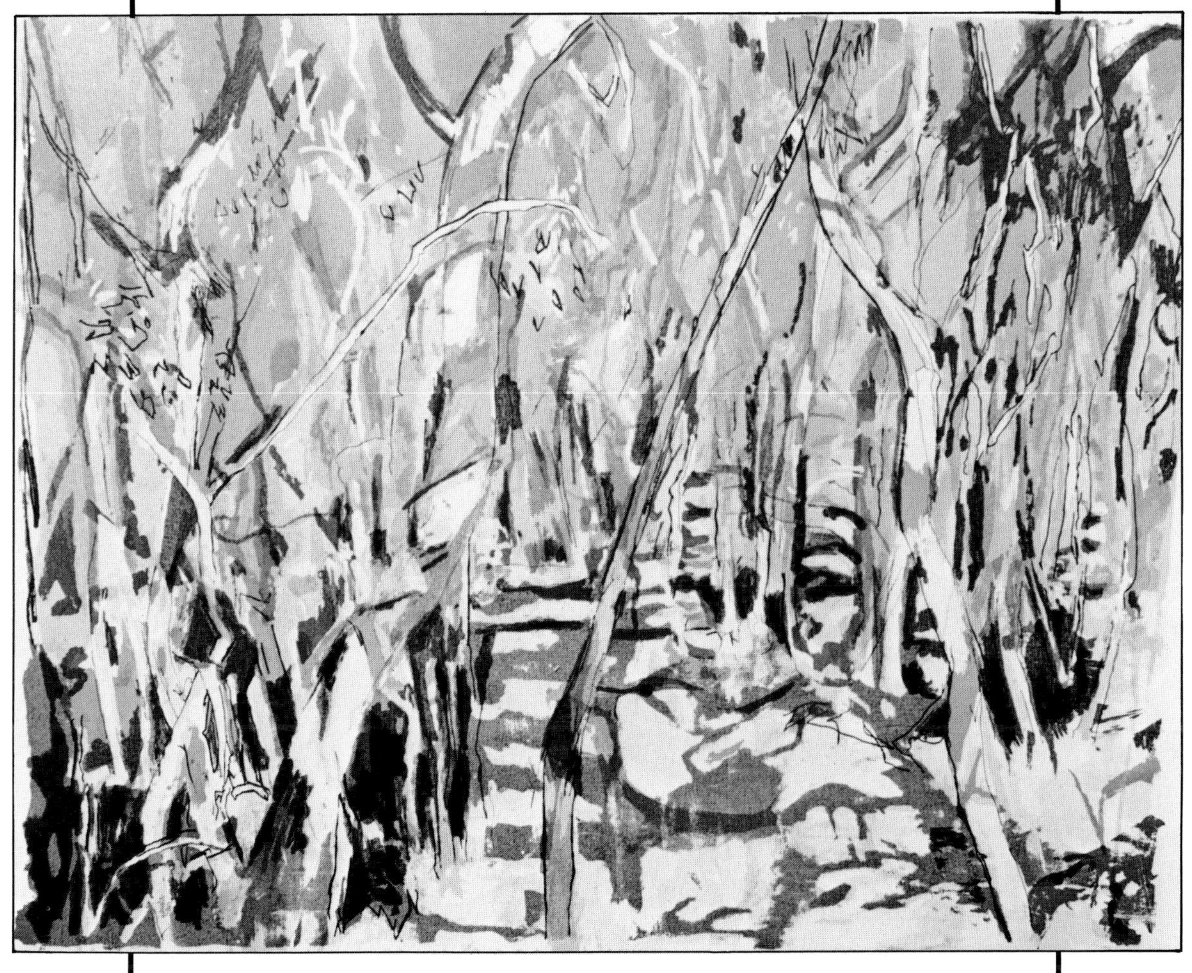

29
David Schlunke
"Mallee Study" 1969

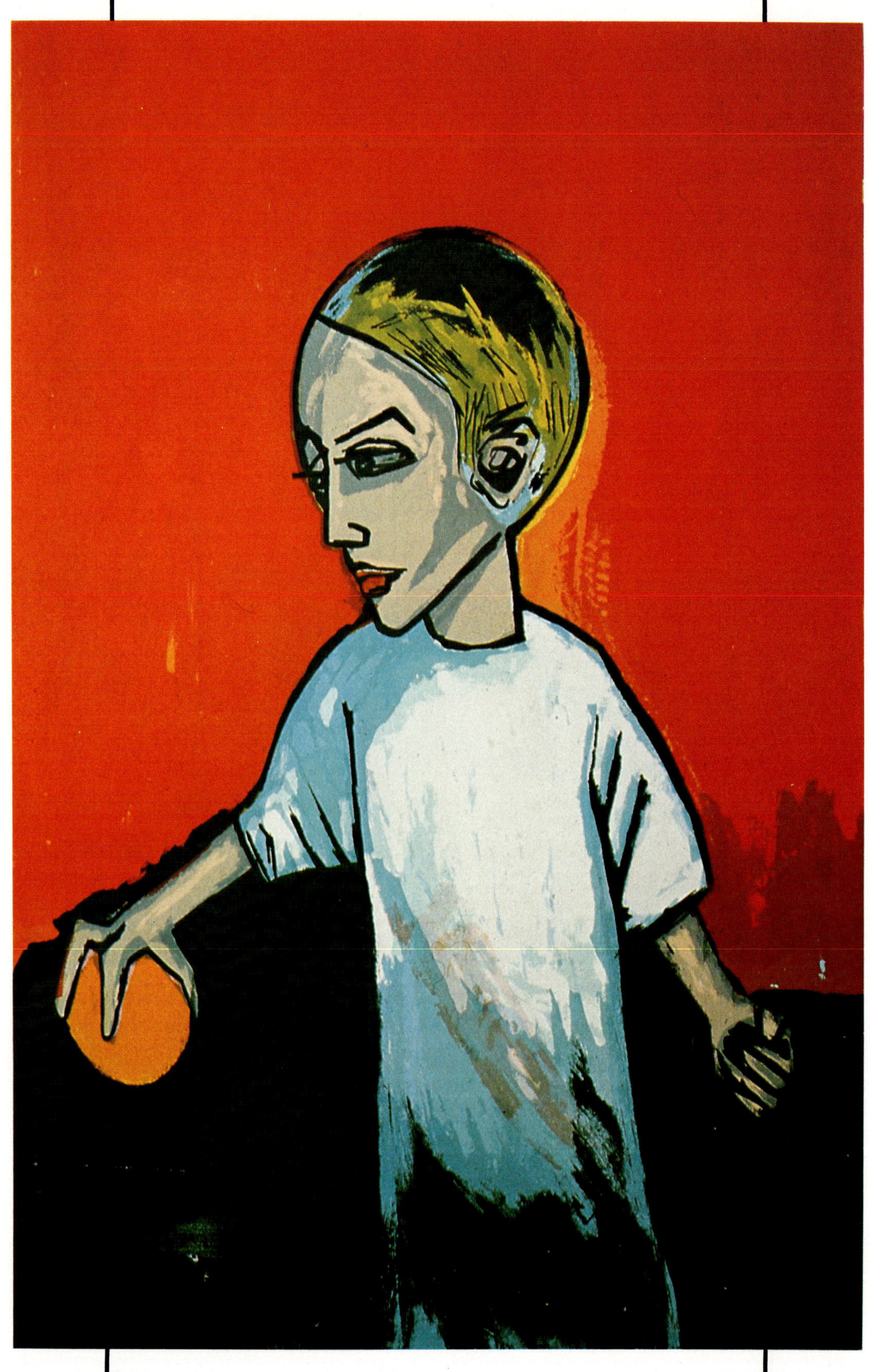

30
Robert Dickerson
"The Orange Ball" 1969

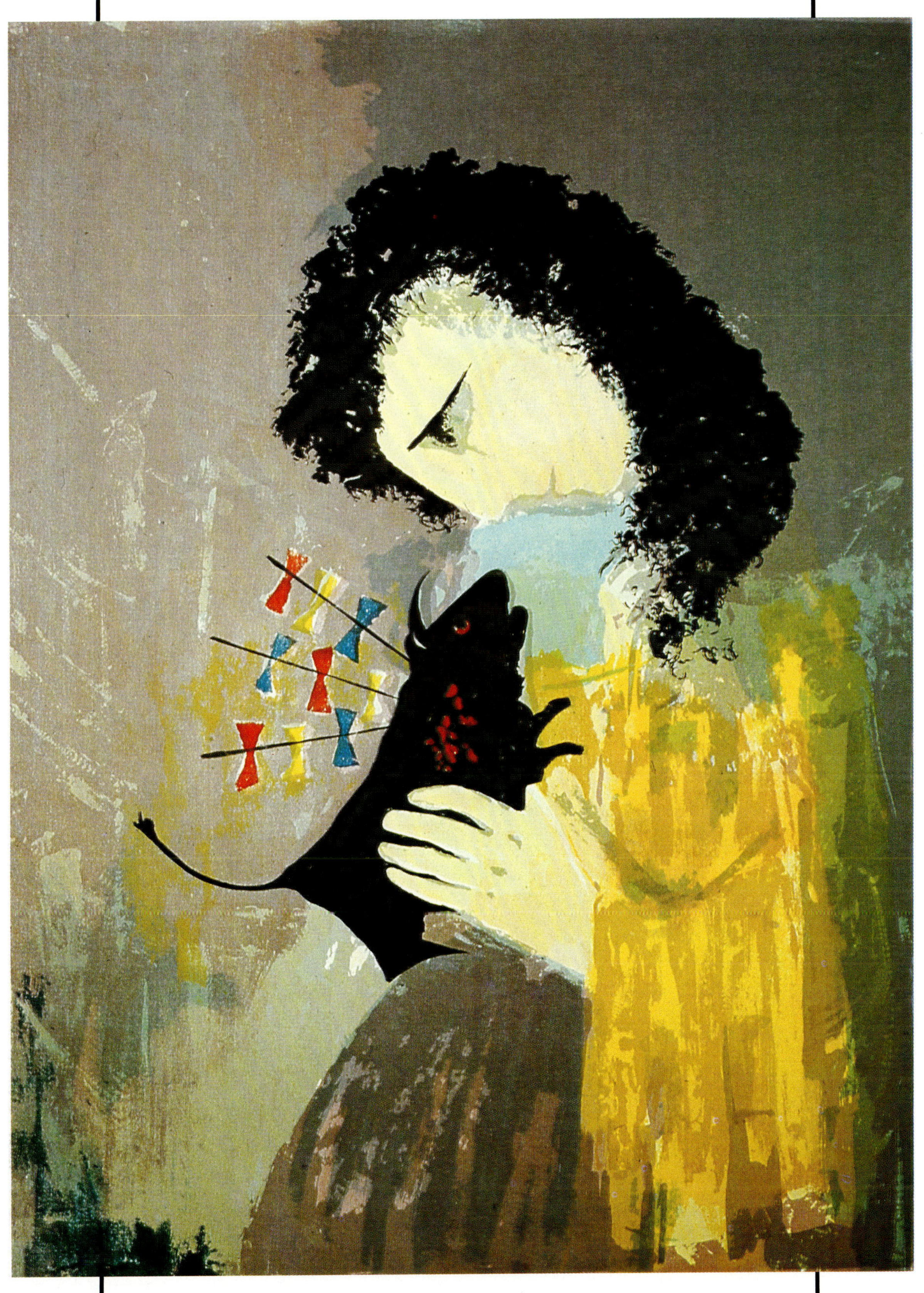

31
David Boyd
"Bull Effigy" 1969

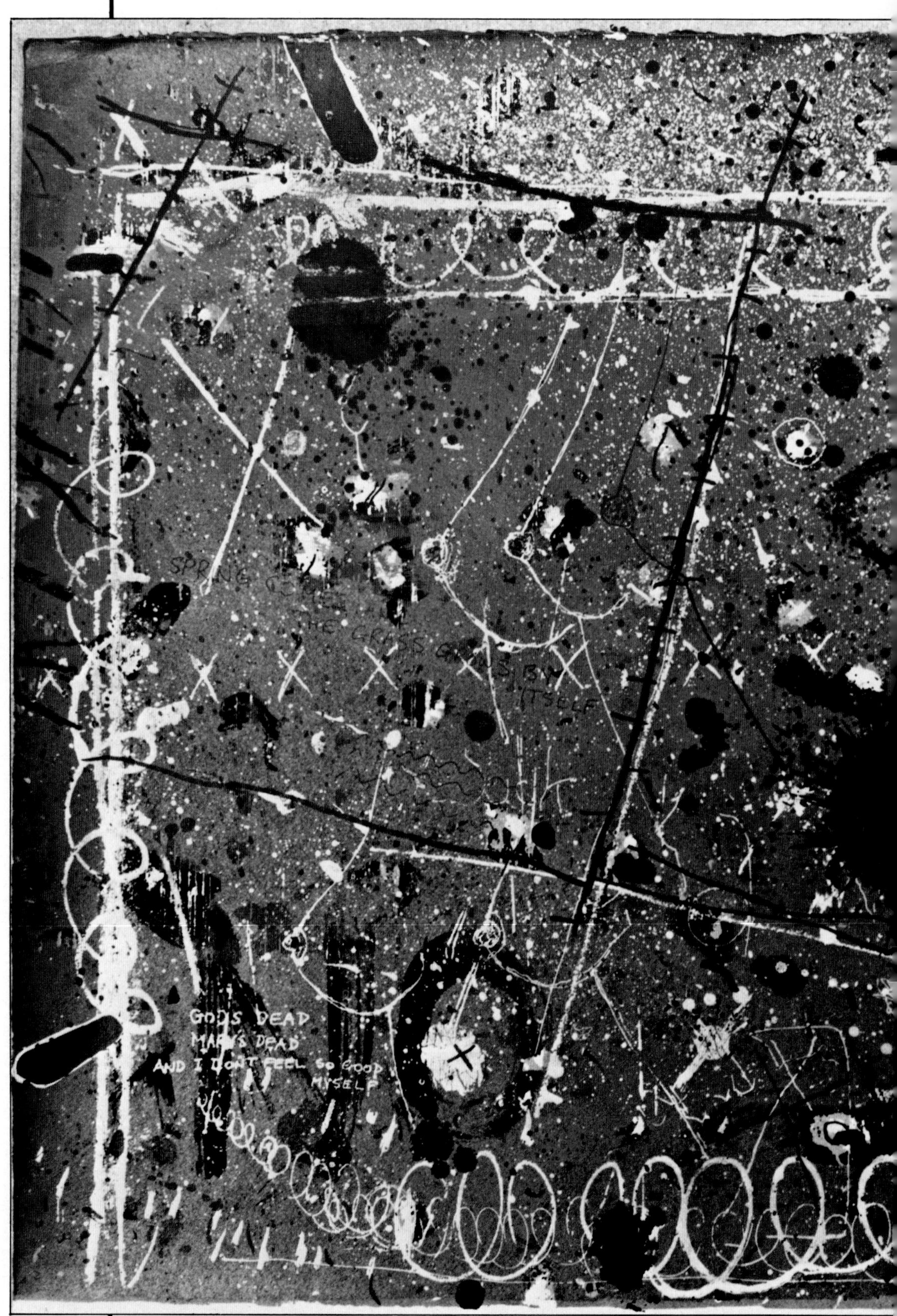

GOD'S DEAD
MARY'S DEAD
AND I DON'T FEEL SO GOOD
MYSELF

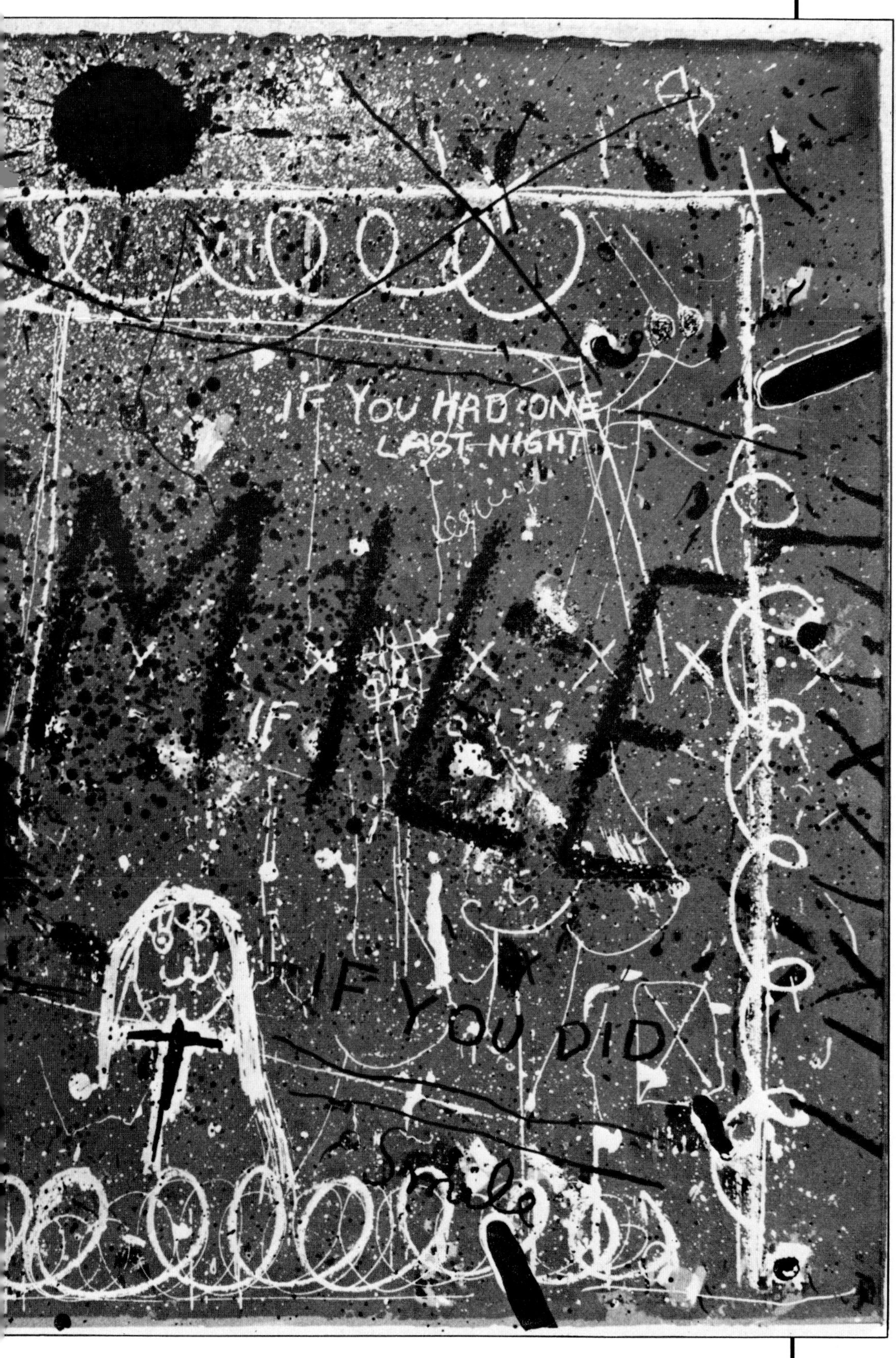

32
Basil Hadley
"Smile" 1979

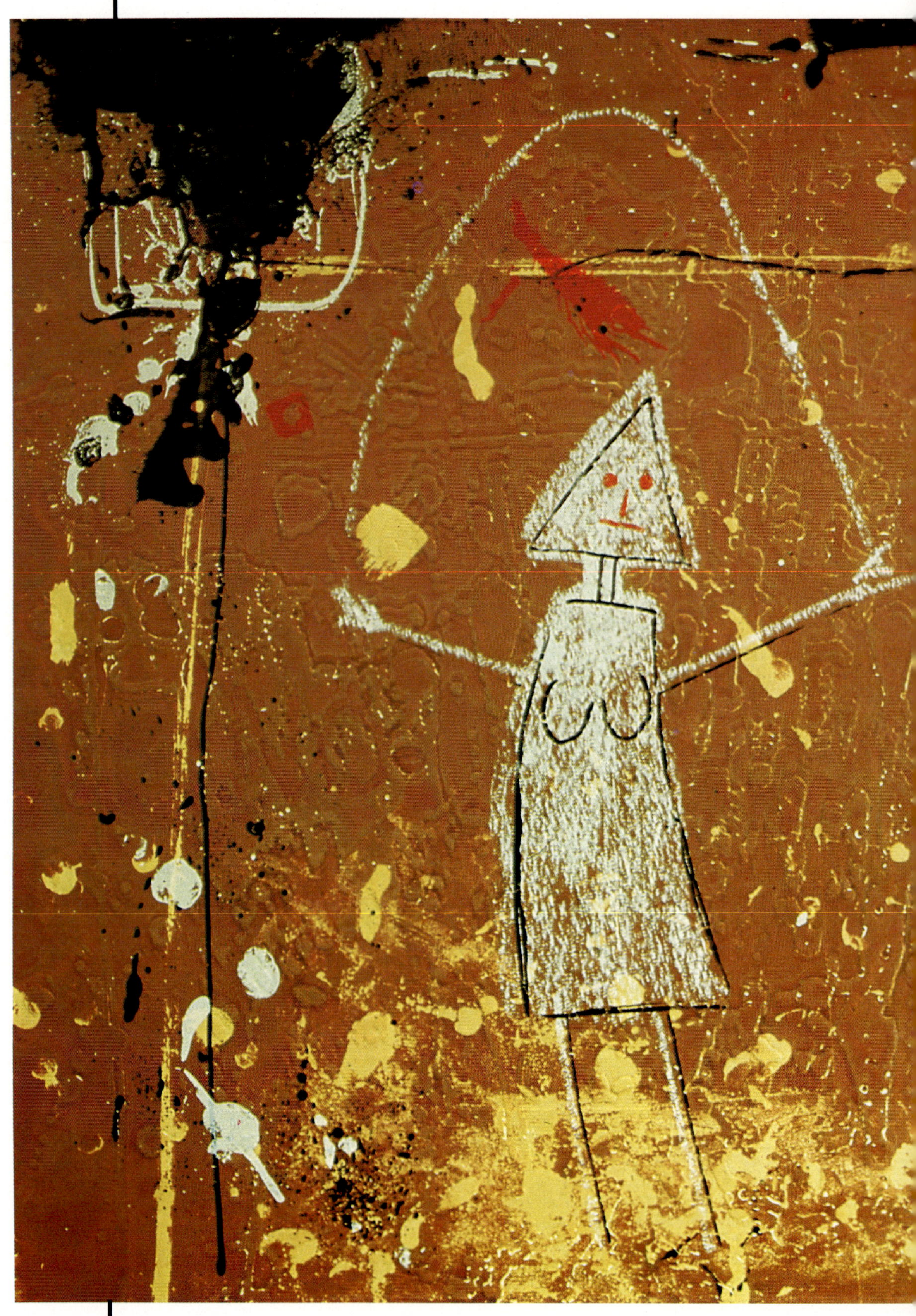

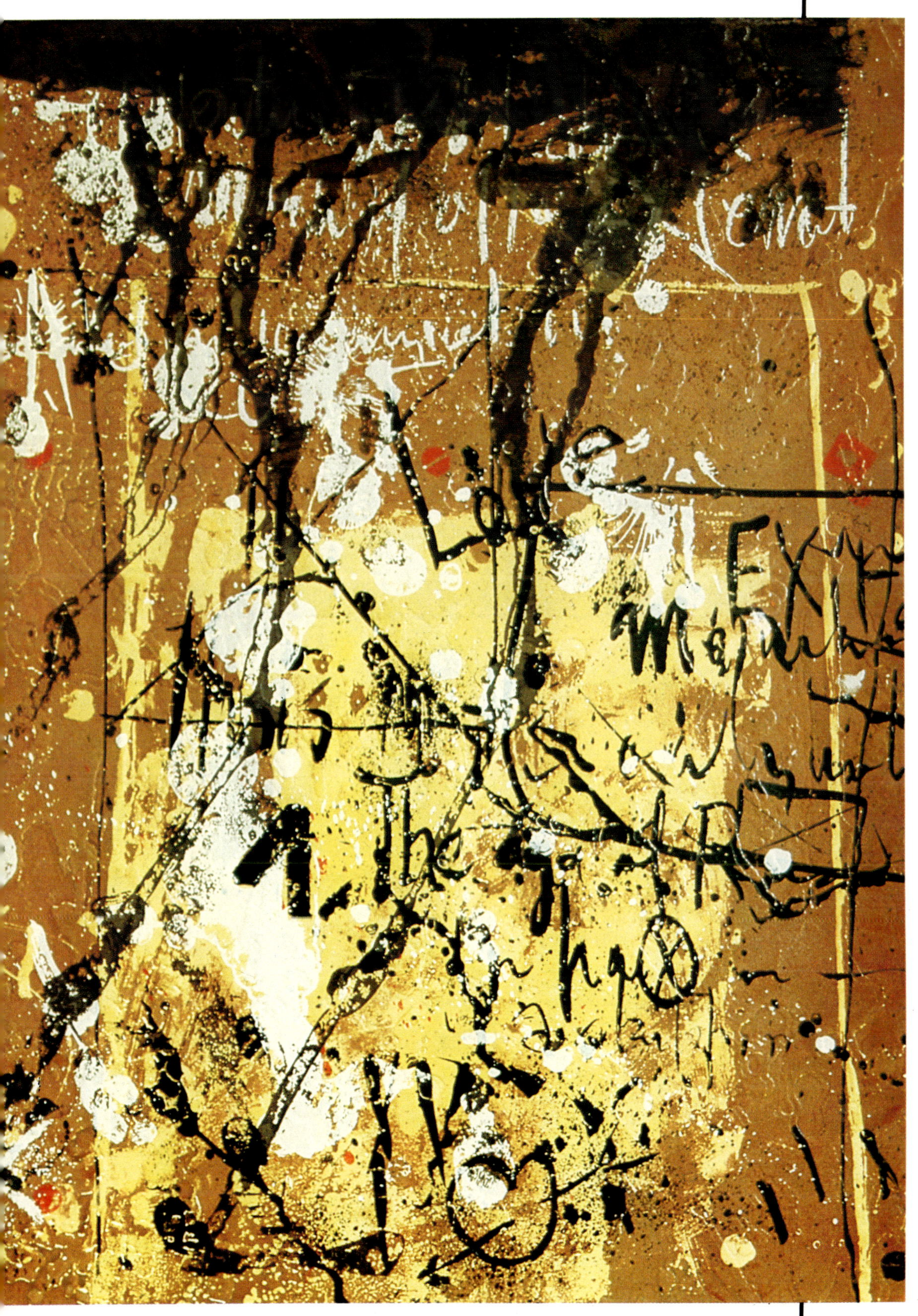

33
Basil Hadley
"Skipping Girl Wall" 1978

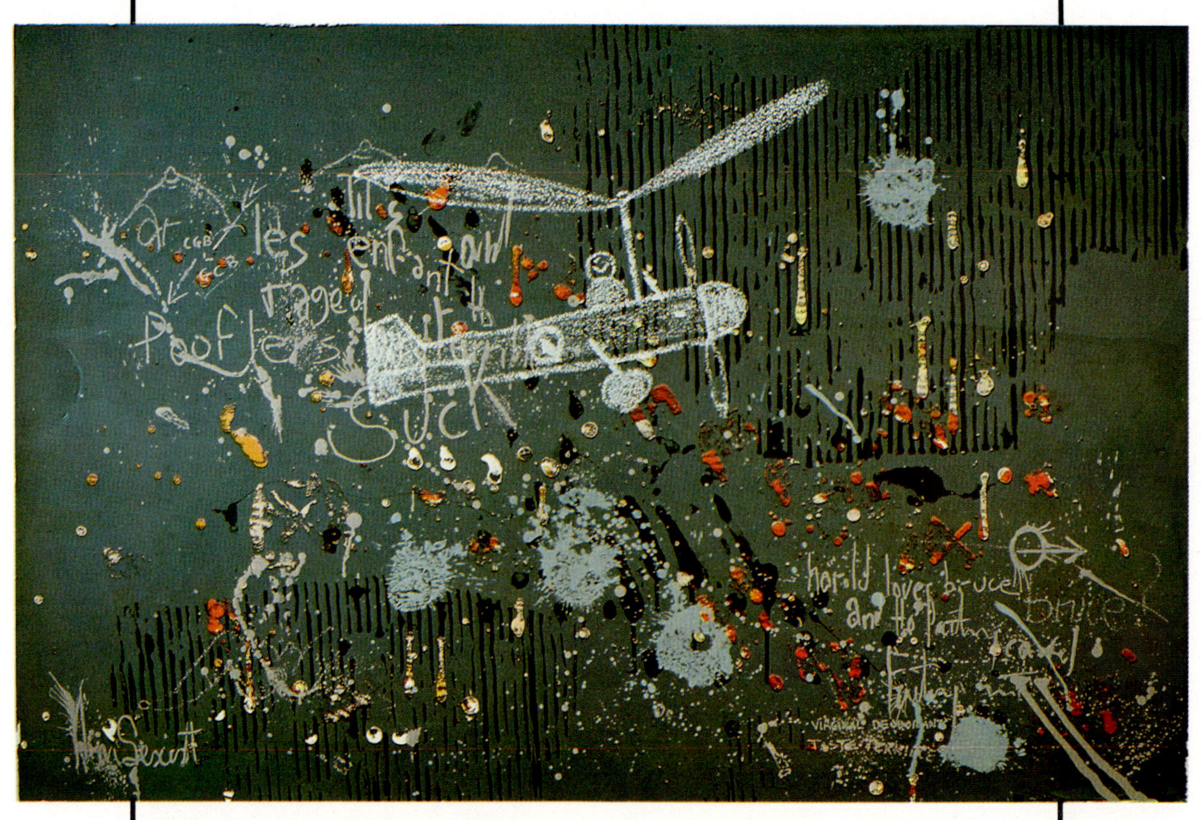

34
Basil Hadley
"Wall Theme VII" 1978

35
Basil Hadley
"Wall Theme VIII" 1978

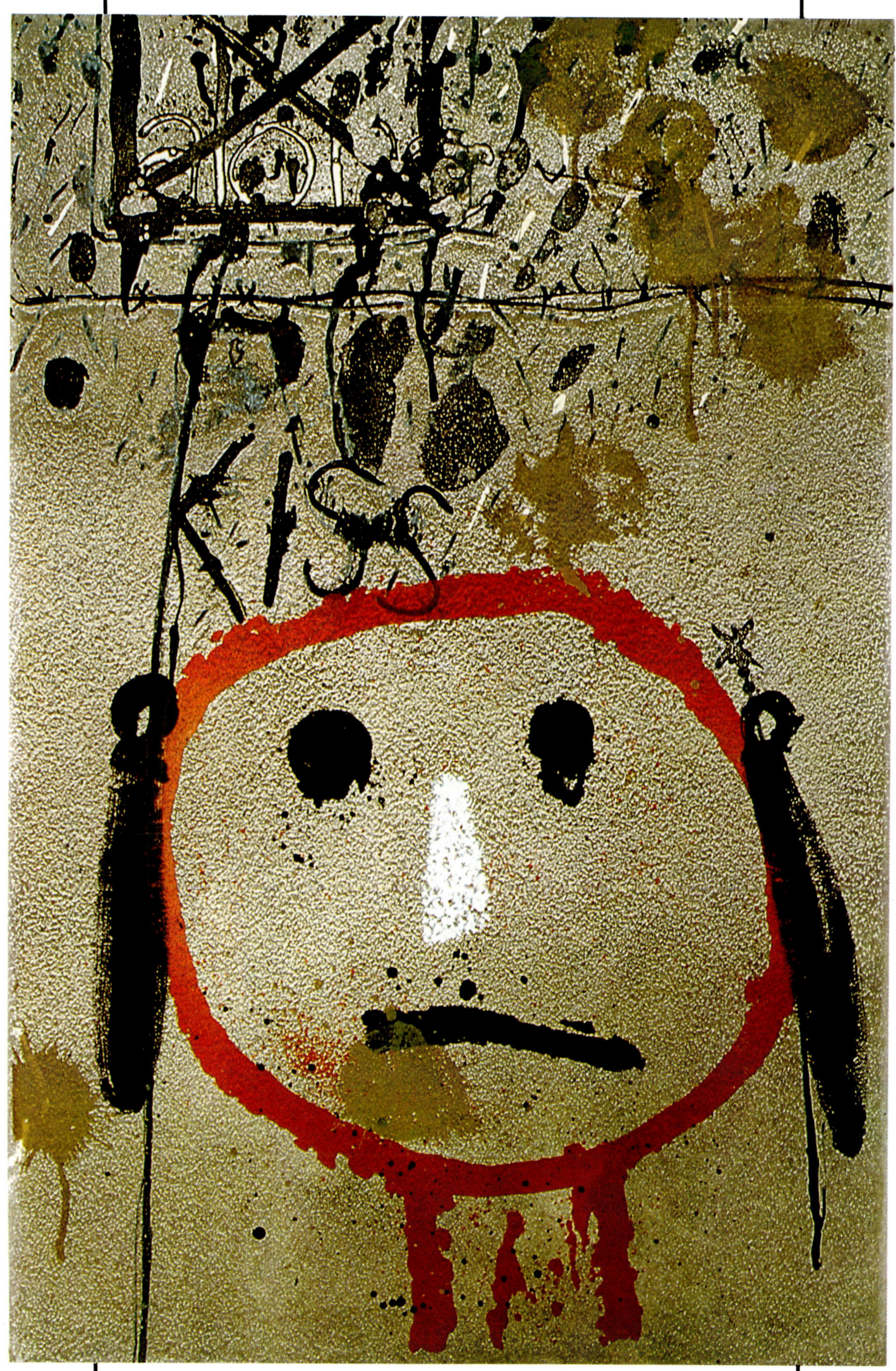

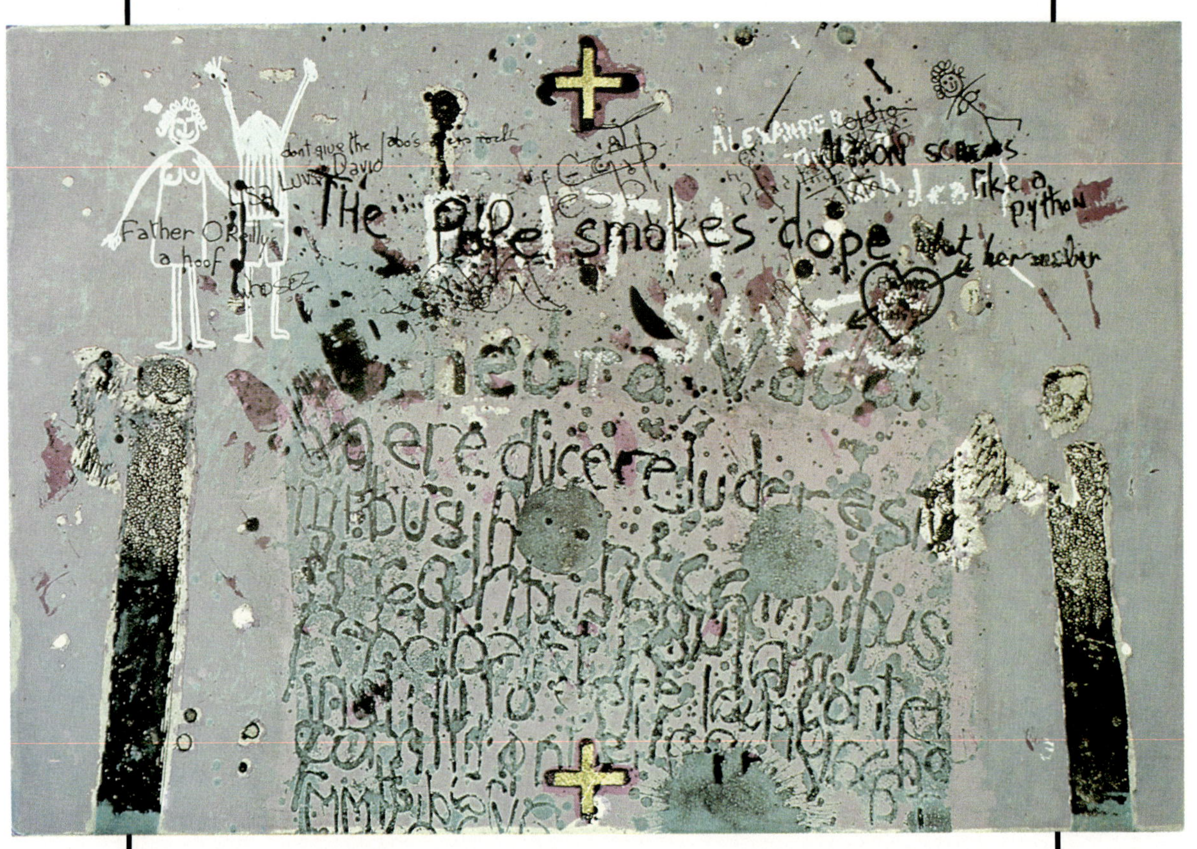

36
Basil Hadley
"Wall Theme IX" 1978

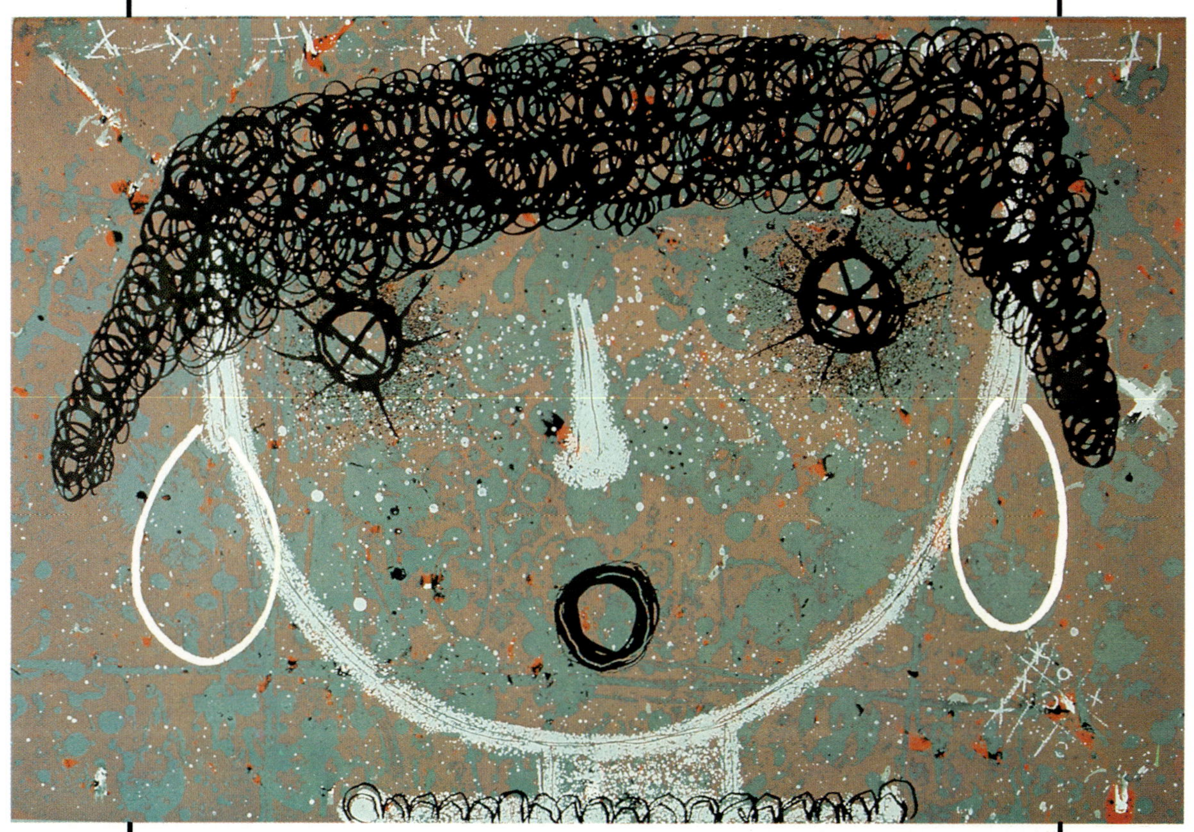

37
Basil Hadley
"Girl with Ear-rings" 1979

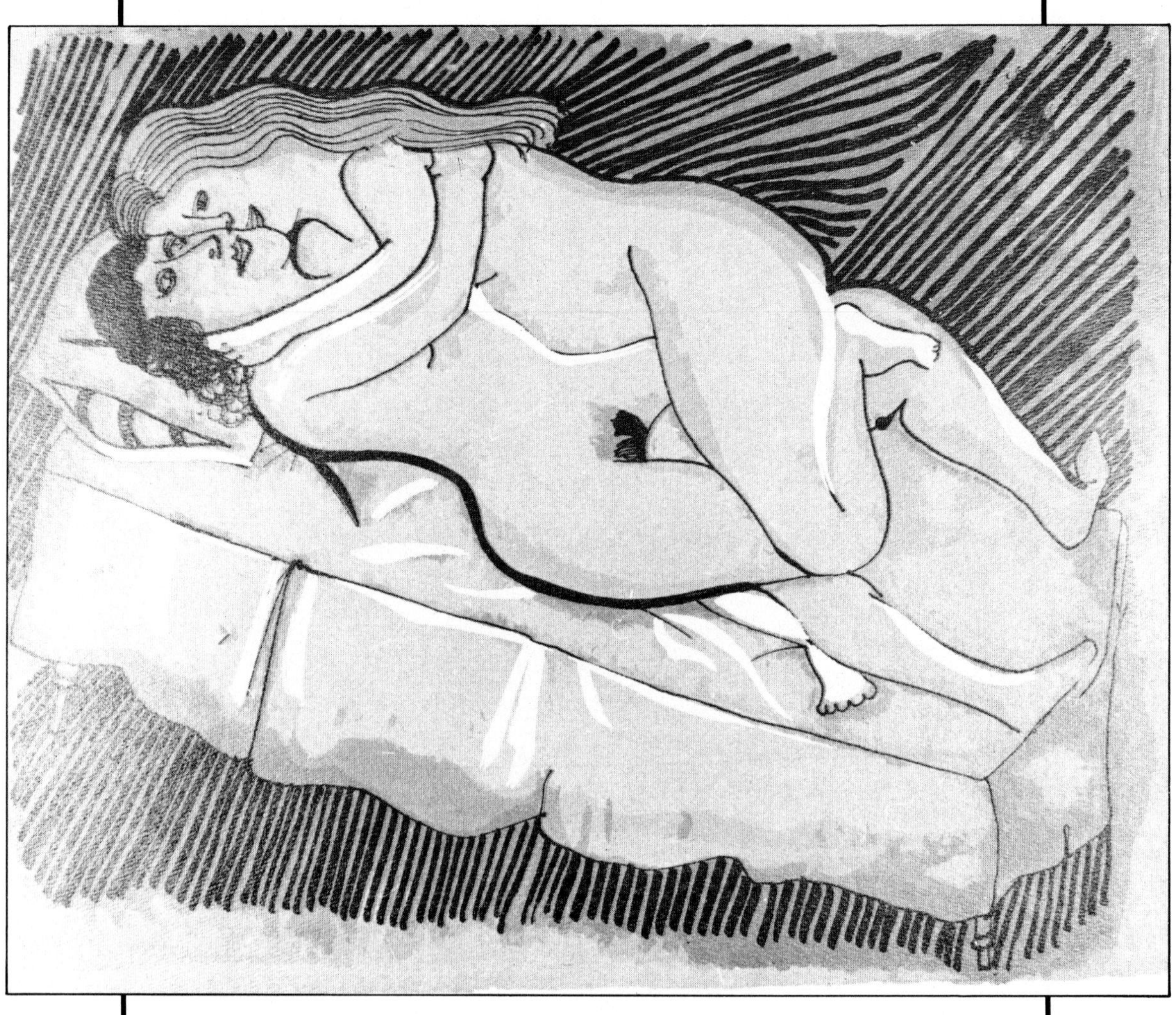

38
Charles Blackman
"The Embrace" 1969

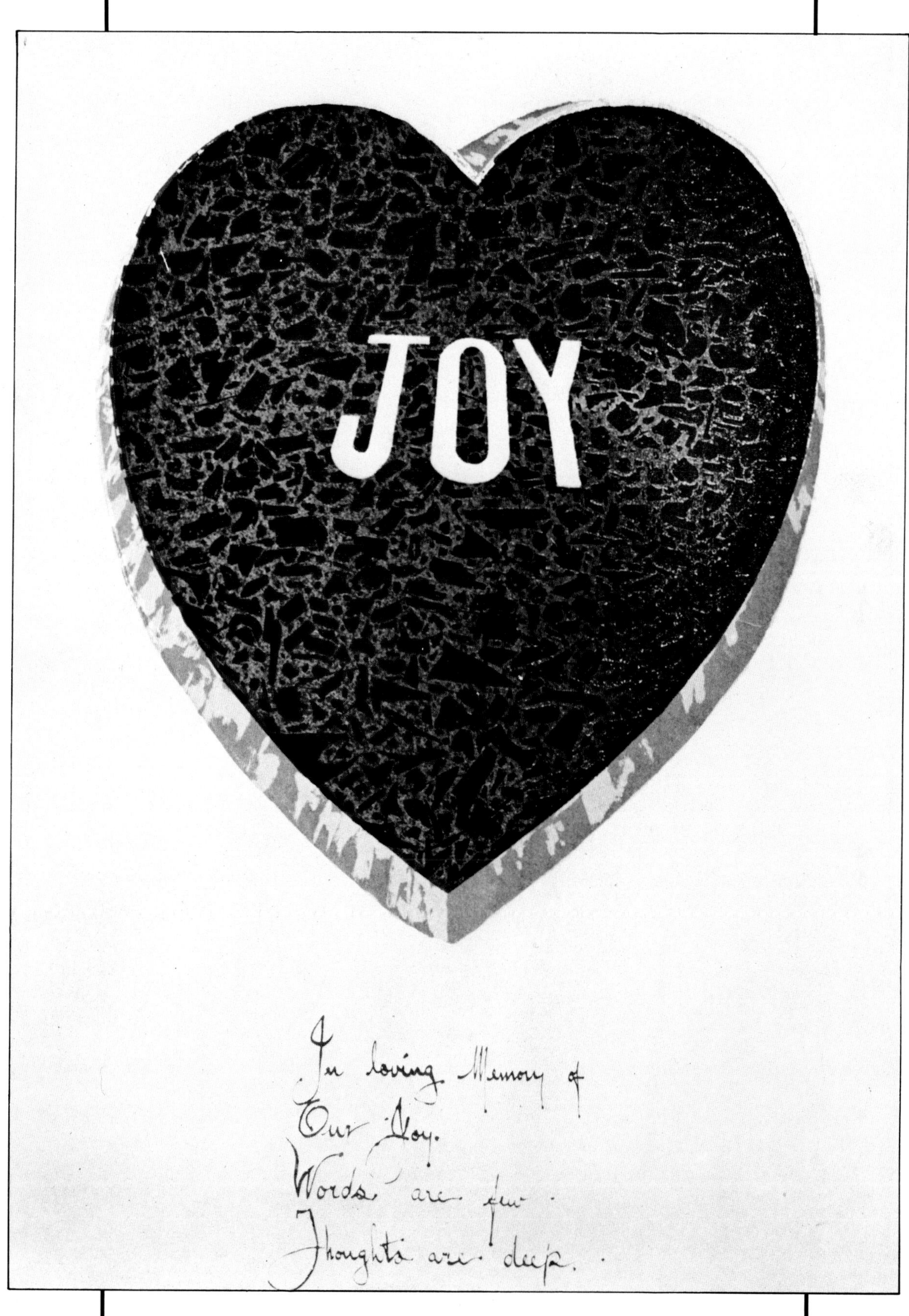

39
Richard Tipping
"Joy" 1978

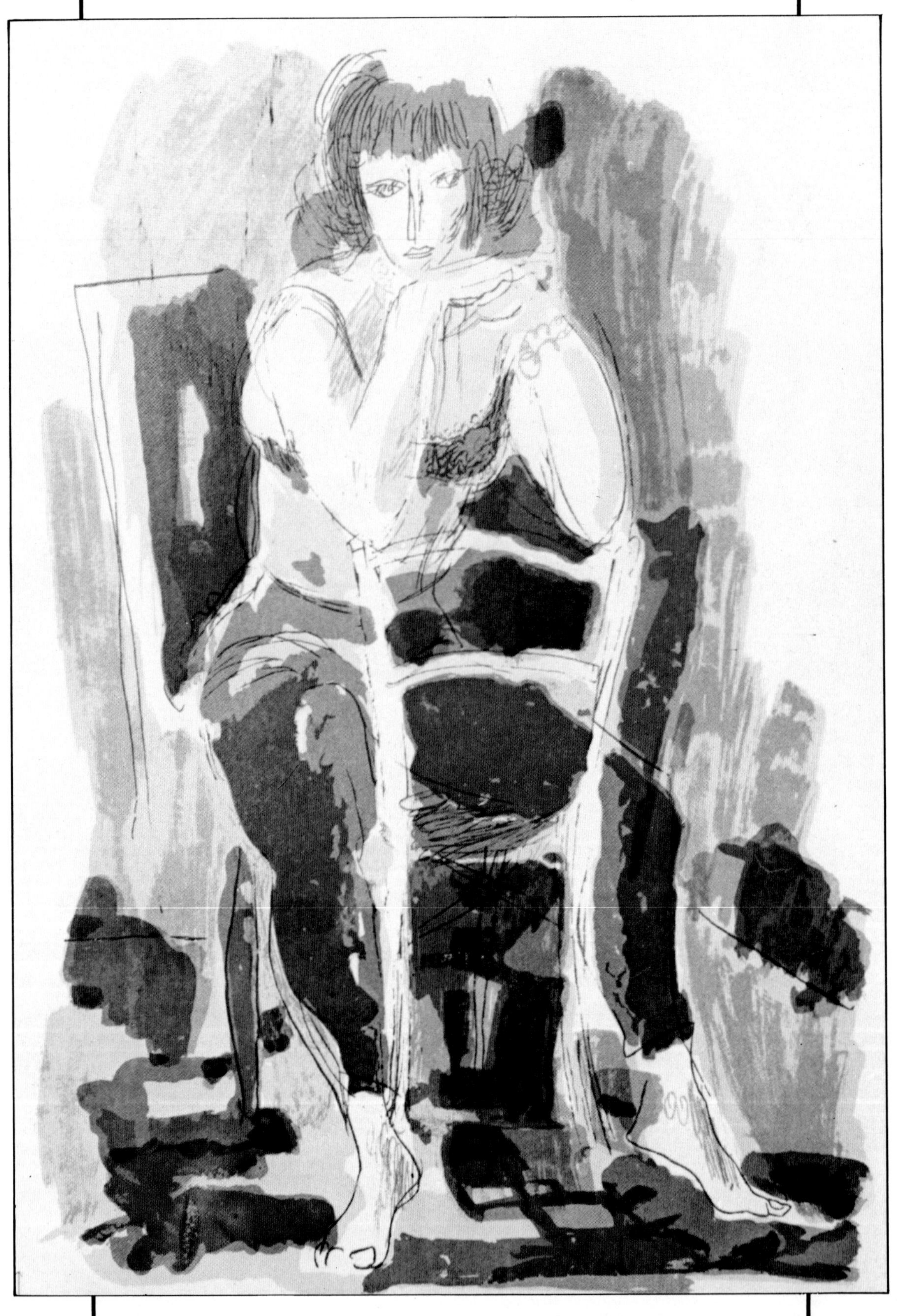

40
Francis Lymburner
''Dancer Resting'' 1968

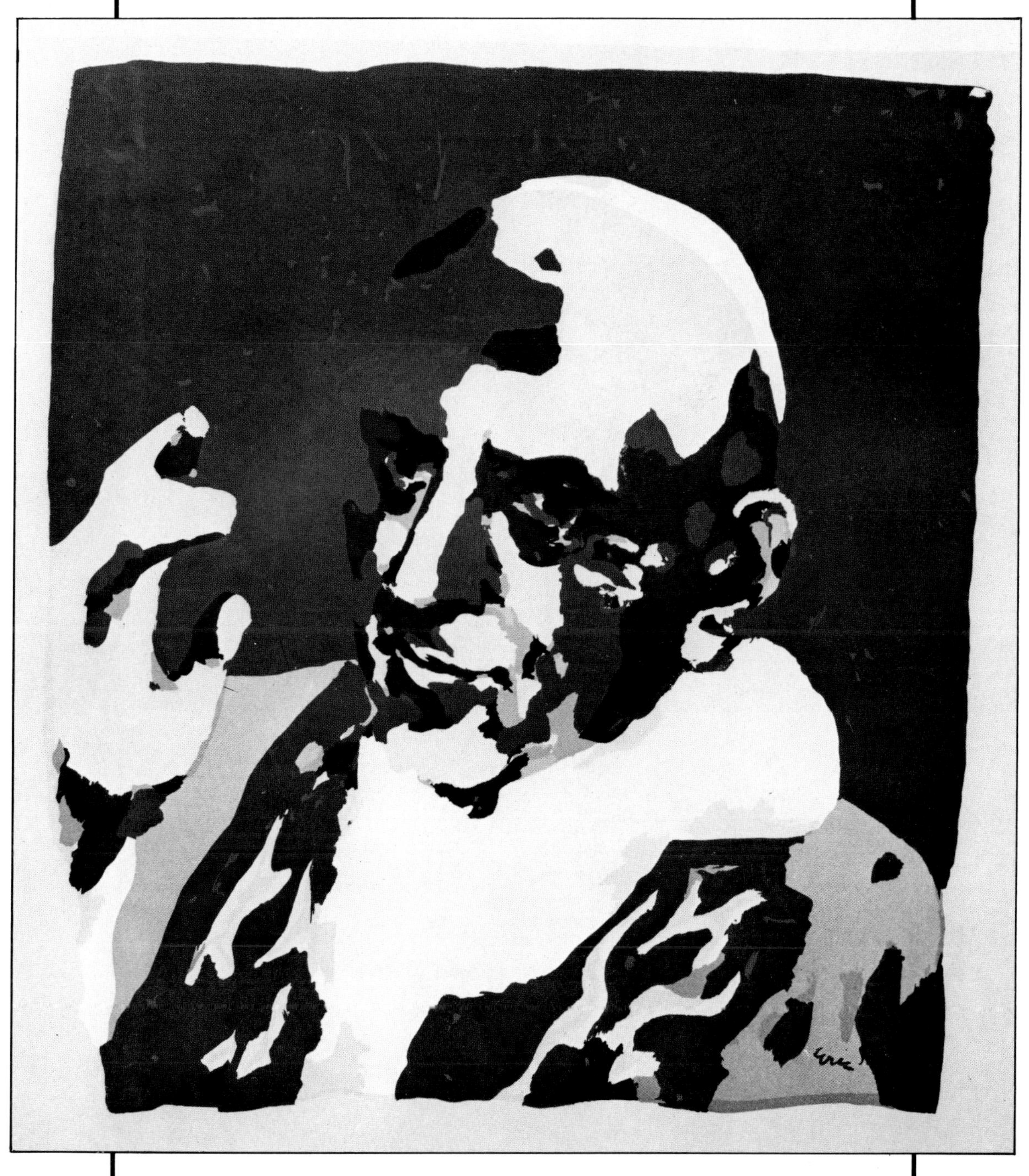

41
Eric Smith
"His Holiness Pope Paul VI" 1970

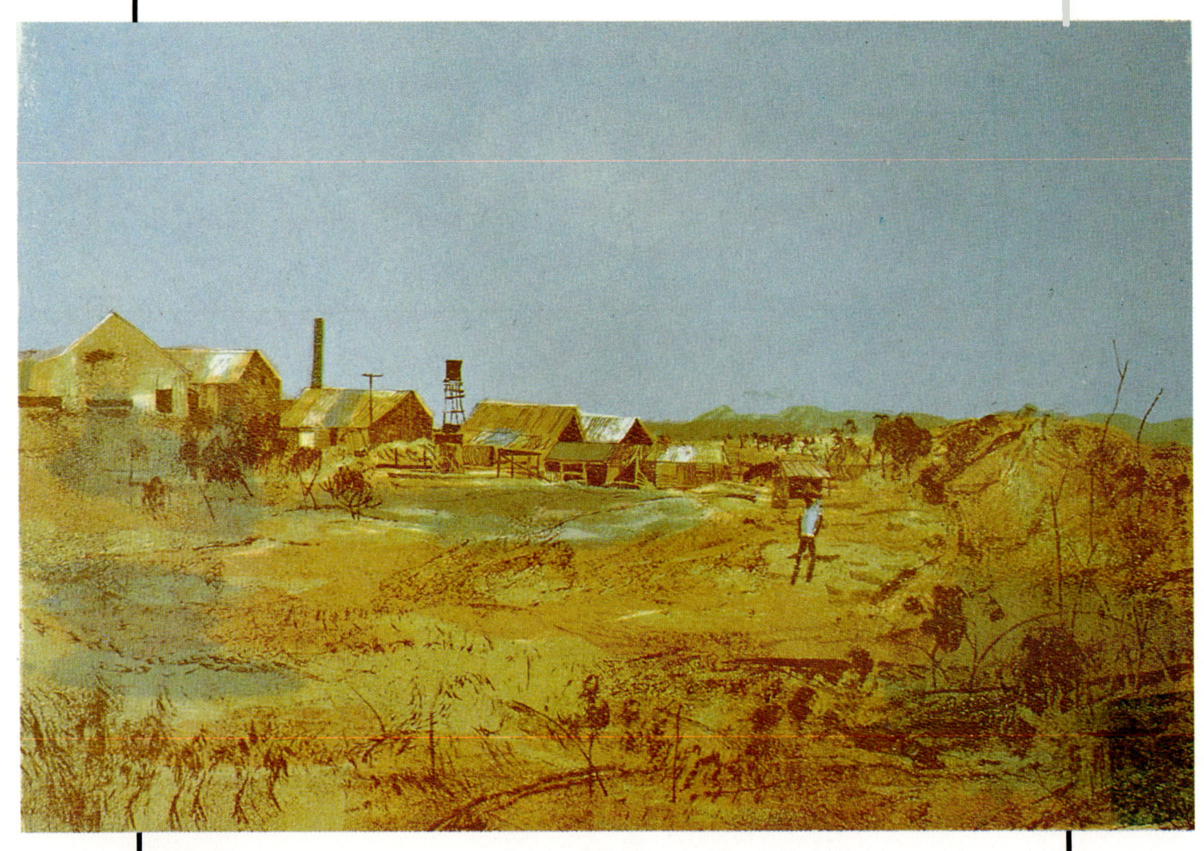

42
Ray Crooke
"Mining Town, North Queensland" 1969

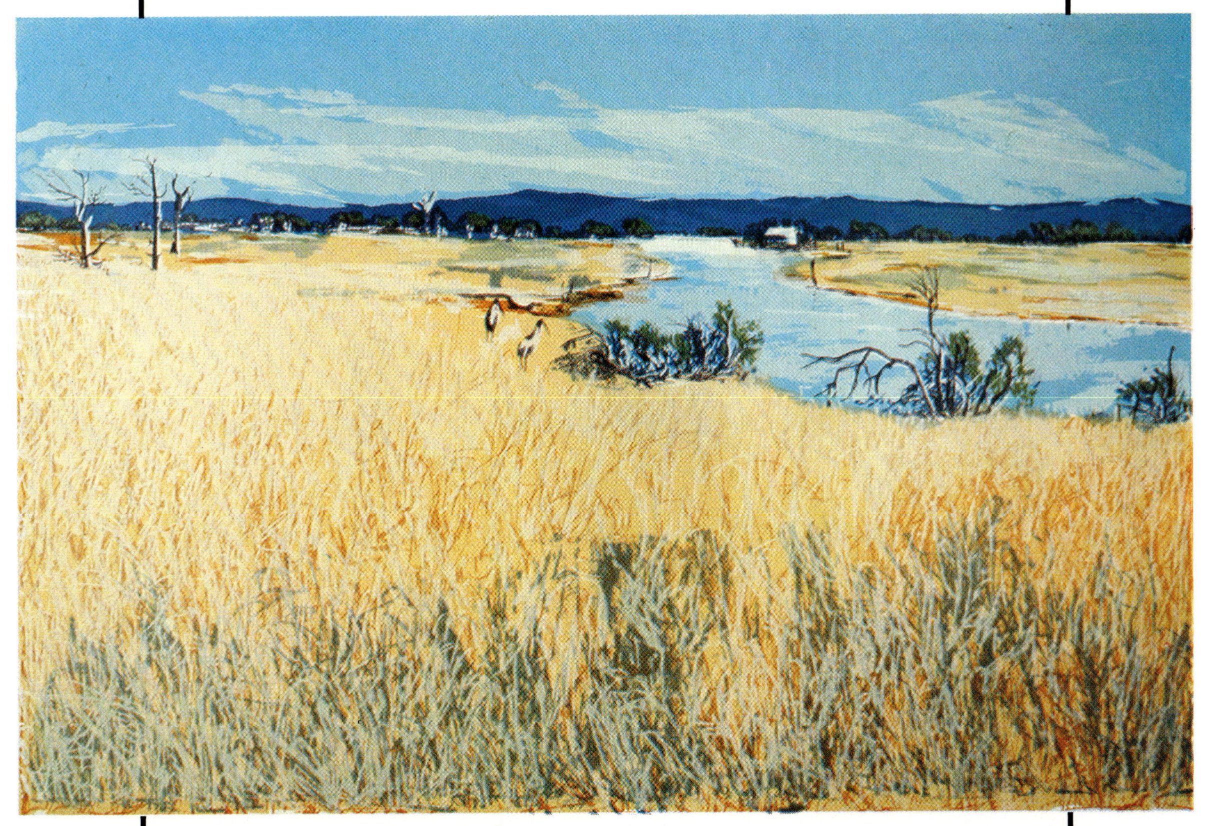

43
David Dridan
"Mundoo Channel" 1976

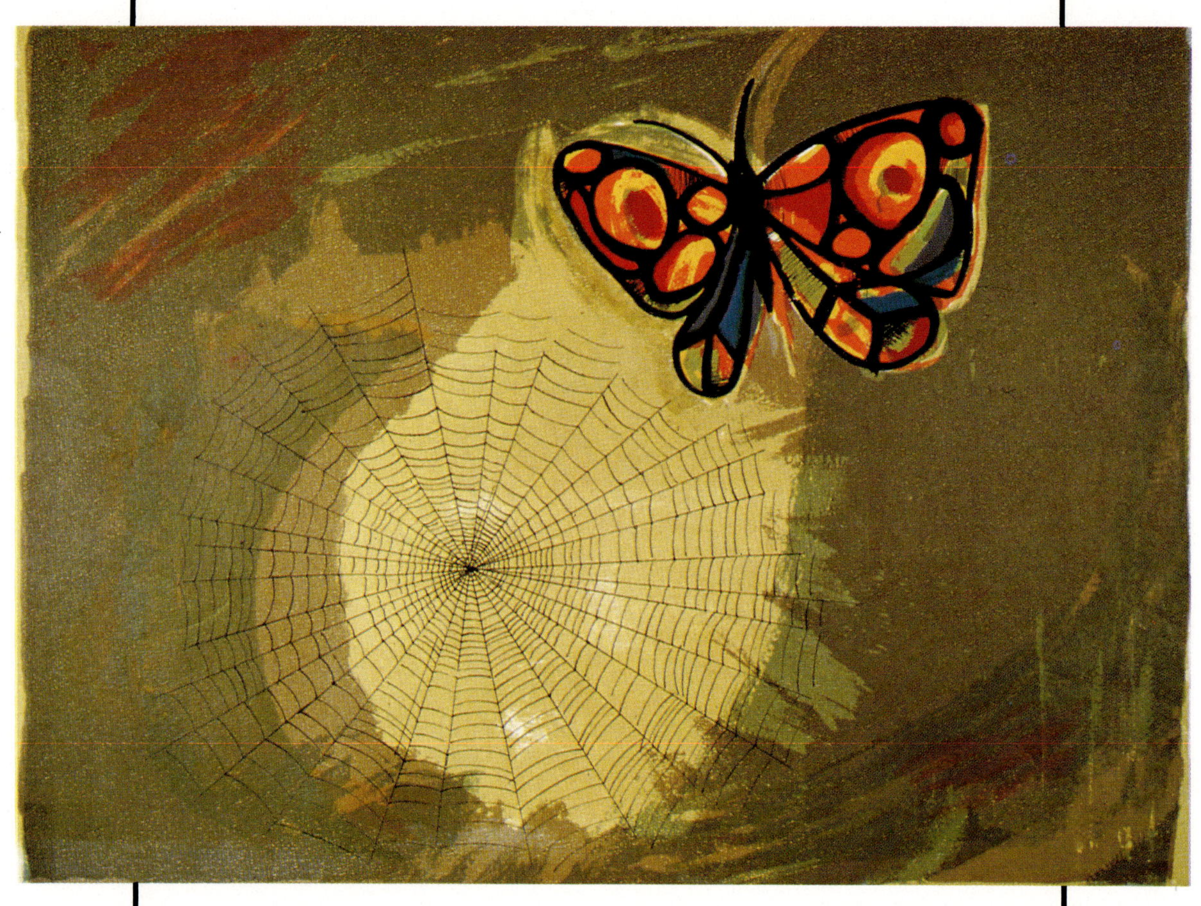

44
Charles Blackman
"The Web" 1970

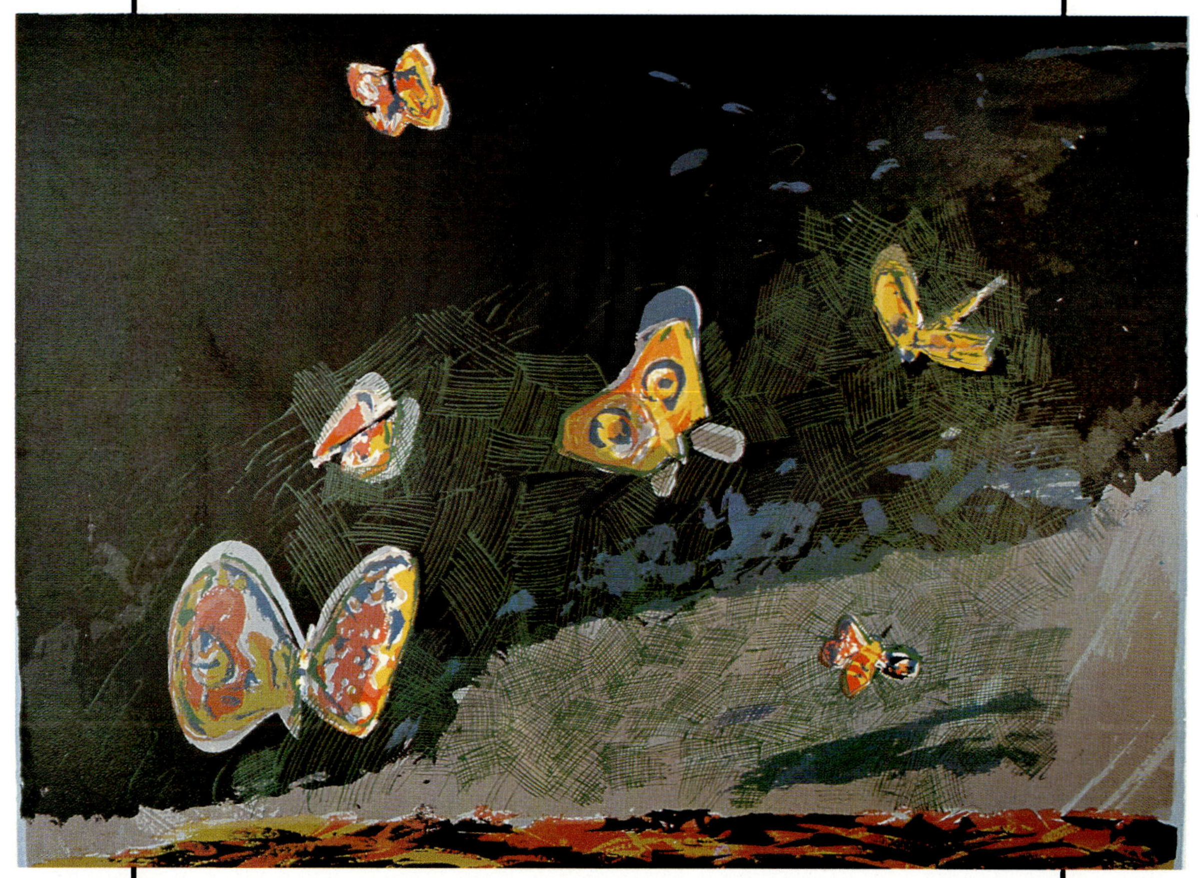

45
Charles Blackman
"Night Flight" 1970

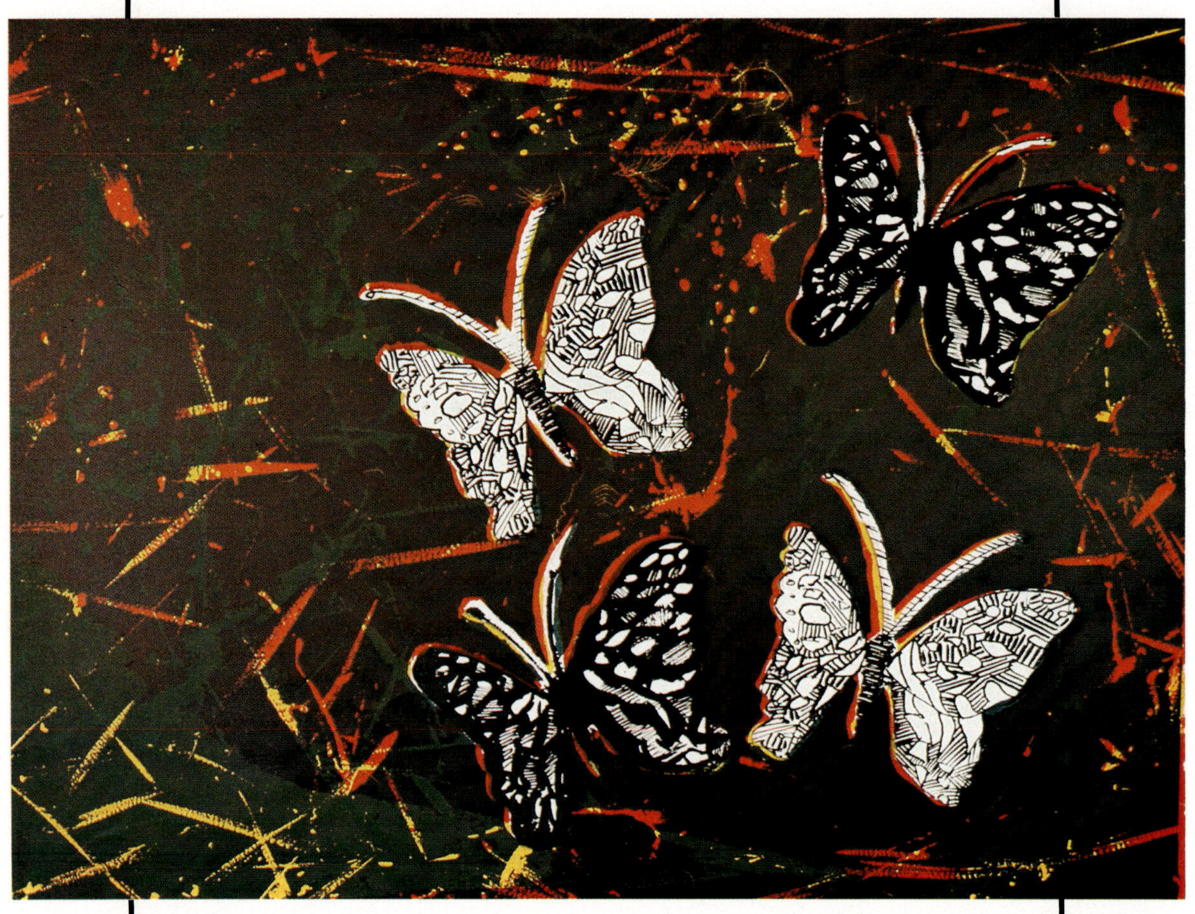

46
Charles Blackman
"The Cavern" 1970

47
Charles Blackman
"Tiger Butterfly" 1970

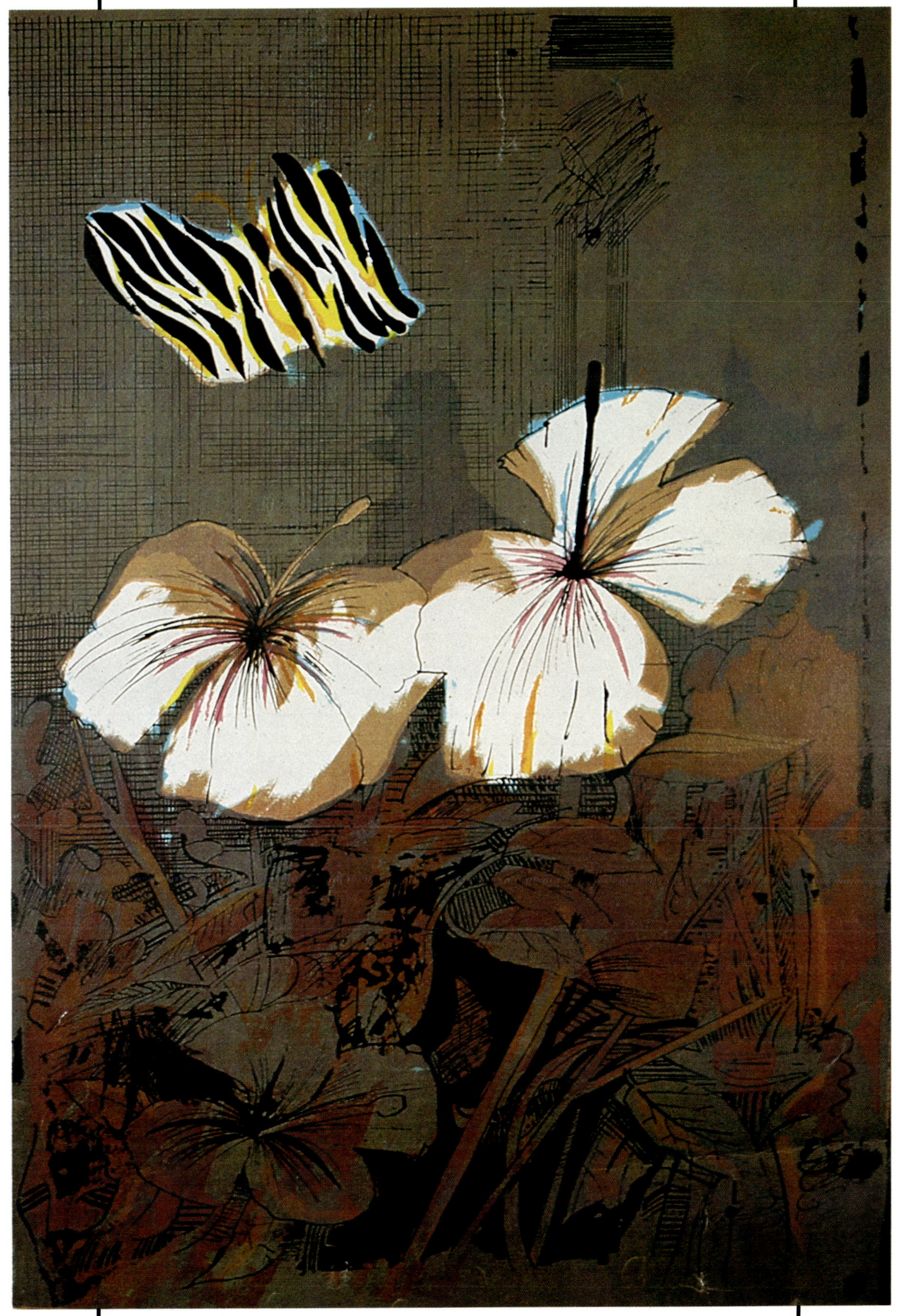

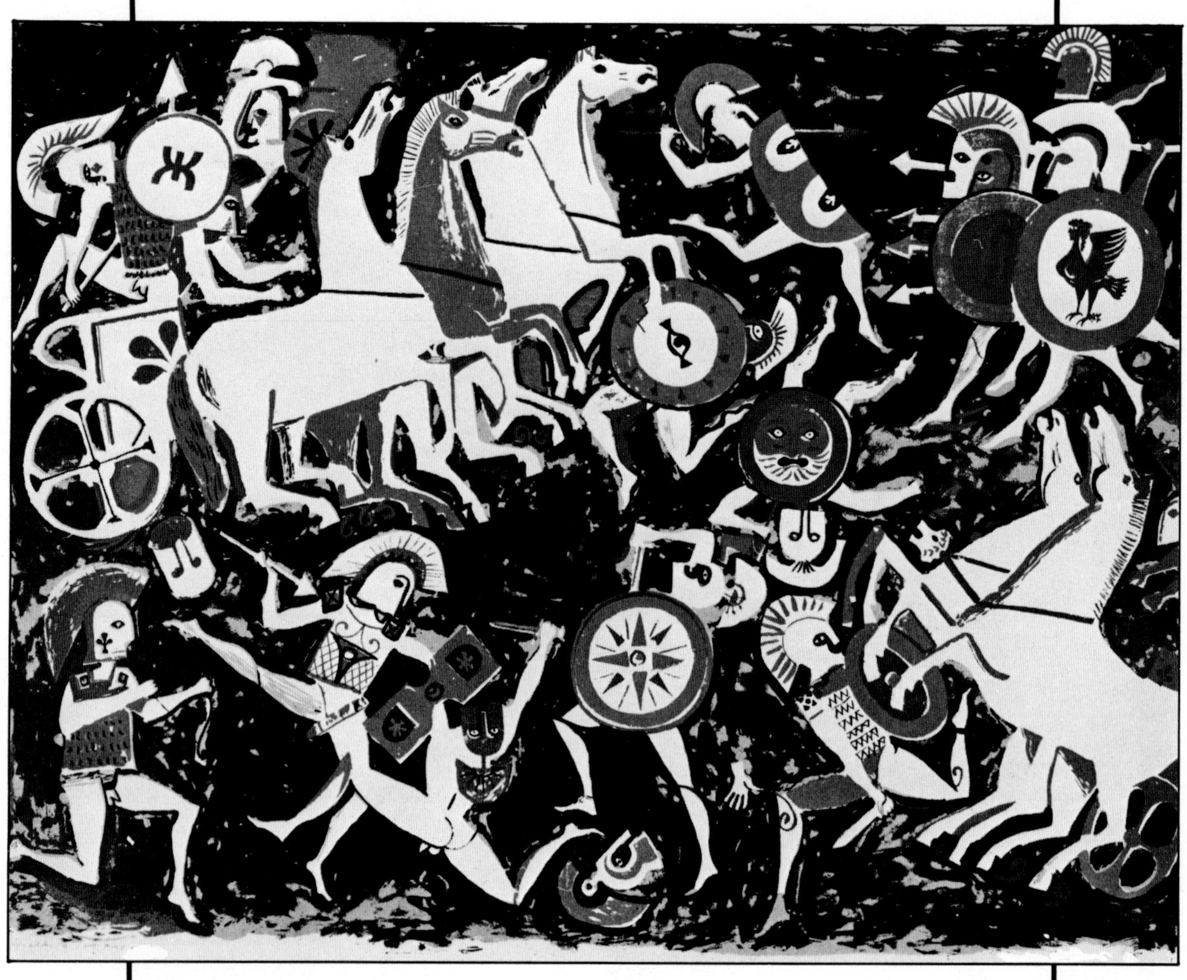

48
Cedric Flower
"Greeks and Trojans" 1968

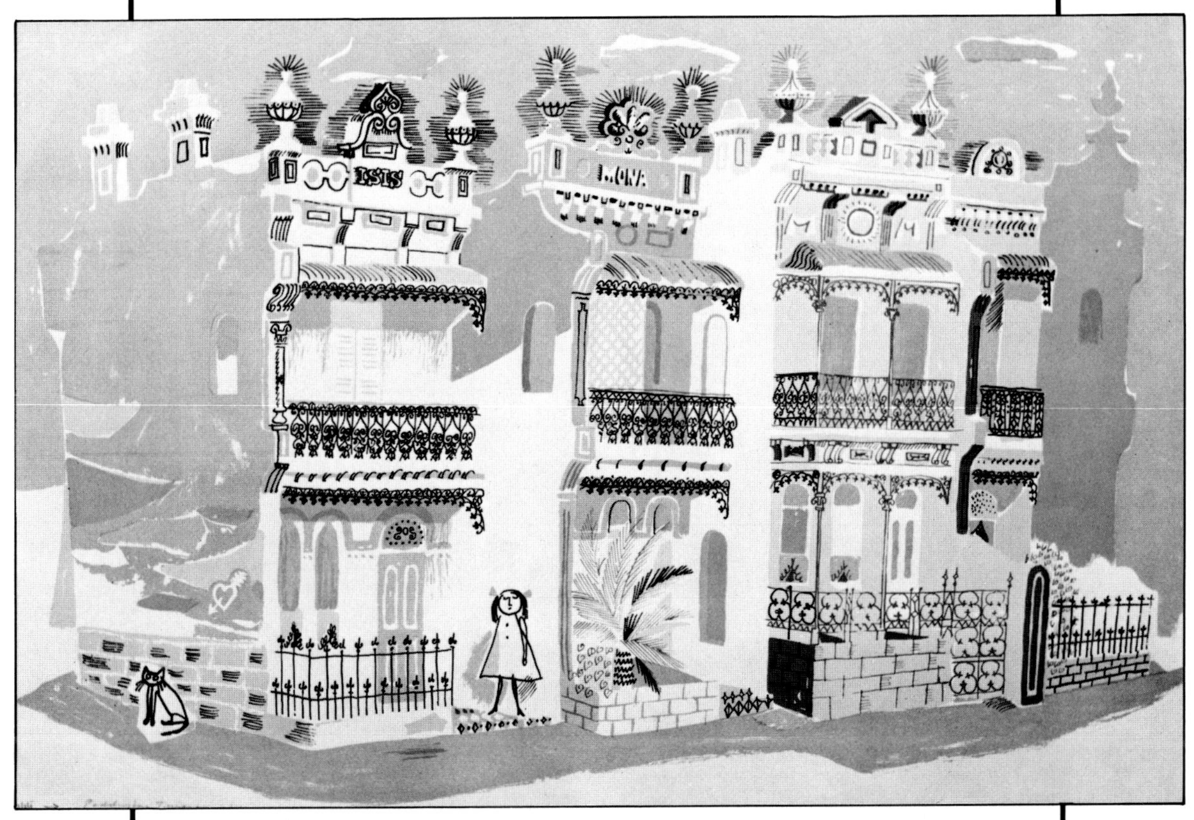

49
Cedric Flower
"Paddington Terrace" 1968

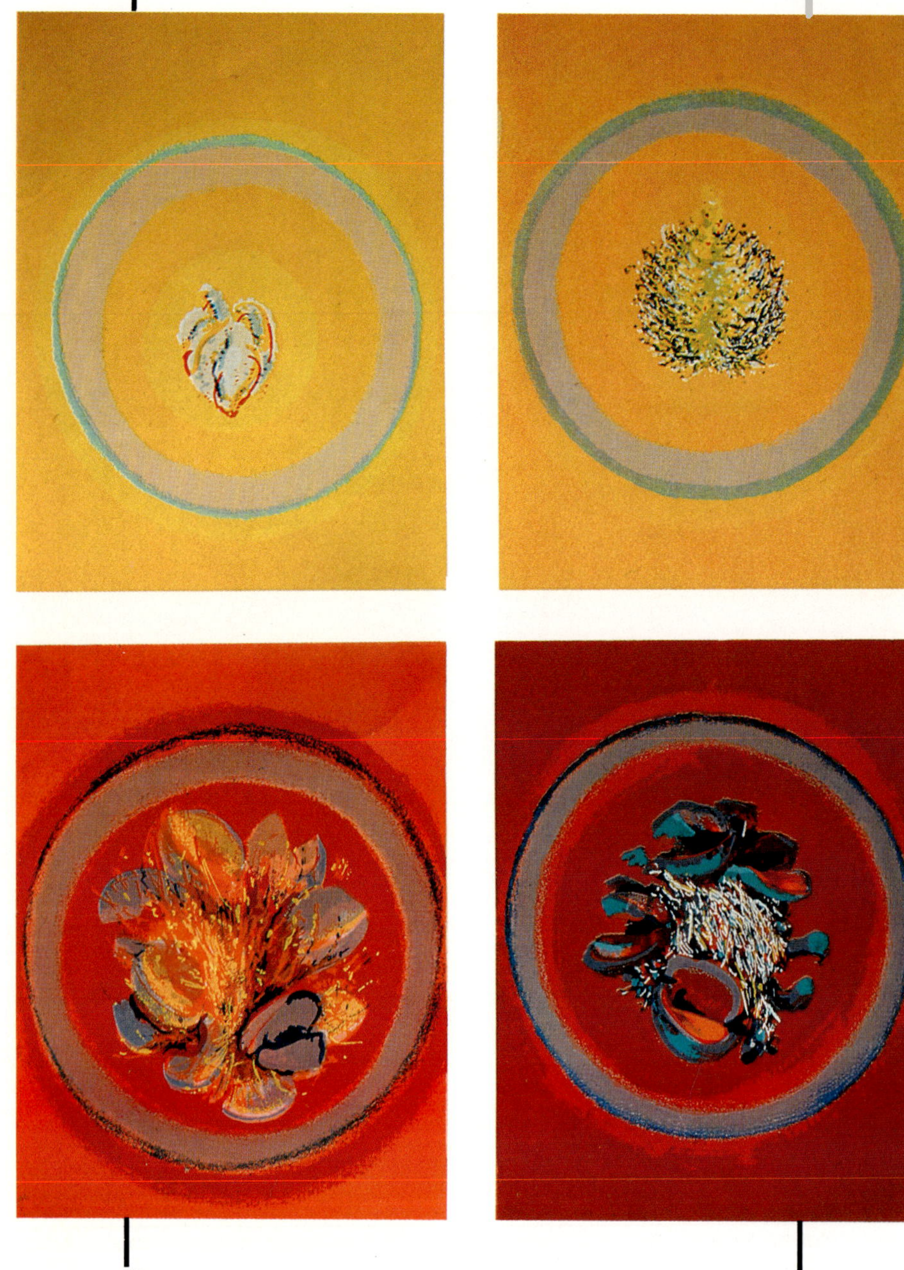

50
Frank Hodgkinson
"Genesis" A 1977

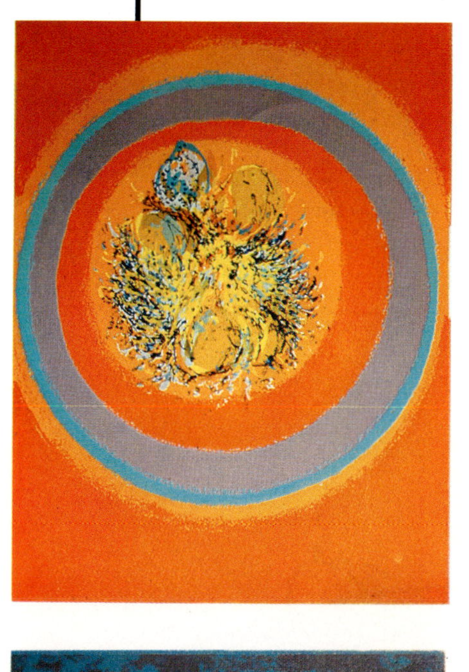
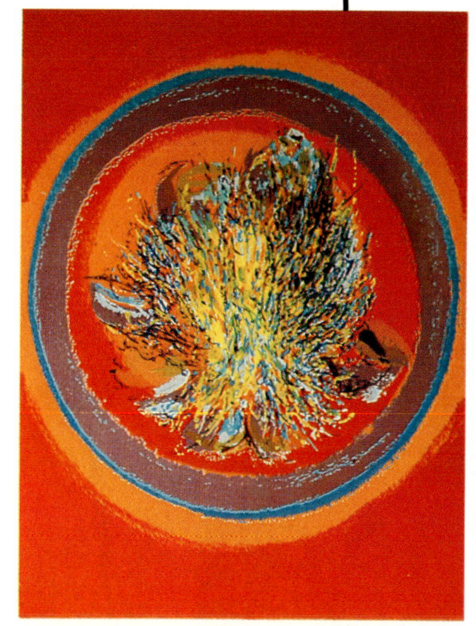
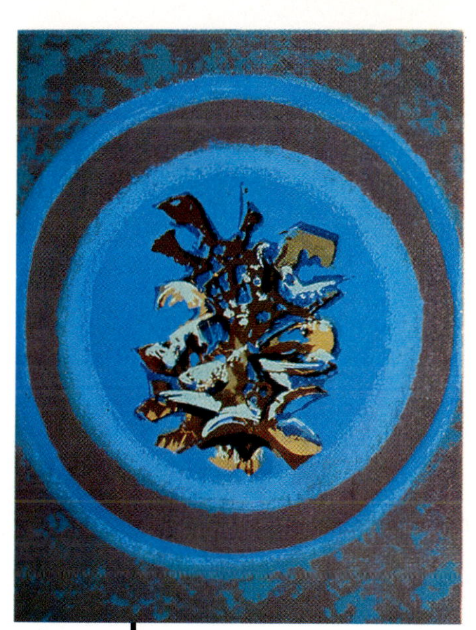
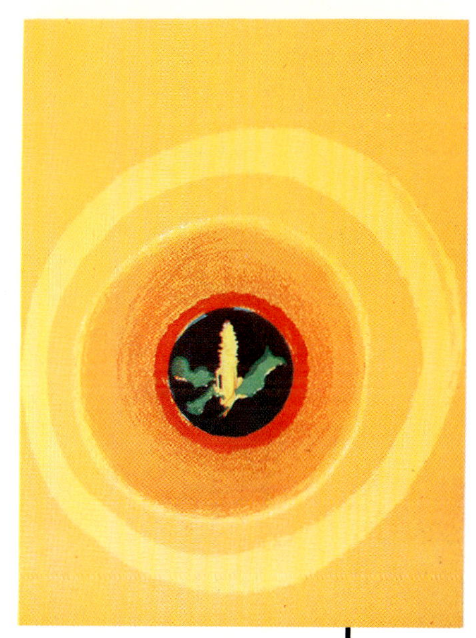

51
Frank Hodgkinson
"Genesis" B 1977

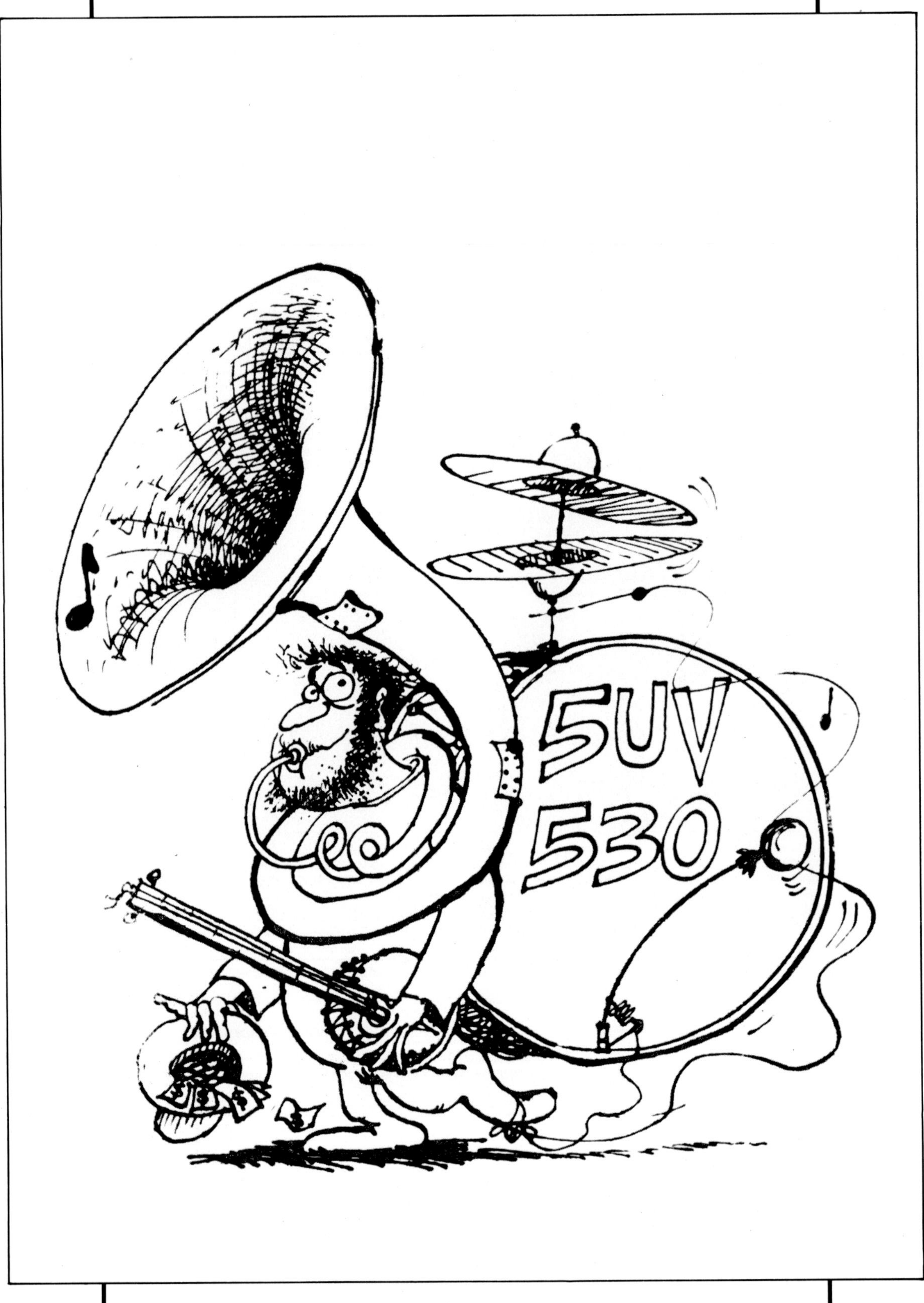

52
Ross Bateup
"Radiothon '77" 1977

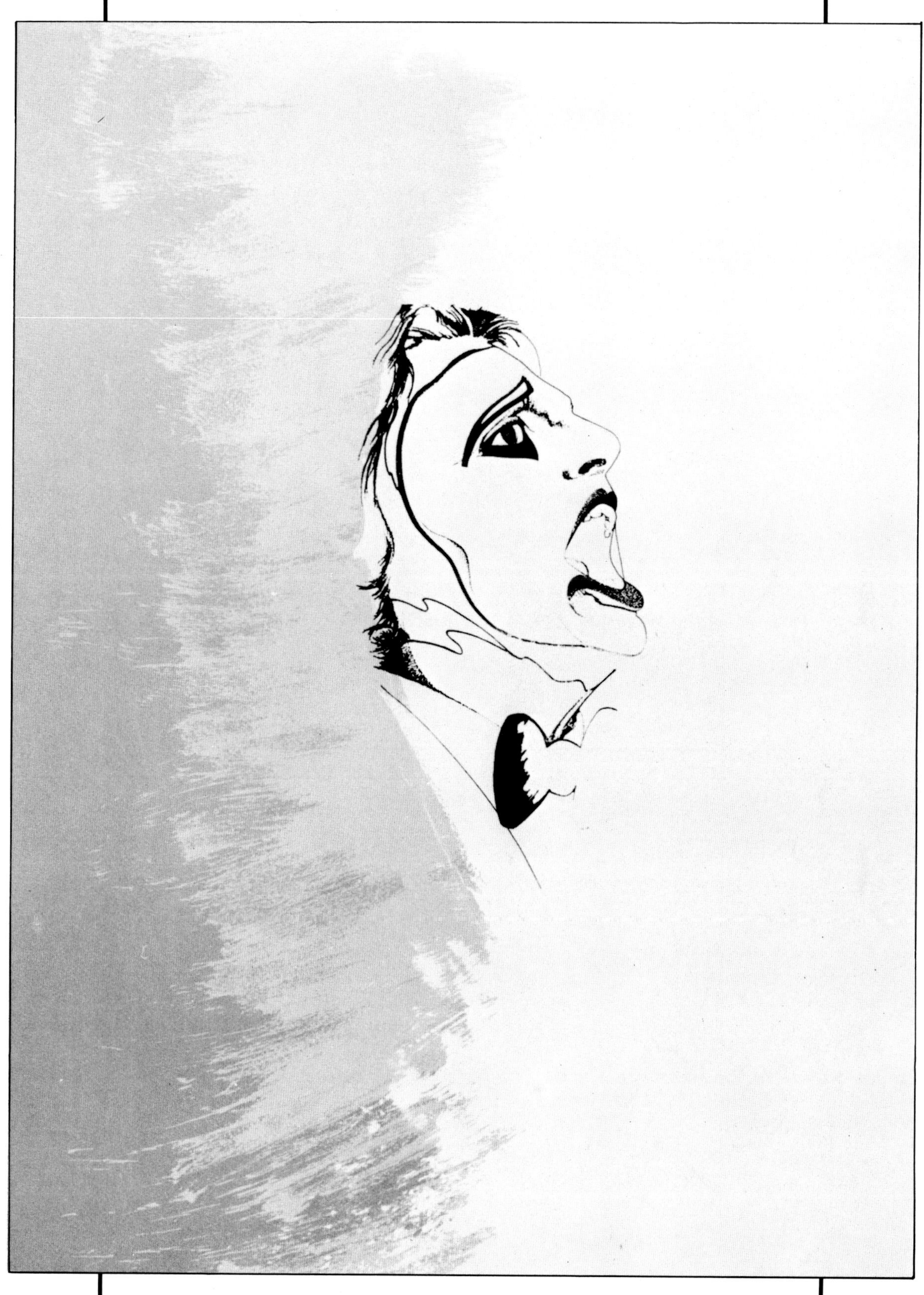

53
Max Mastrosavis
"Beckett on Love" 1980

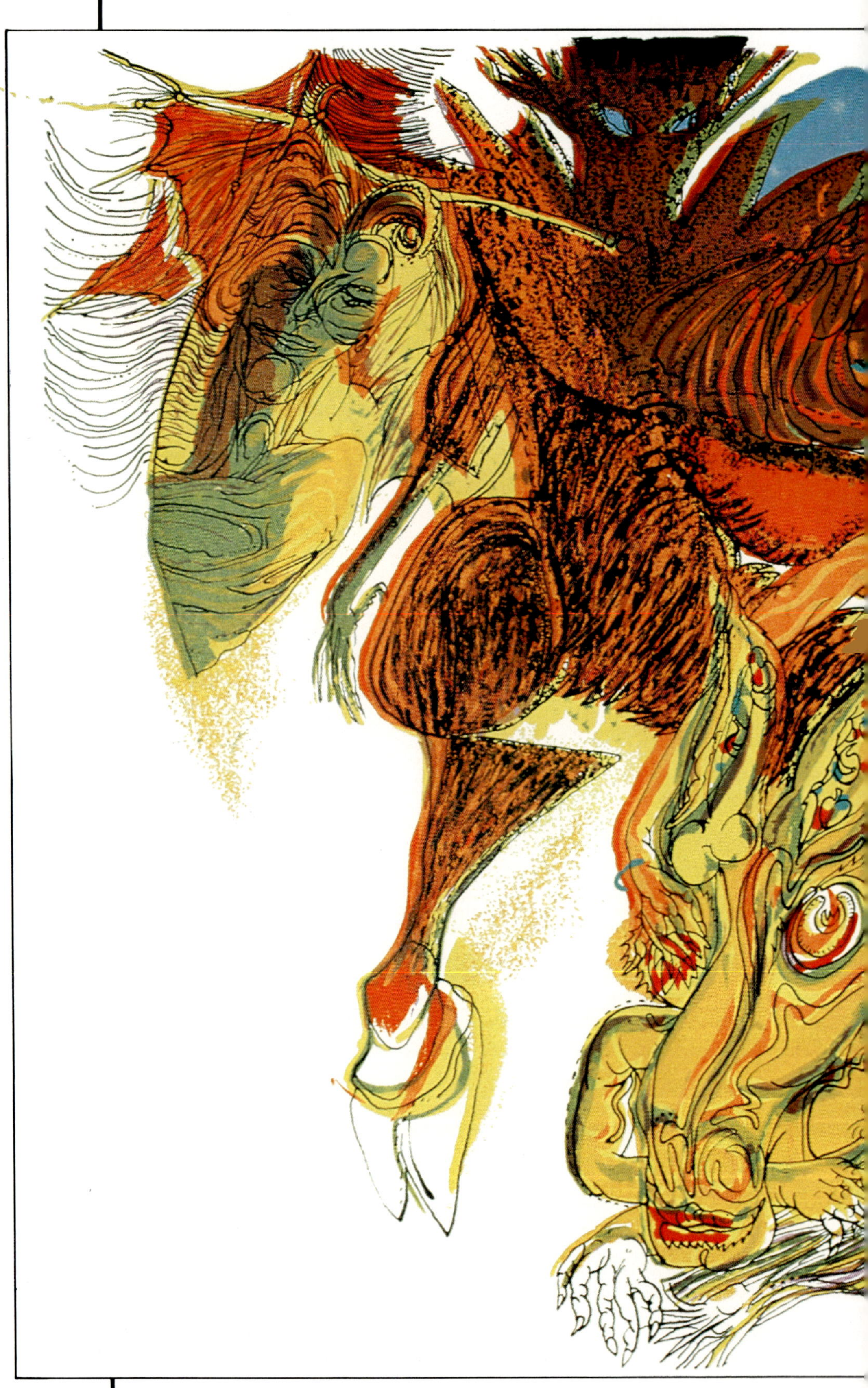

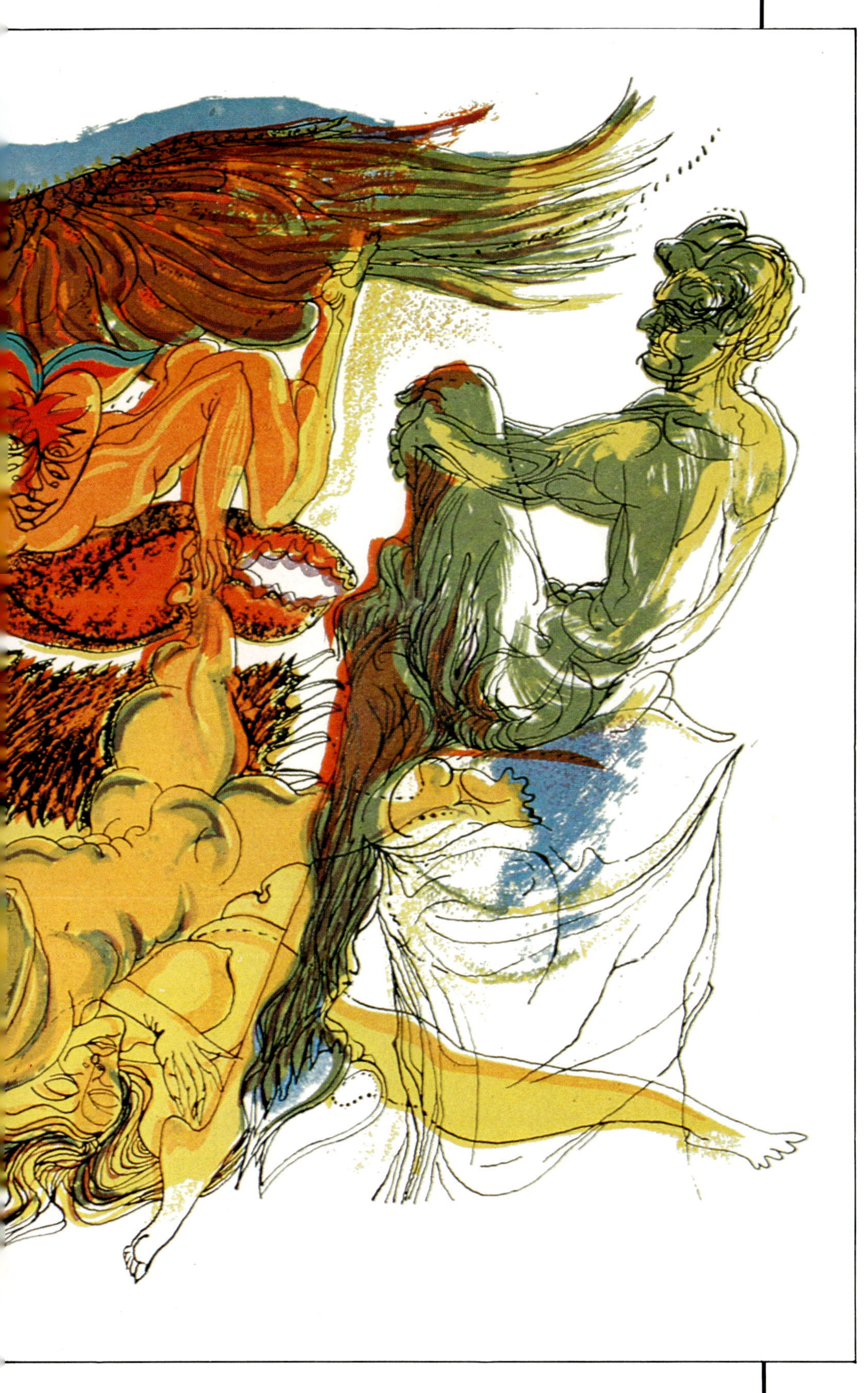

54

John Aland

"Midsummer Night's Dream" 1981

125

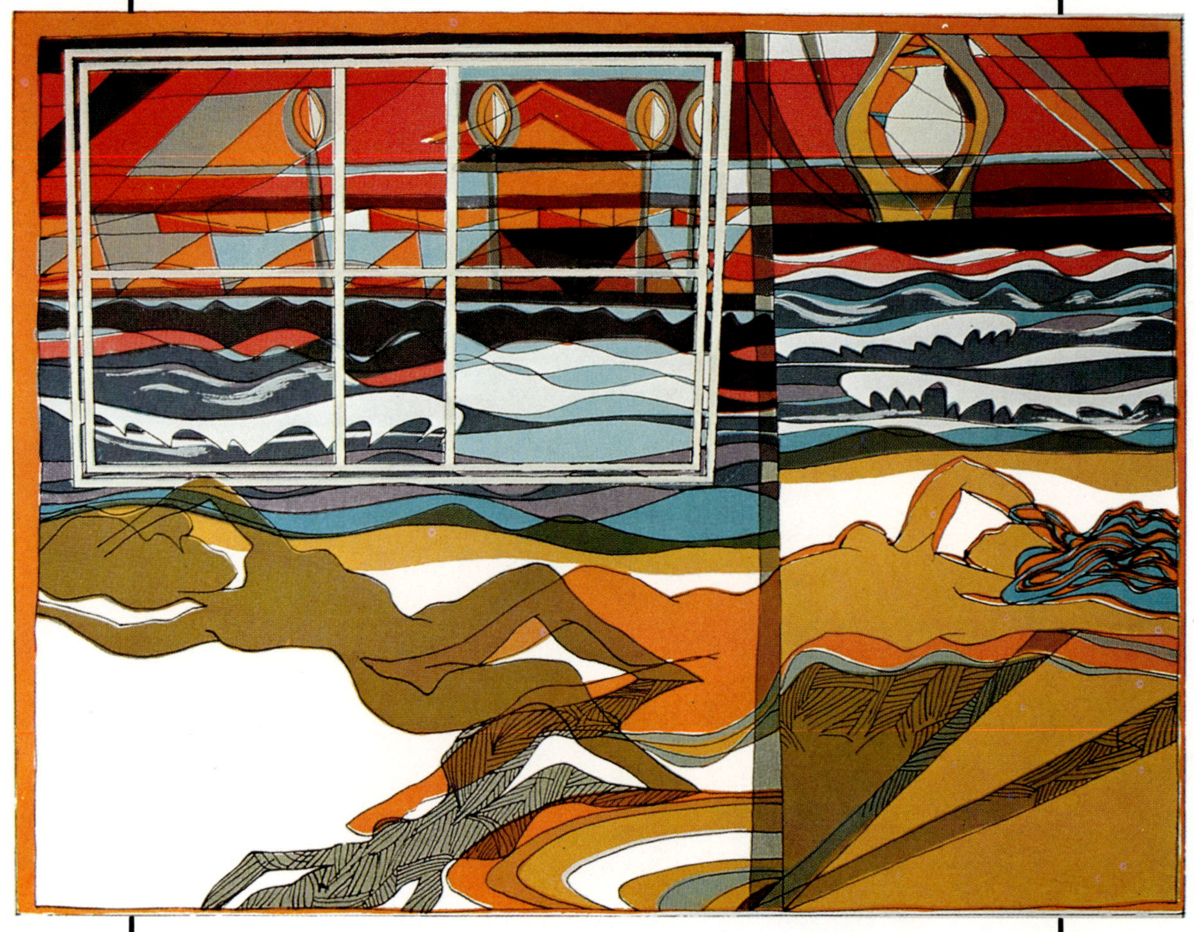

55
John Aland
"Heatwaves — Nocturne" 1970

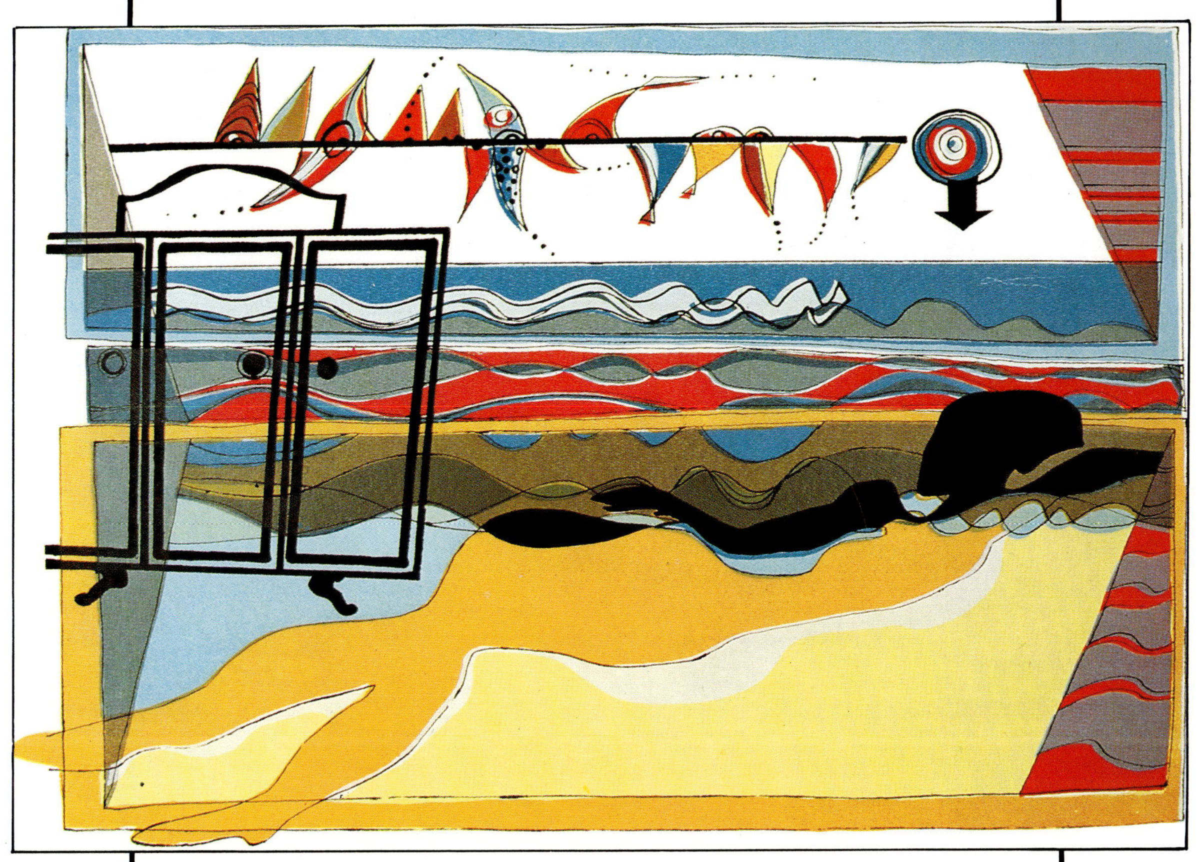

56
John Aland
"Bureau on St Kilda Beach — Morning" 1970

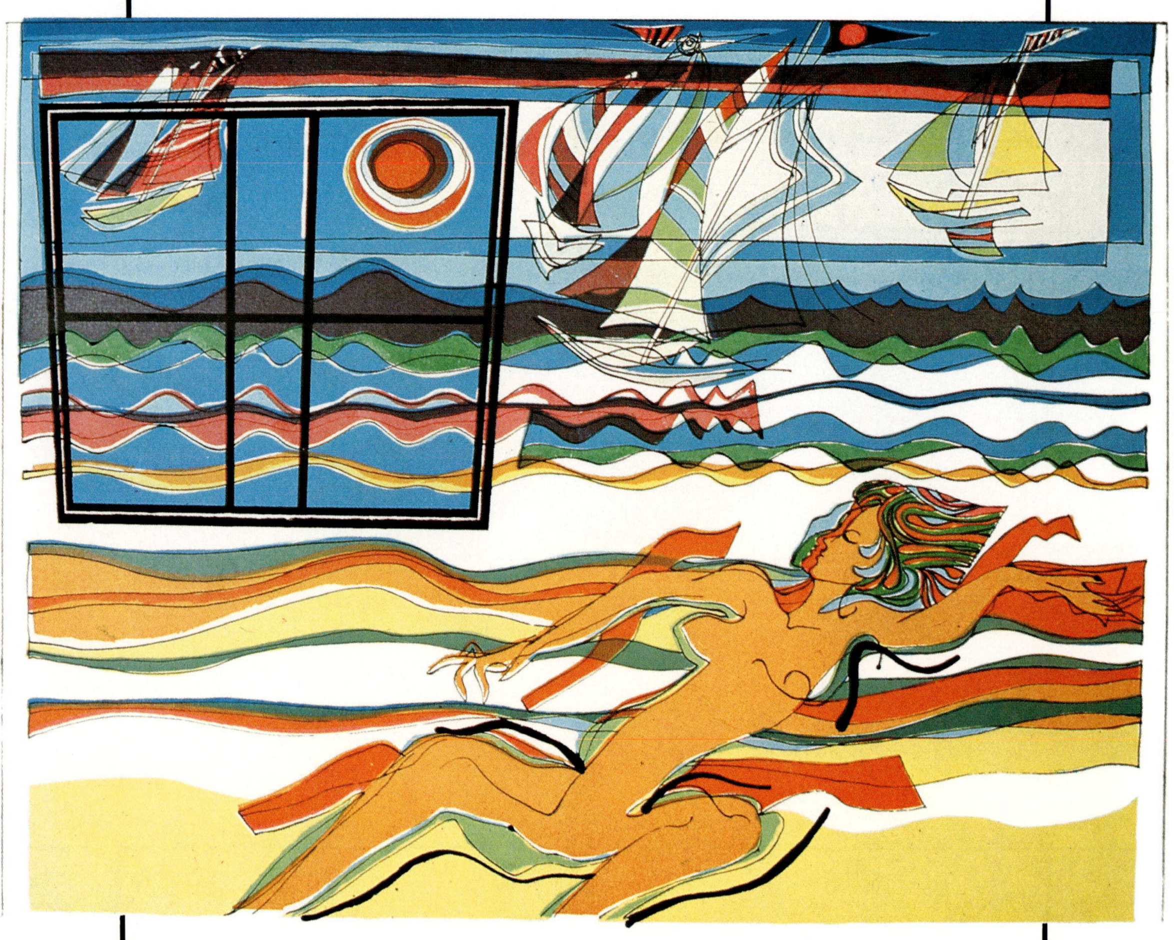

57
John Aland
"Noon — St Kilda Beach" 1970

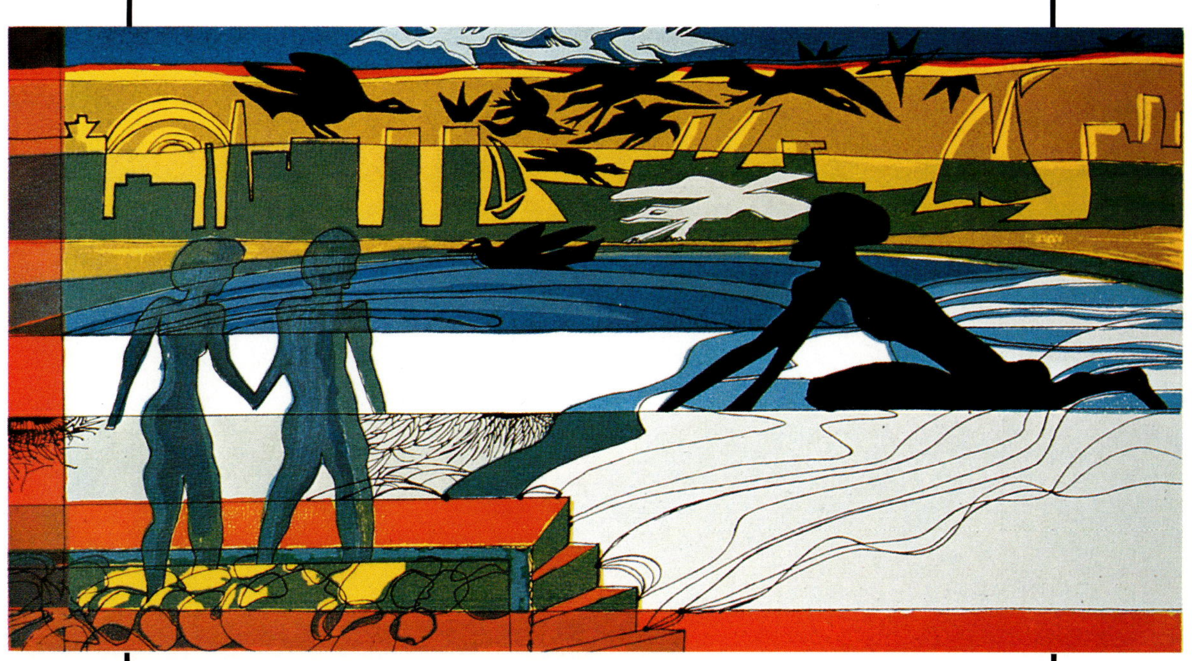

58
John Aland
"Surfrider — Summer Twilight" 1970

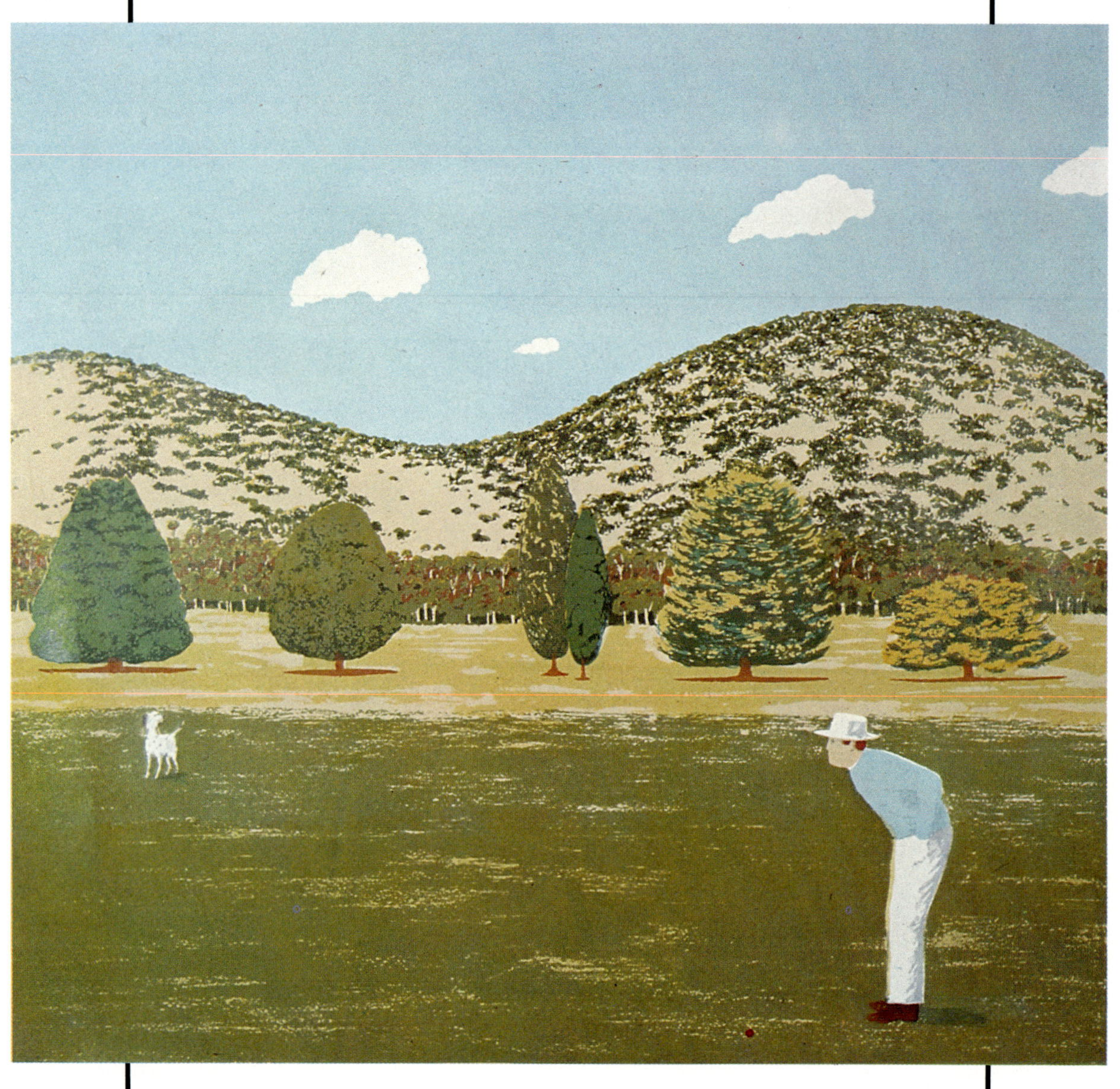

59
Keith Cowlam
"A Man and his Dog" 1982

THE CATALOGUE

The Catalogue

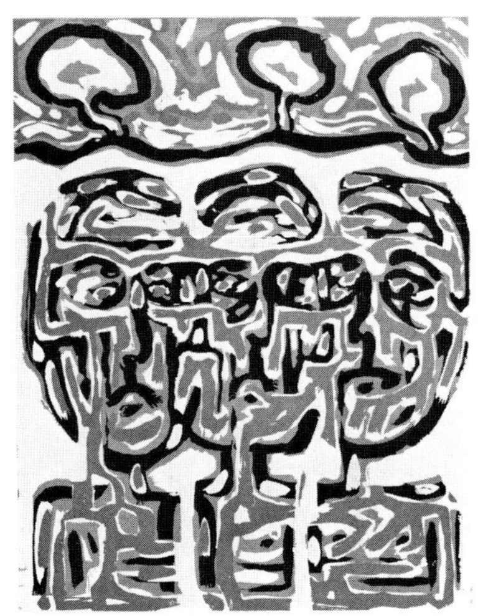

MILGATE, Rodney
"Human Image"
640mm × 510mm
Edition: 60
Paper: Kent

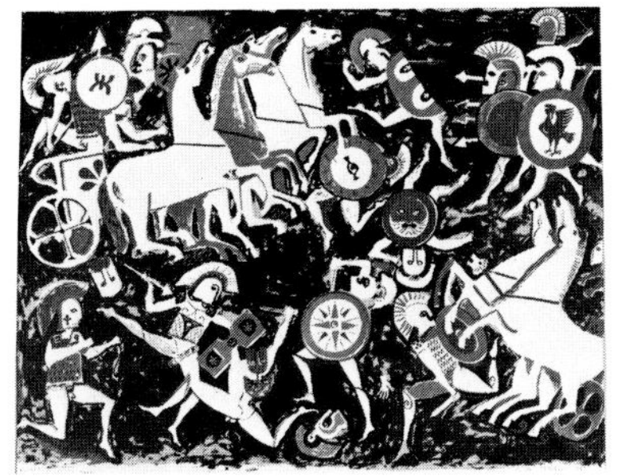

FLOWER, Cedric
"Greeks and Trojans"
490mm × 645mm
Edition: 100
Paper: Kent

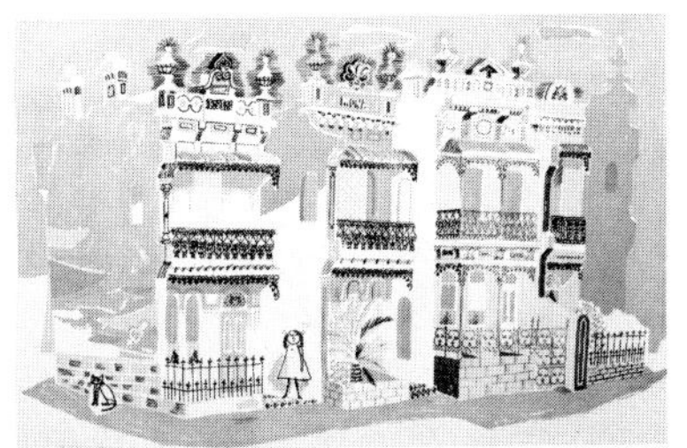

FLOWER, Cedric
"Paddington Terrace"
445mm × 685mm
Edition: 100
Paper: Handmade Hayle Mill 16

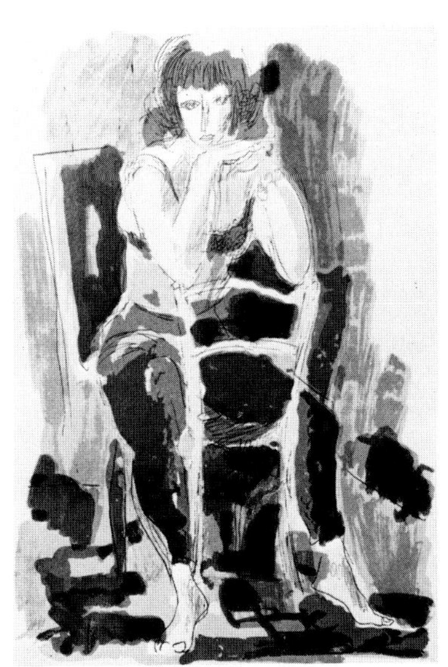

LYMBURNER, Francis
"Dancer Resting"
500mm × 350mm
Edition: 100
Paper: Kent

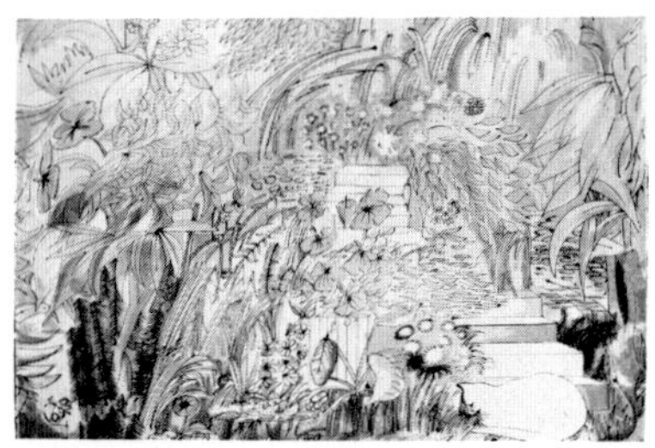

BLACKMAN, Charles
"The Garden"
685mm × 995mm
Edition: 75
Paper: Kent

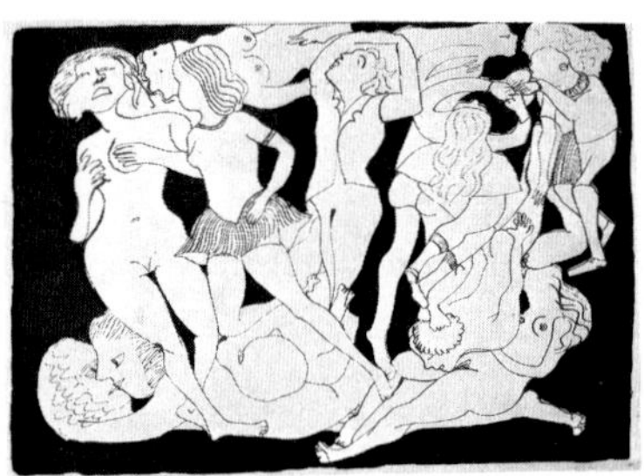

BLACKMAN, Charles
"I Love Tom Jones"
405mm × 565mm
Edition: 4 × 25
Paper: Kent

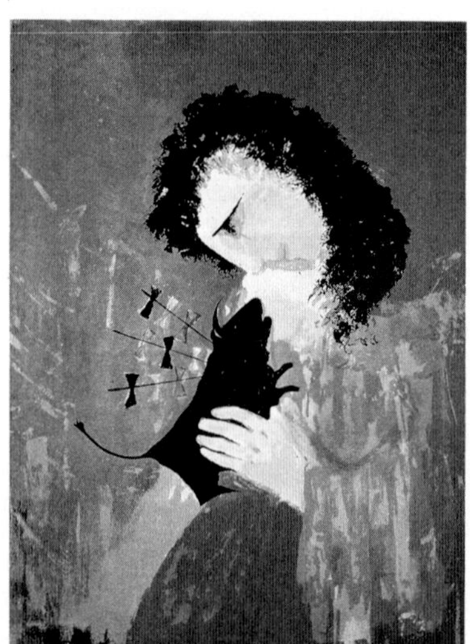

BOYD, David
"Bull Effigy"
835mm × 620mm
Edition: 60
Paper: Lavis Montgolfier

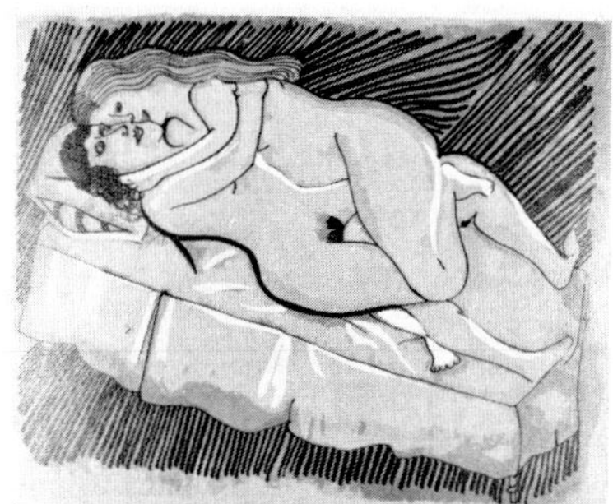

BLACKMAN, Charles
"The Embrace"
420mm × 520mm
Edition: 75
Paper: Lavis Montgolfier

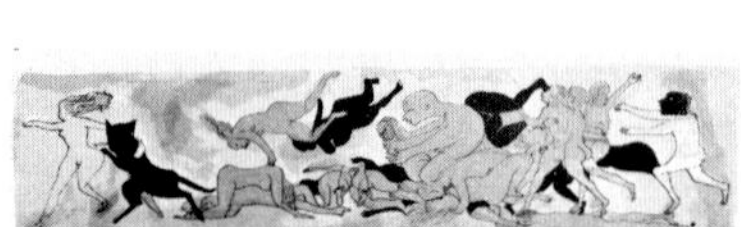

BLACKMAN, Charles
"Witches Sabbath"
245mm × 1000mm
Edition: 60
Paper: Kent

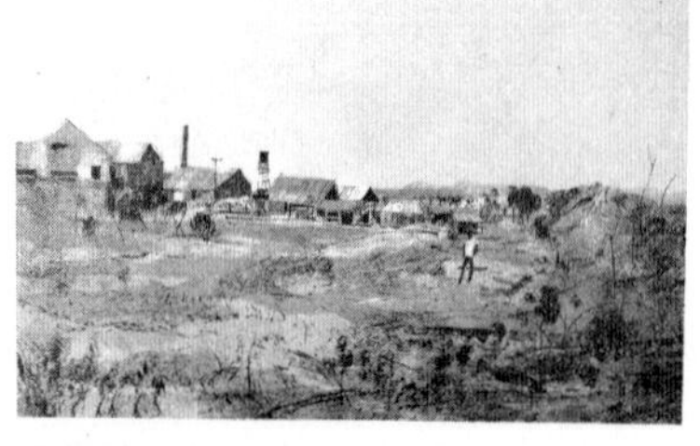

CROOKE, Ray
"Mining Town, North Queensland"
380mm × 560mm
Edition: 60
Paper: Lavis Montgolfier

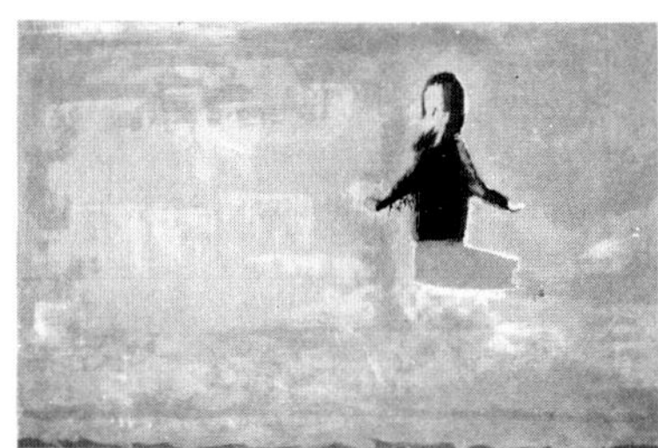

BLACKMAN, Charles
"Girl on a Beach"
490mm × 705mm
Edition: 60
Paper: Handmade

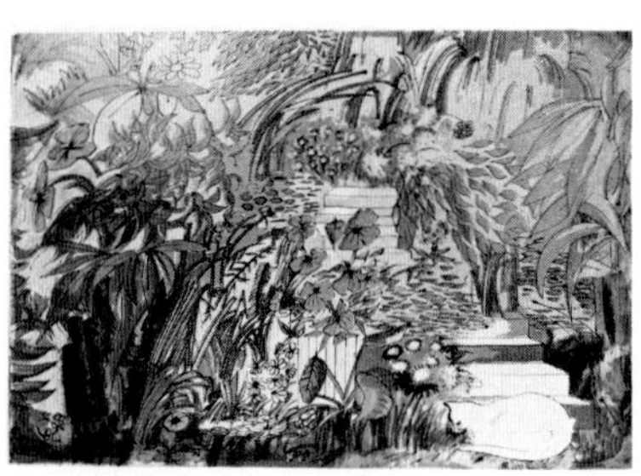

BLACKMAN, Charles
"White Cat's Garden"
685mm × 995mm
Edition: 75
Paper: Kent

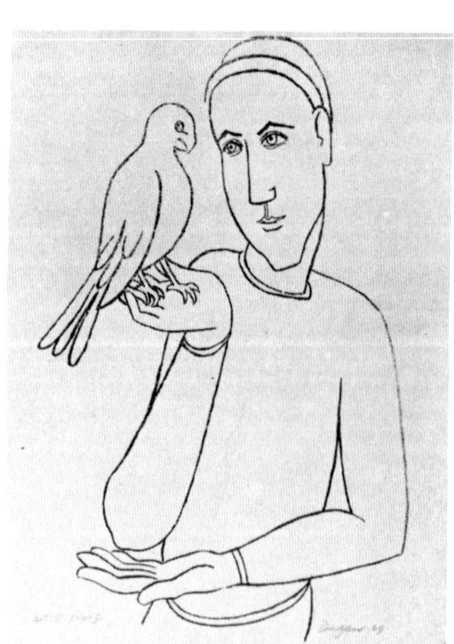

DEGAN, William
"Boy with a Bird"
720mm × 420mm
Edition: 60
Paper: Handmade porridge paper

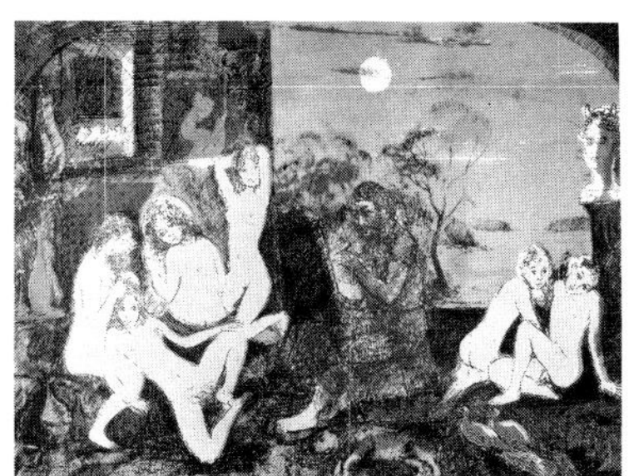

DELPRAT, Paul
"Artist's Studio"
430mm × 580mm
Edition: 2 × 30
Paper: Handmade Hayle Mill 16

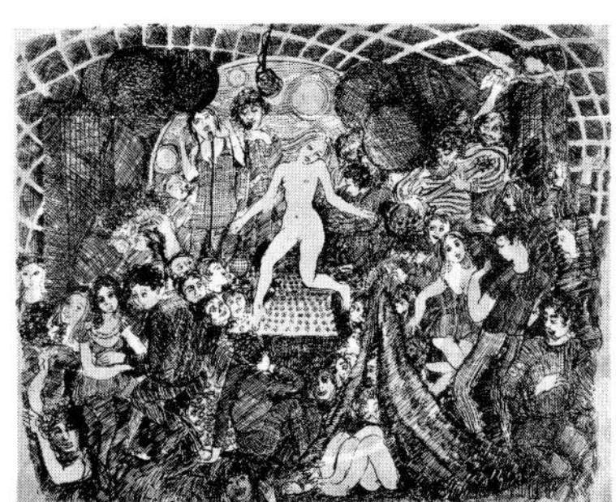

DELPRAT, Paul
"Discotheque"
430mm × 535mm
Edition: 2 × 30
Paper: Lavis Montgolfier

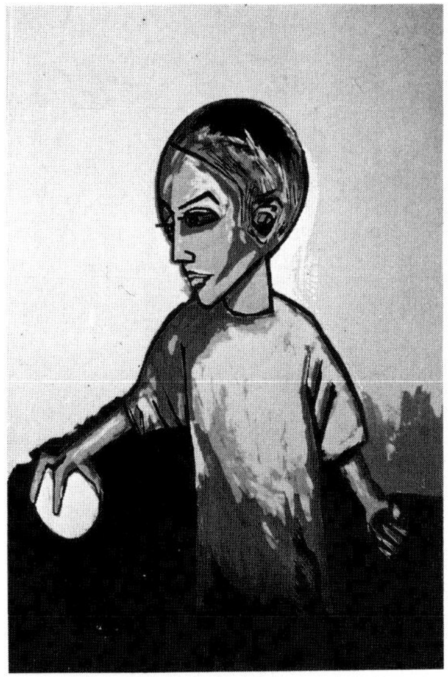

DICKERSON, Robert
"The Orange Ball"
920mm × 610mm
Edition: 60
Paper: Kent

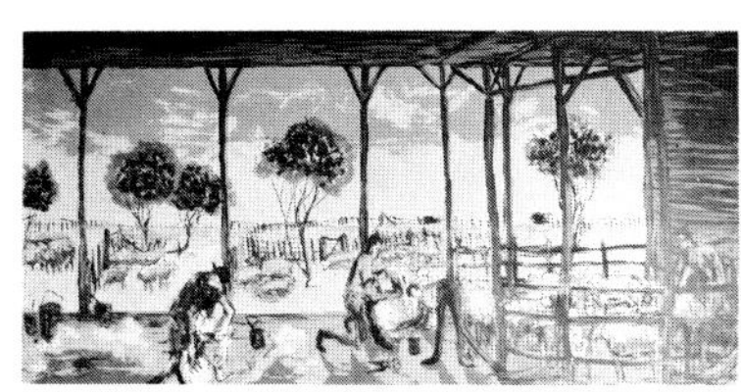

HART, Pro
"The Blade Shearers"
450mm × 915mm
Edition: 60
Paper: Lavis Montgolfier

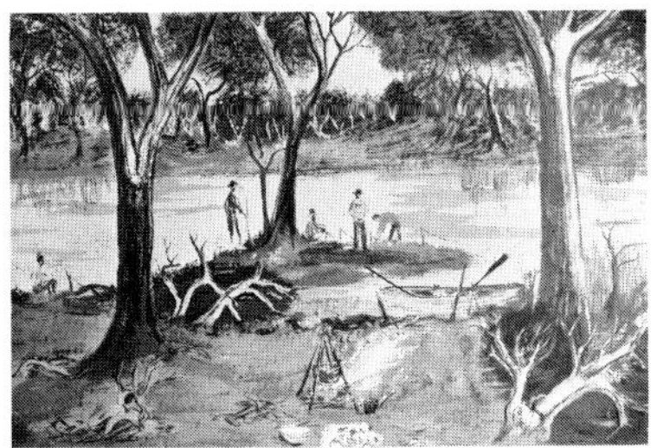

HART, Pro
"Cook Discovering Yabbies"
615mm × 900mm
Edition: 60
Paper: Lavis Montgolfier

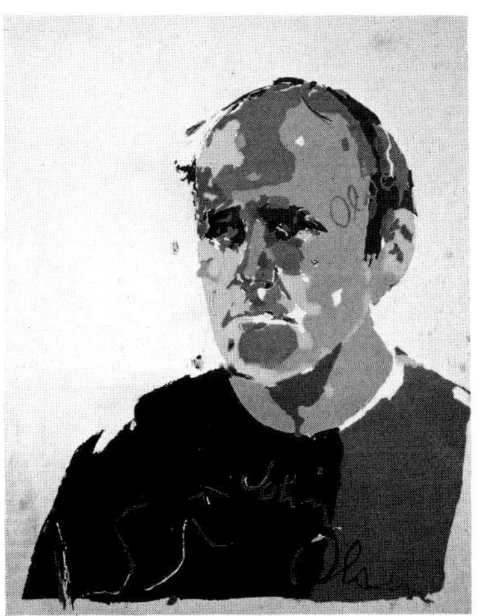

SMITH, Eric
"Portrait of John Olsen"
755mm × 605mm
Edition: 60
Paper: Lavis Montgolfier

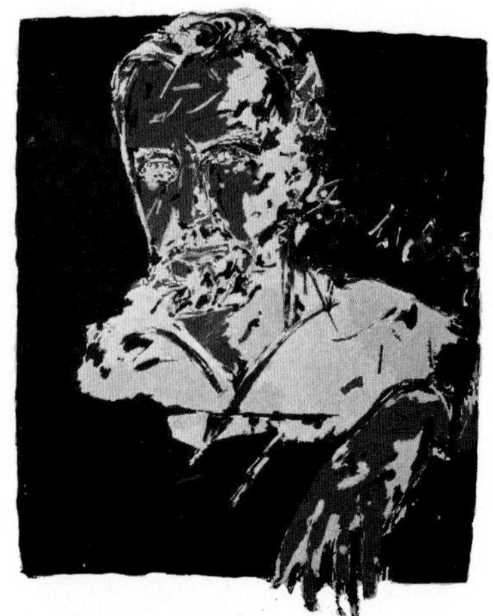

SMITH, Eric
"Portrait of Jon Molvig"
725mm × 565mm
Edition: 60
Paper: Lavis Montgolfier

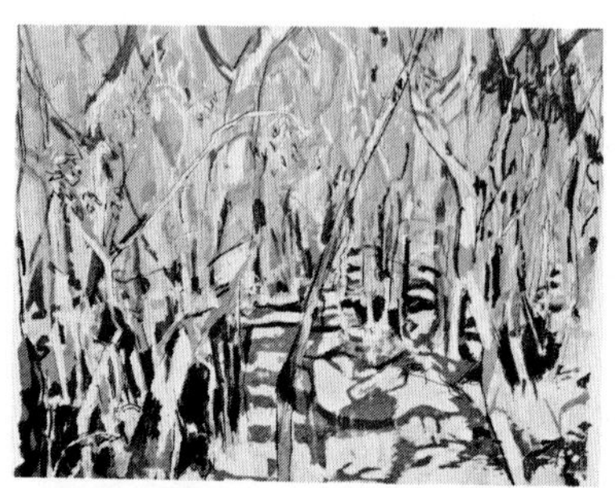

SCHLUNKE, David
"Mallee Study"
540mm × 695mm
Edition: 60
Paper: Lavis Montgolfier

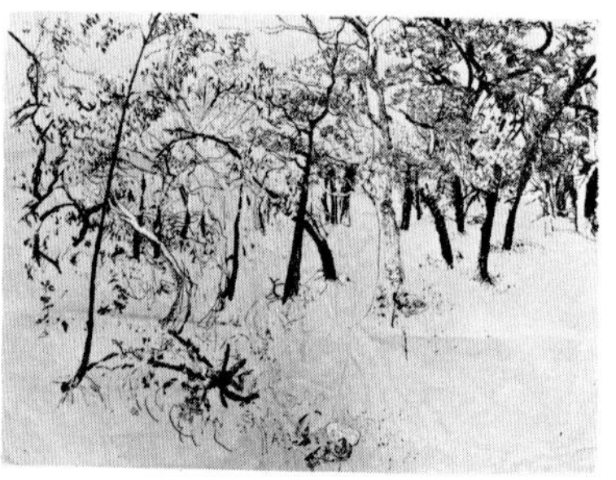

SCHLUNKE, David
"Summer Bush"
620mm × 840mm
Edition: 50
Paper: Lavis Montgolfier

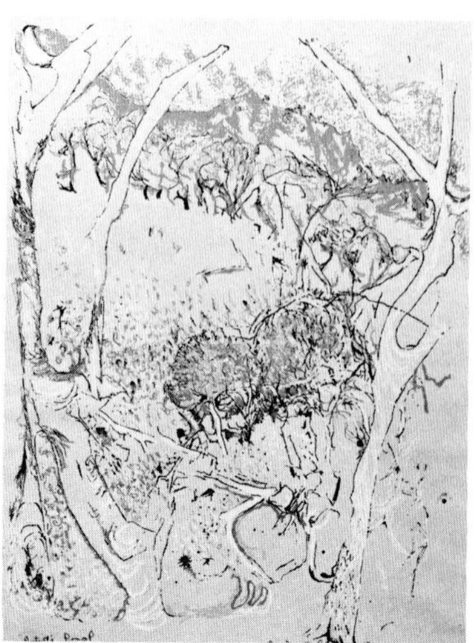

SCHLUNKE, David
"Temora"
590mm × 450mm
Edition: 60
Paper: Handmade

1970

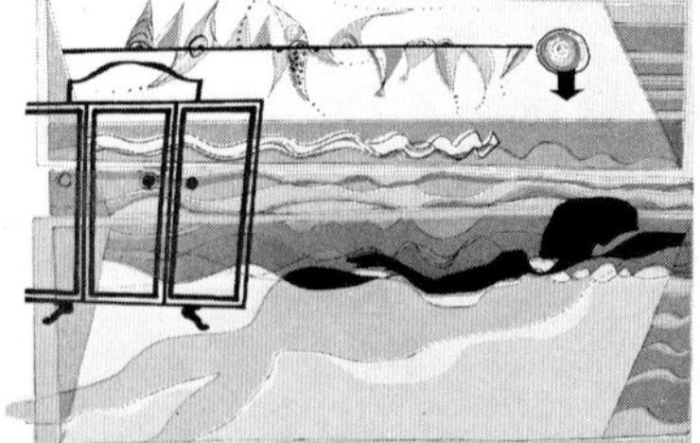

ALAND, John
"Bureau on St Kilda Beach
— Morning"
420mm × 615mm
Edition: 100
Paper: Lavis Montgolfier

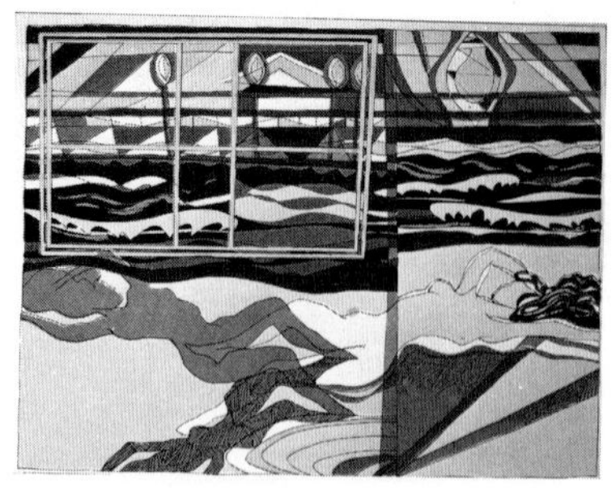

ALAND, John
"Heatwaves — Nocturne"
535mm × 720mm
Edition: 100
Paper: Lavis Montgolfier

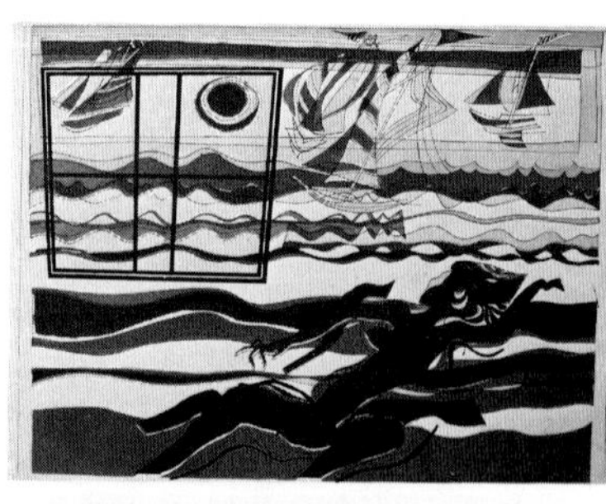

ALAND, John
"Noon — St Kilda Beach"
535mm × 715mm
Edition: 100
Paper: Lavis Montgolfier

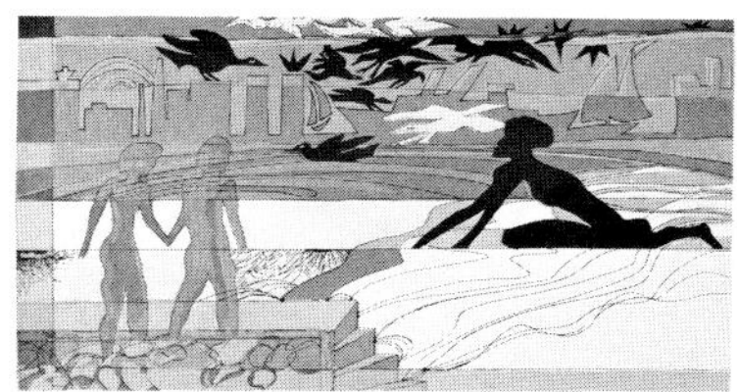

ALAND, John
"Surfrider — Summer Twilight"
400mm × 775mm
Edition: 100
Paper: Lavis Montgolfier

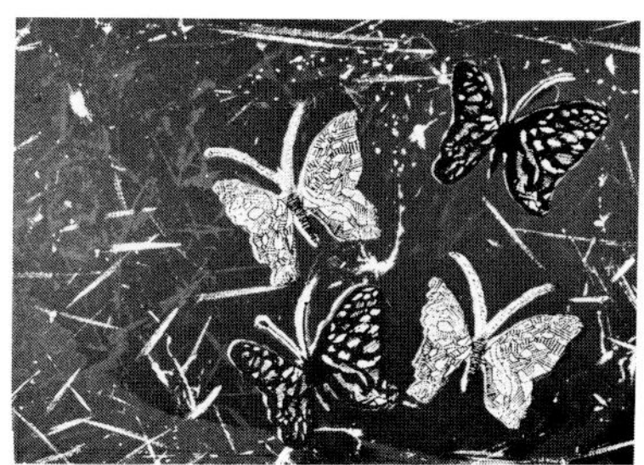

BLACKMAN, Charles
"The Cavern"
470mm × 630mm
Edition: 100
Paper: Kent

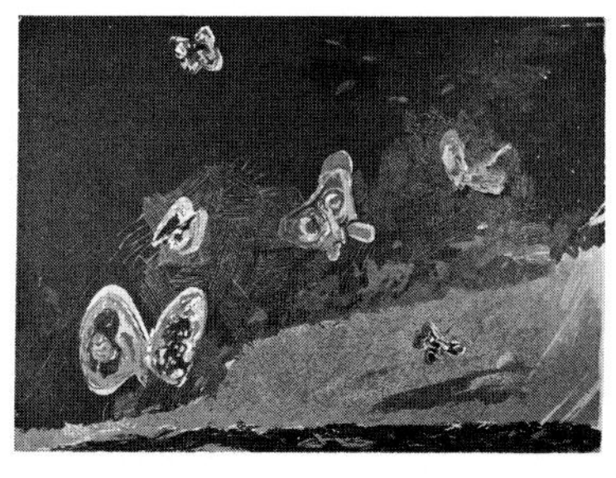

BLACKMAN, Charles
"Night Flight"
550mm × 760mm
Edition: 75
Paper: Kent

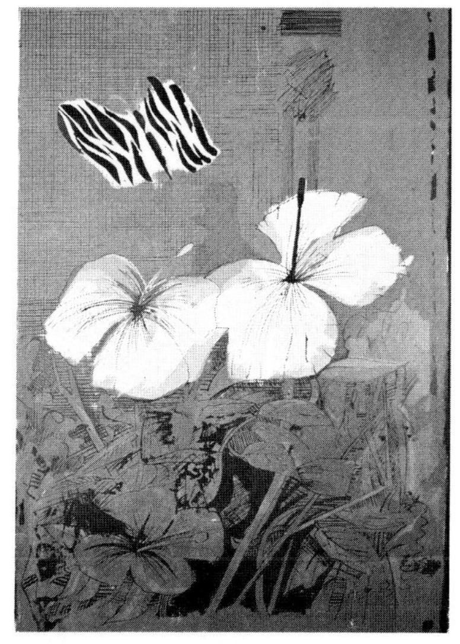

BLACKMAN, Charles
"Tiger Butterfly"
755mm × 540mm
Edition: 100
Paper: Lavis Montgolfier

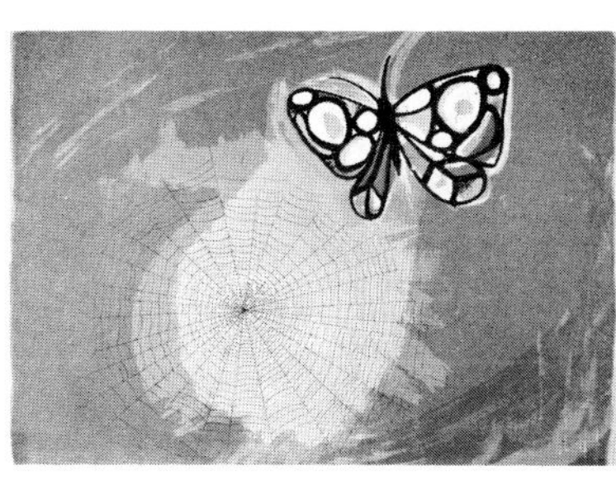

BLACKMAN, Charles
"The Web"
510mm × 700mm
Edition: 75
Paper: Lavis Montgolfier

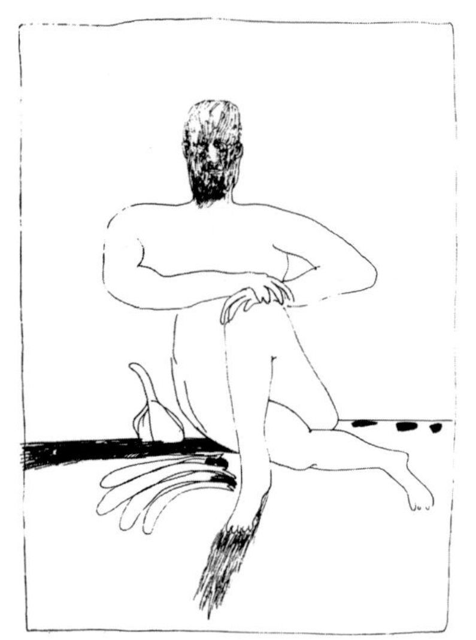

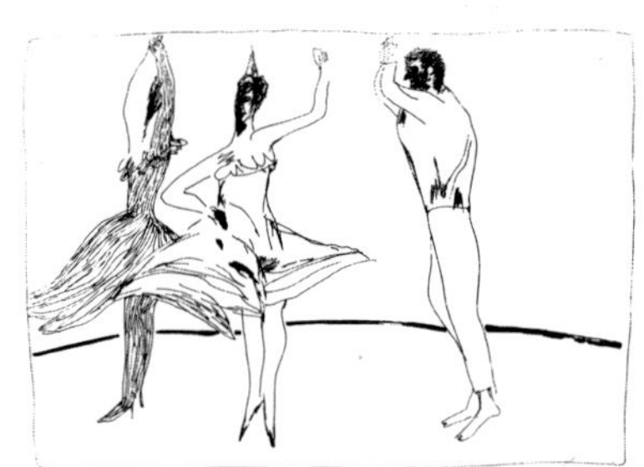

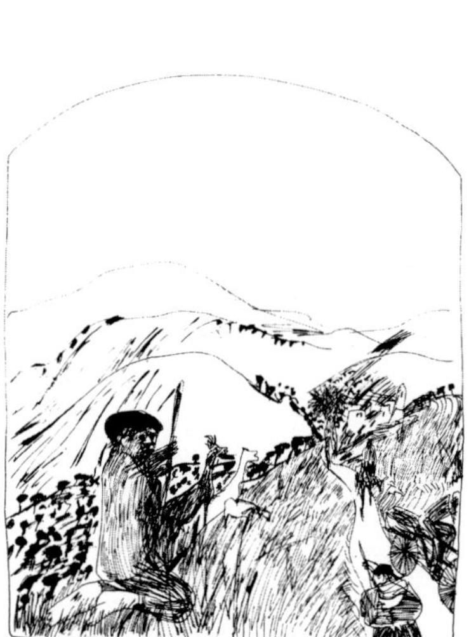

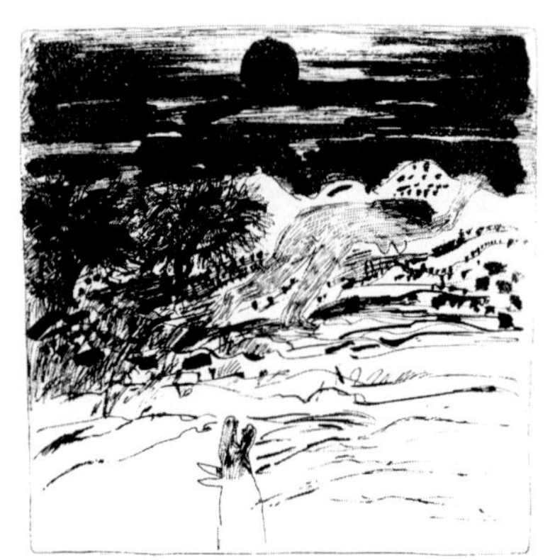

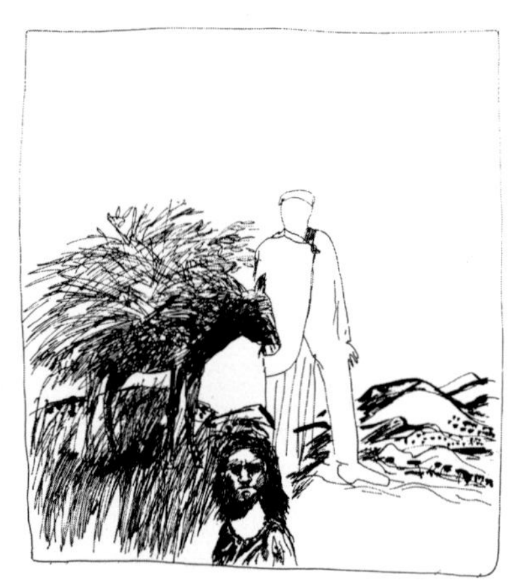

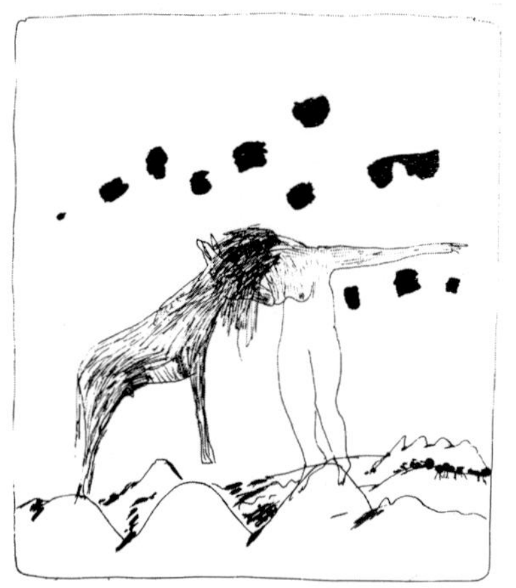

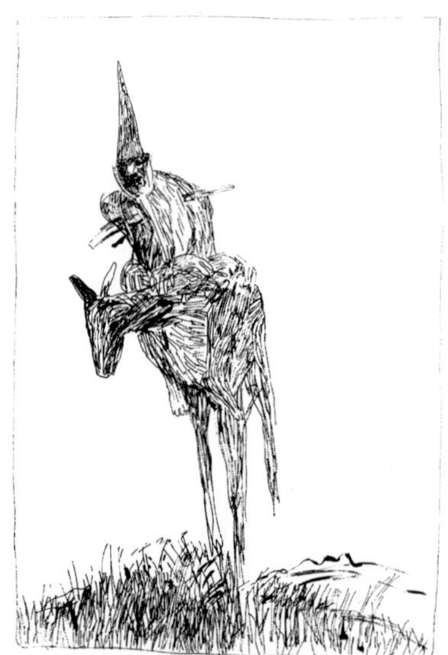

CONNOR, Kevin
"Andalusian Portfolio"
(7 graphics)
Various sizes
Edition: 50 folios
Paper: Handmade Hayle Mill

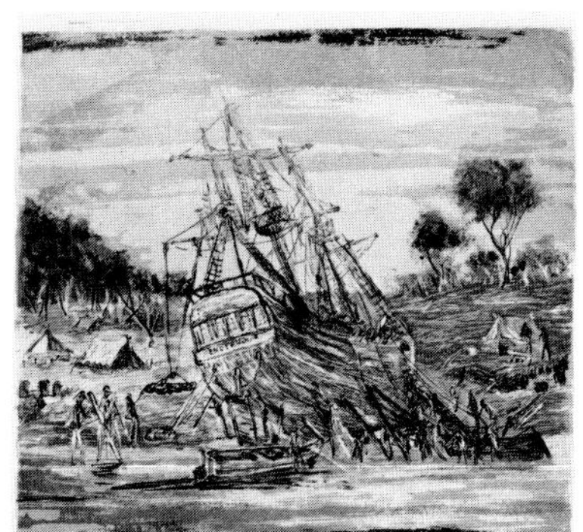

HART, Pro
(the Captain Cook series)
"Careening The Endeavour"
660mm × 715mm
Edition: 60
Paper: Lavis Montgolfier

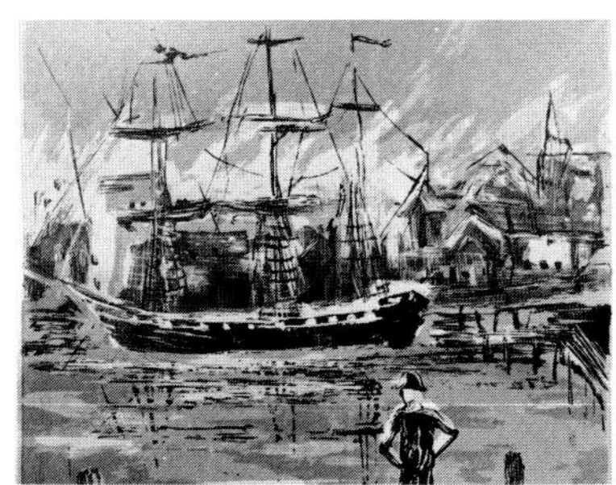

HART, Pro
"Cook at Whitby"
410mm × 460mm
Edition: 100
Paper: Lavis Montgolfier

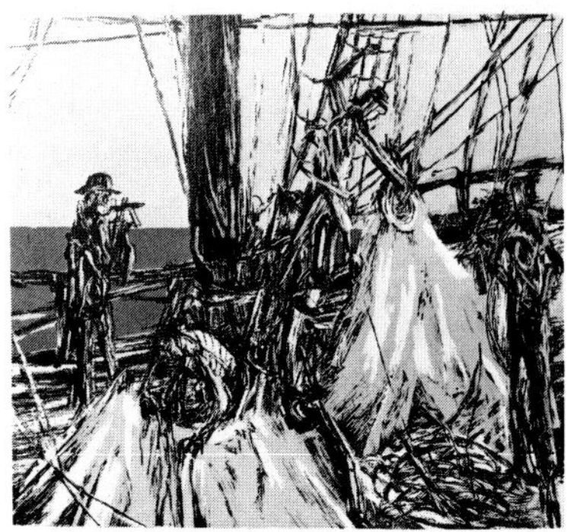

HART, Pro
"Cook Drying Sails"
500mm × 560mm
Edition: 50
Paper: Lavis Montgolfier

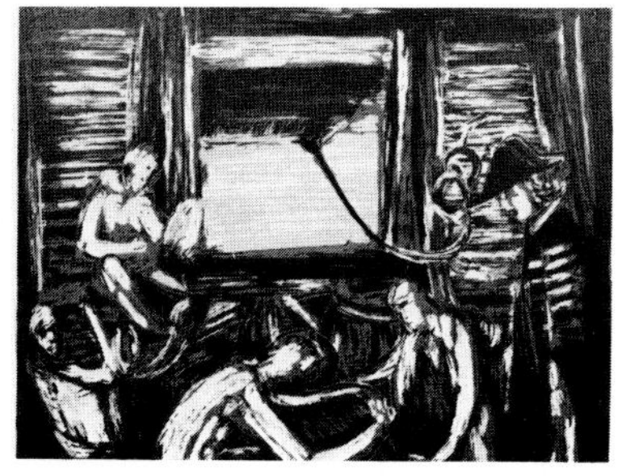

HART, Pro
"Cook Loading Stores"
445mm × 455mm
Edition: 100
Paper: Lavis Montgolfier

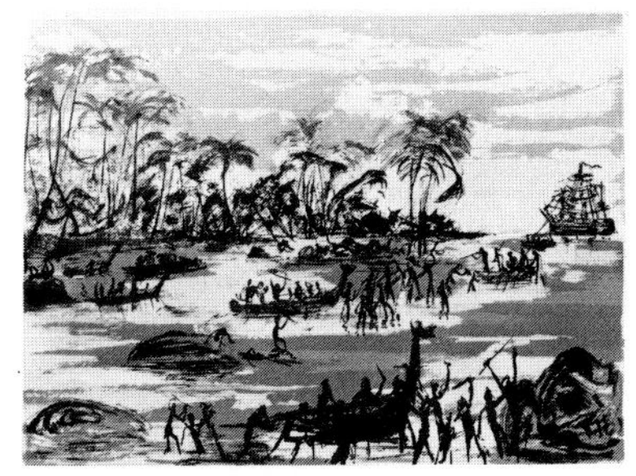

HART, Pro
"Death of Cook"
525mm × 715mm
Edition: 100
Paper: Lavis Montgolfier

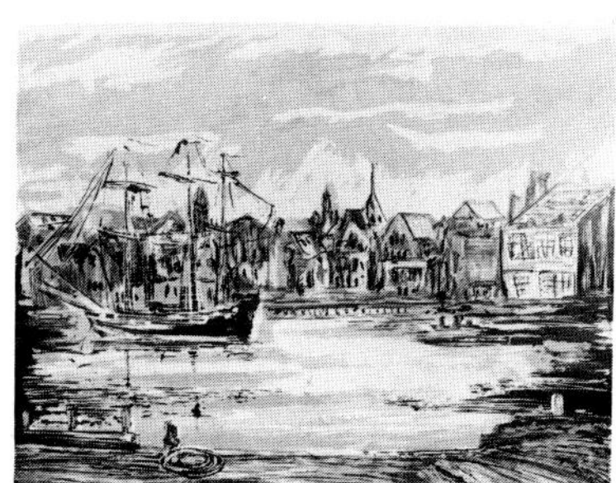

HART, Pro
"The Endeavour at Whitby"
460mm × 610mm
Edition: 100
Paper: Lavis Montgolfier

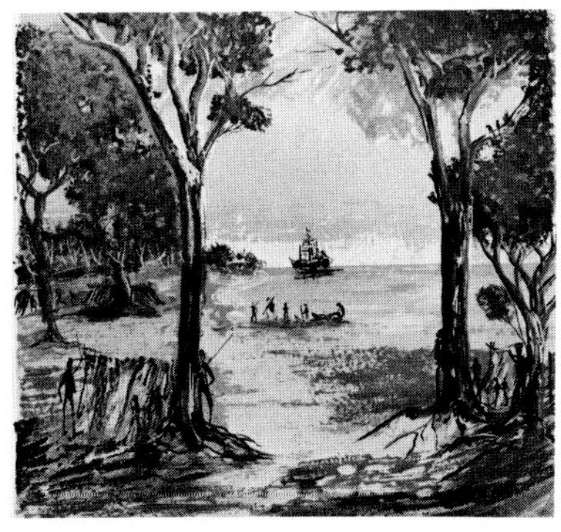

HART, Pro
"The Landing"
655mm × 720mm
Edition: 100
Paper: Lavis Montgolfier

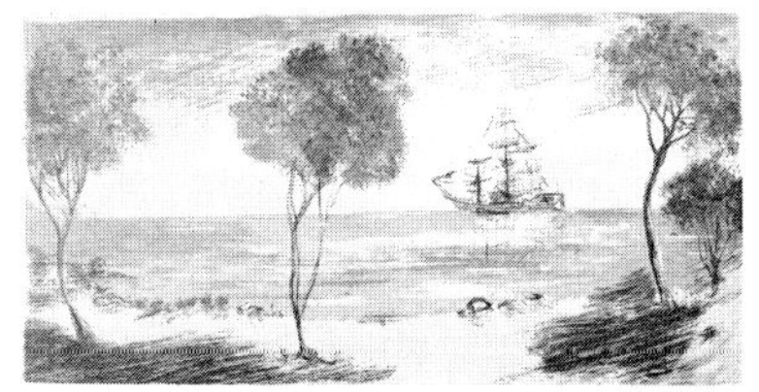

HART, Pro
"Off Kurnell"
300mm × 595mm
Edition: 100
Paper: Lavis Montgolfier

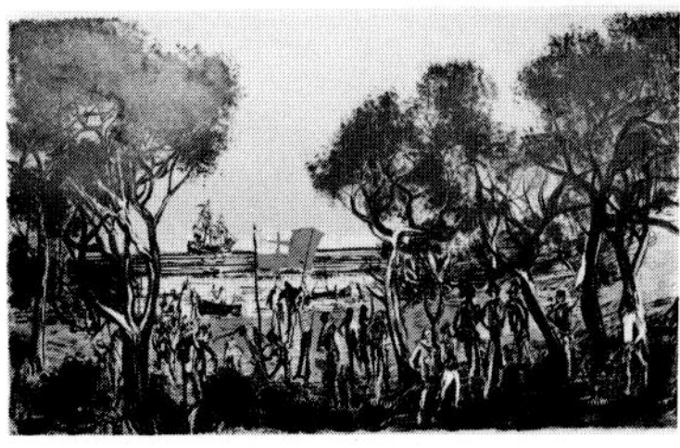

HART, Pro
"Study for Cook Landing"
565mm × 940mm
Edition: 60
Paper: Lavis Montgolfier

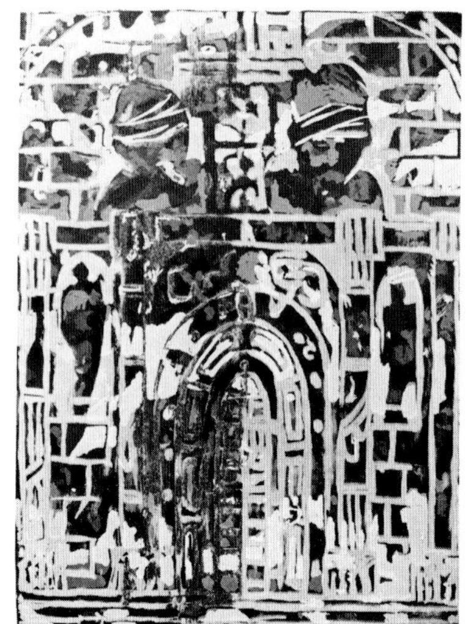

MILGATE, Rodney
"Dilemma"
610mm × 460mm
Edition: 60
Paper: Kent

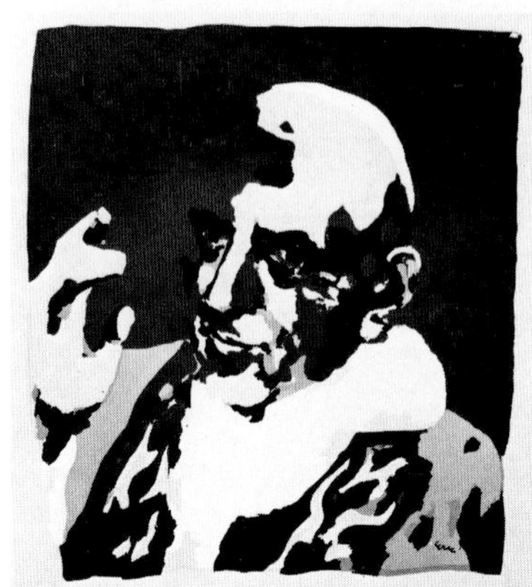

SMITH, Eric
"His Holiness Pope Paul VI"
600mm × 560mm
Edition: 5000
Paper: Kent

1971

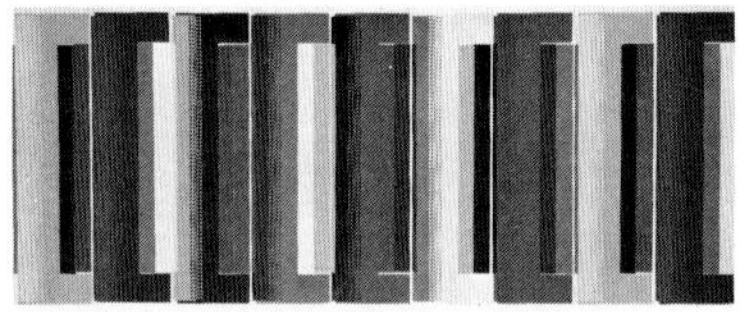

NICHOLSON, Michael
"Modular Strip Art-oons"
Blue series/
yellow-orange/yellow (8 graphics)
1200mm × 610mm
Edition: 25
Paper: Kent

1976

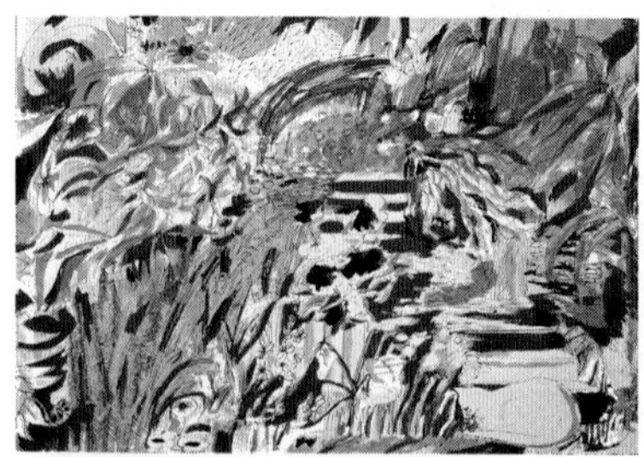

BLACKMAN, Charles
"Eclipse
in the White Cat's Garden"
685mm × 995mm
Edition: 60
Paper: Velin Cuve BFK Rives

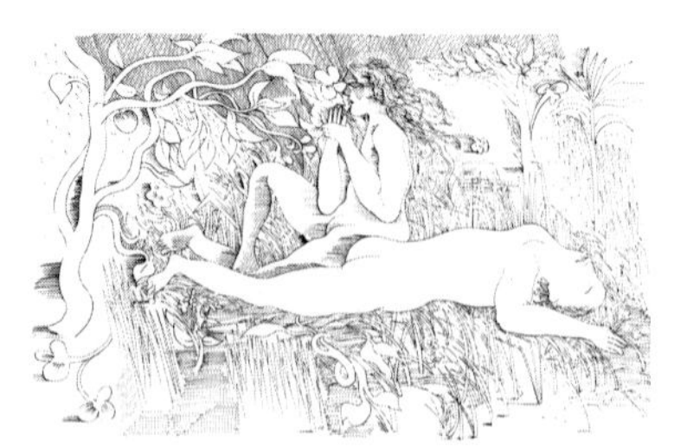

BLACKMAN, Charles
"Paradise Garden"
635mm × 995mm
Edition: 75
Paper: Arches Cuve

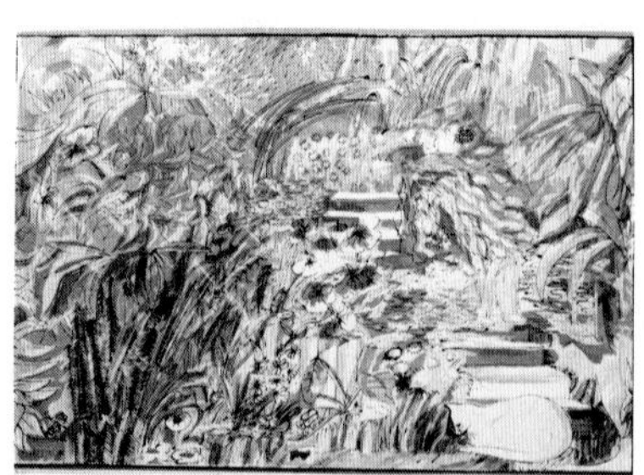

BLACKMAN, Charles
"Passing Clouds
in the White Cat's Garden"
685mm × 995mm
Edition: 60
Paper: Velin Cuve BFK Rives

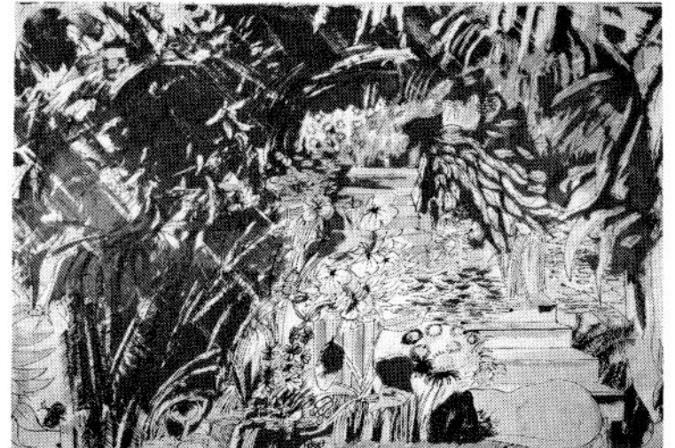

BLACKMAN, Charles
"Summer
in the White Cat's Garden"
685mm × 995mm
Edition: 90
Paper: Velin Cuve BFK Rives

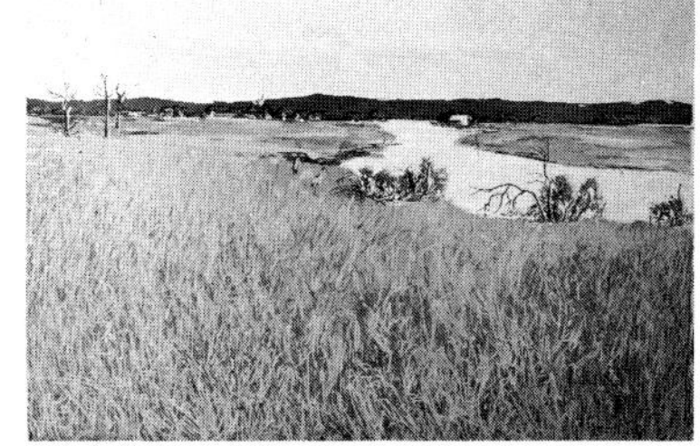

DRIDAN, David
"Mundoo Channel'
510mm × 760mm
Edition: 60
Paper: Arches

1977

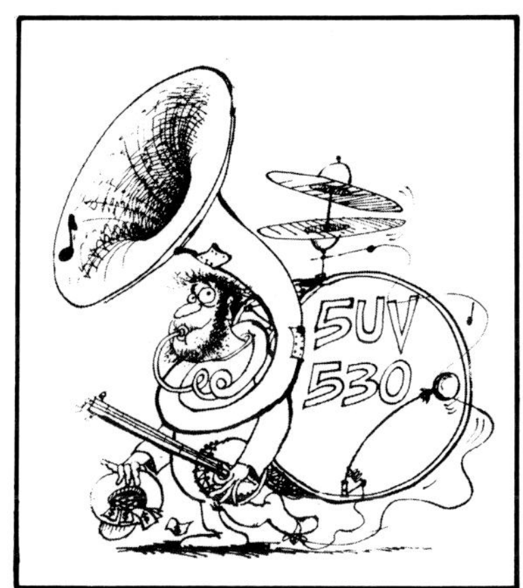

BATEUP, Ross
"Radiothon '77"
360mm × 340mm
Edition: 25
Paper: Handmade

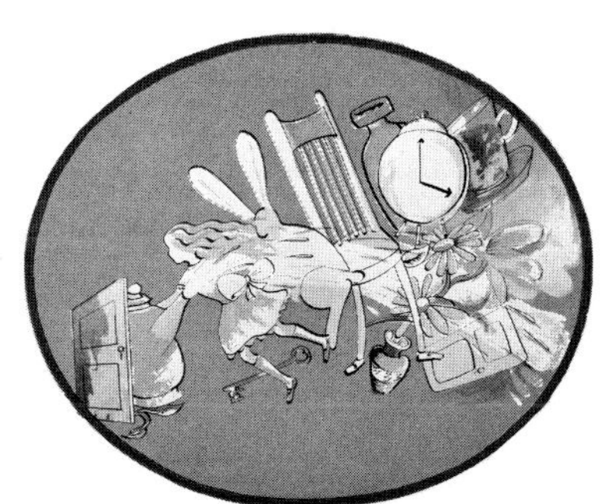

BLACKMAN, Charles
"Alice in Wonderland"
675mm × 830mm (oval format)
Edition: 75
Paper: Velin Arches Blanc

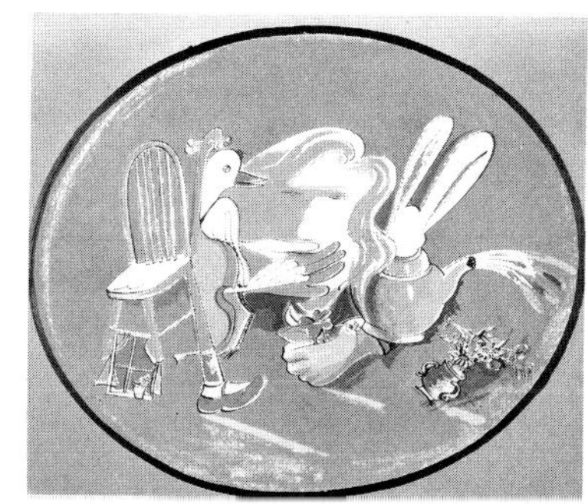

BLACKMAN, Charles
"Alice Through the Looking Glass"
695mm × 935mm (oval format)
Edition: 75
Paper: Velin Arches Blanc

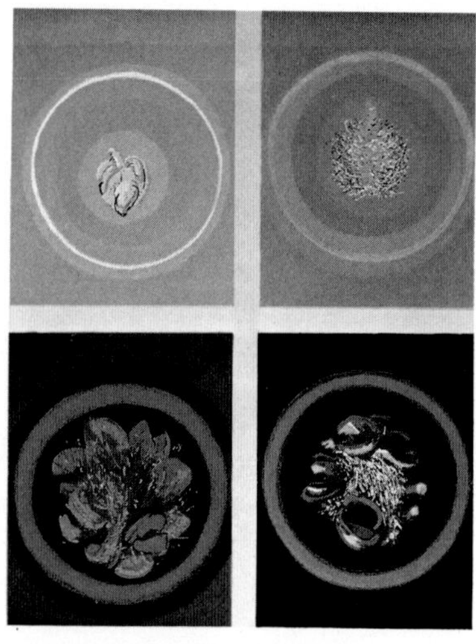

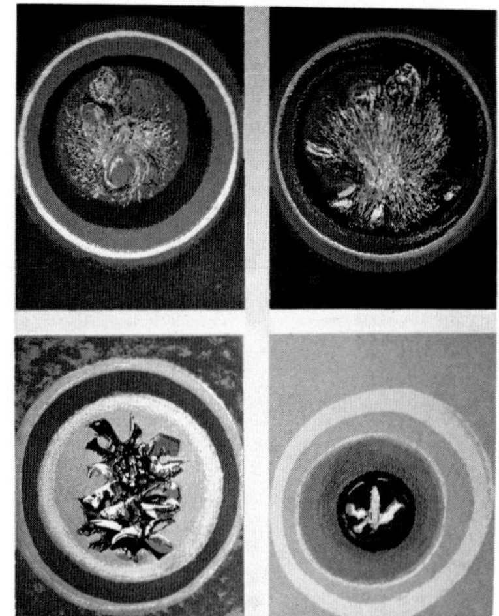

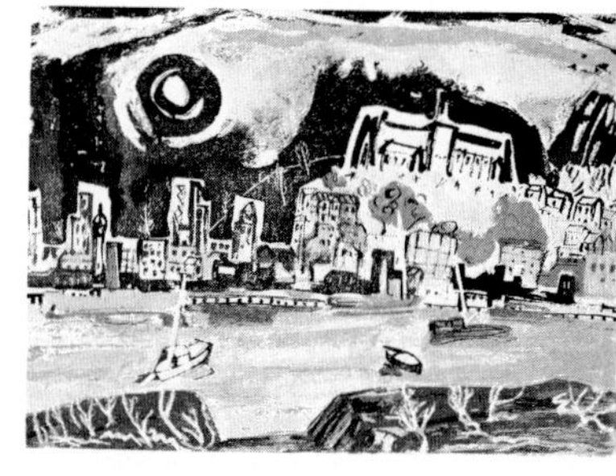

HODGKINSON, Frank
"Genesis" (A and B)
840mm × 650mm
Edition: 100
Paper: Arches

SMITH, Mervyn
"Newcastle"
545mm × 760mm
Edition: 75
Paper: Arches

1978

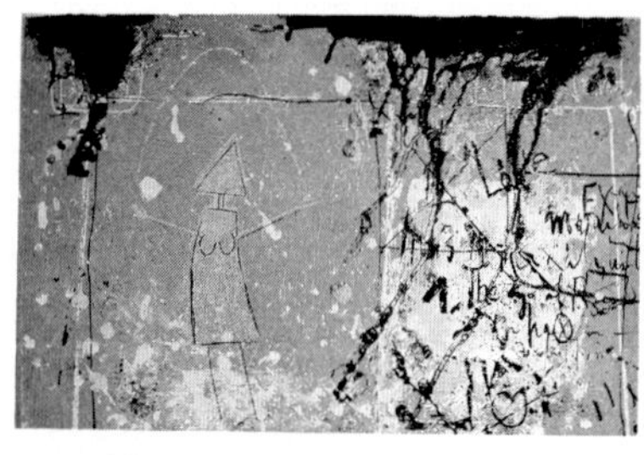

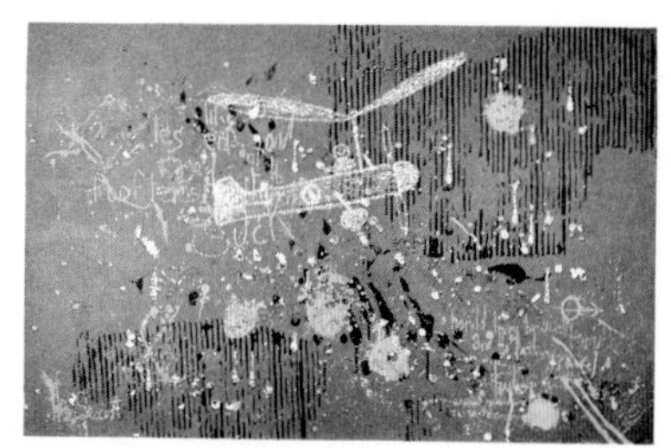

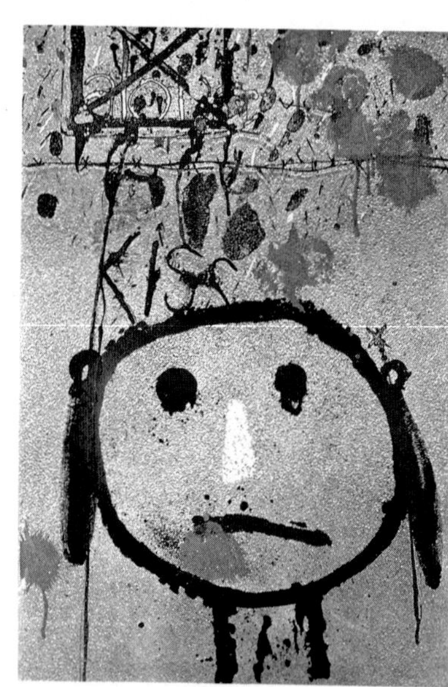

HADLEY, Basil
"Skipping Girl Wall"
505mm × 755mm
Edition: 30
Paper: Arches 88

HADLEY, Basil
"Wall Theme VII"
605mm × 925mm
Edition: 30
Paper: Arches

HADLEY, Basil
"Wall Theme VIII"
750mm × 500mm
Edition: 25
Paper: Arches 88

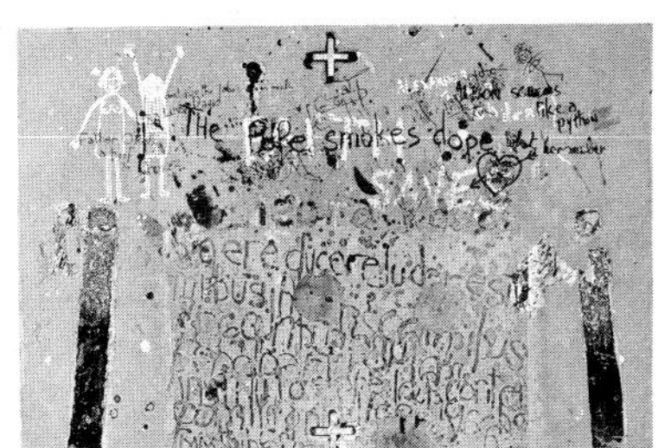

HADLEY, Basil
"Wall Theme IX"
530mm × 770mm
Edition: 25
Paper: Arches

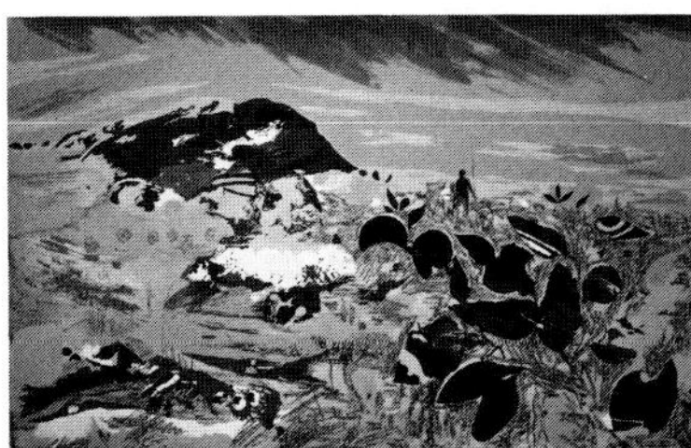

JUNIPER, Robert
"Alcheringa"
580mm × 905mm
Edition: 75
Paper: Arches

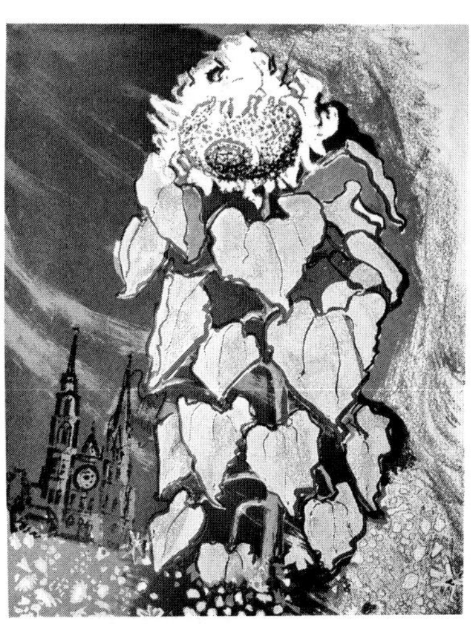

SMITH, Mervyn
"Sunflower with Cathedral"
980mm × 715mm
Edition: 35
Paper: Arches

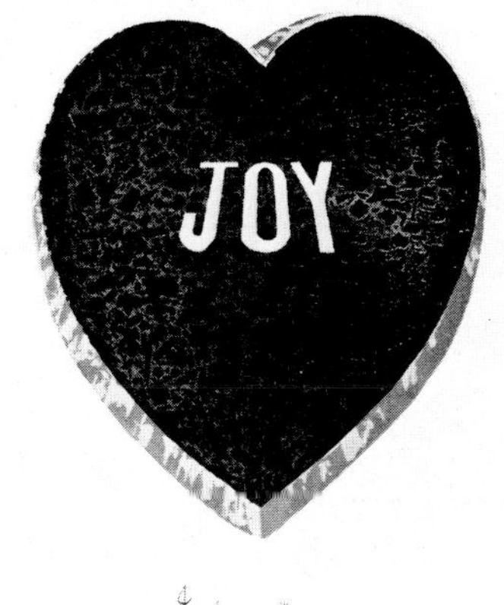

TIPPING, Richard
"Joy"
570mm × 360mm
Edition: 30
Paper: Arches 88

1979

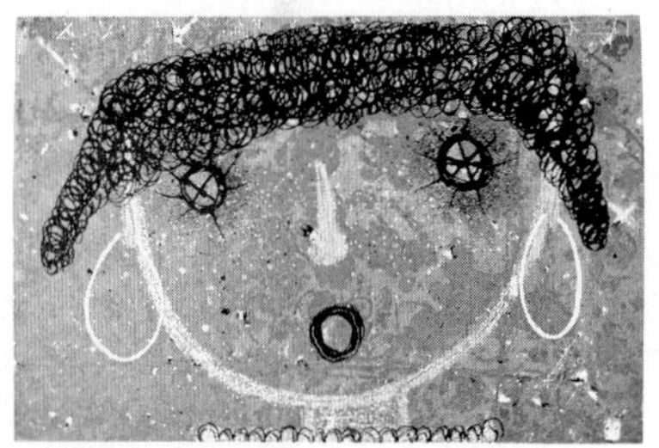

HADLEY, Basil
"Girl with Ear-rings"
510mm × 760mm
Edition: 50
Paper: Arches 88

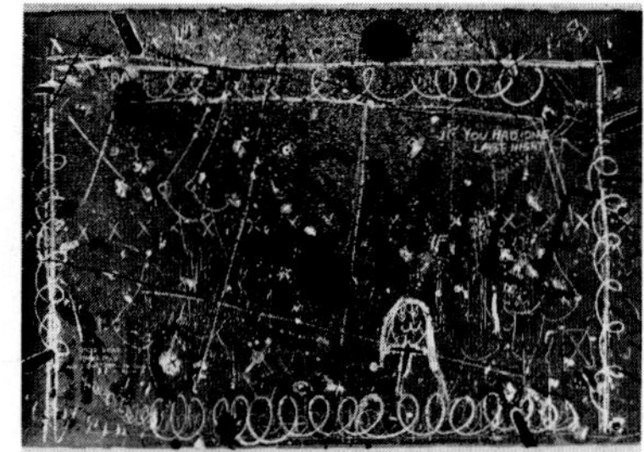

HADLEY, Basil
"Smile"
570mm × 765mm
Edition: 50
Paper: Arches 88

1980

1981

1982

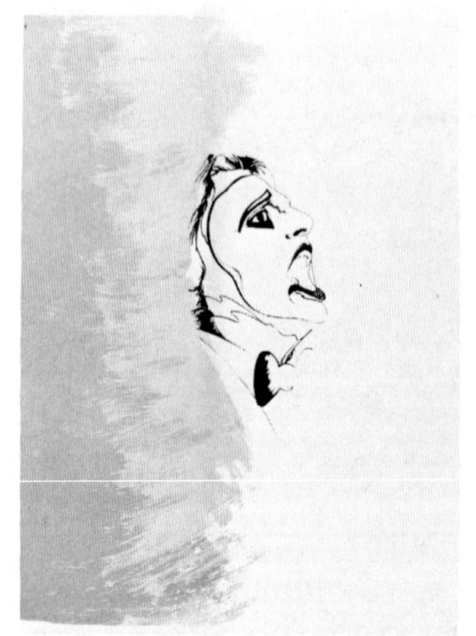

MASTROSAVIS, Max
"Beckett on Love"
610mm × 460mm
Edition: 50
Paper: Arches-Dessin

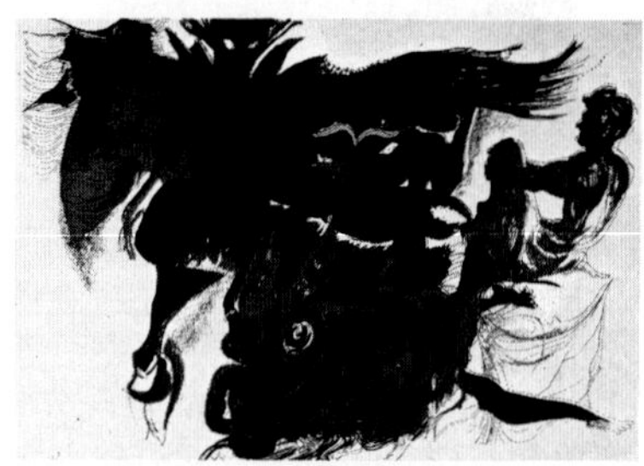

ALAND, John
"Midsummer Night's Dream"
560mm × 770mm
Edition: 50
Paper: Stonehenge-Rising

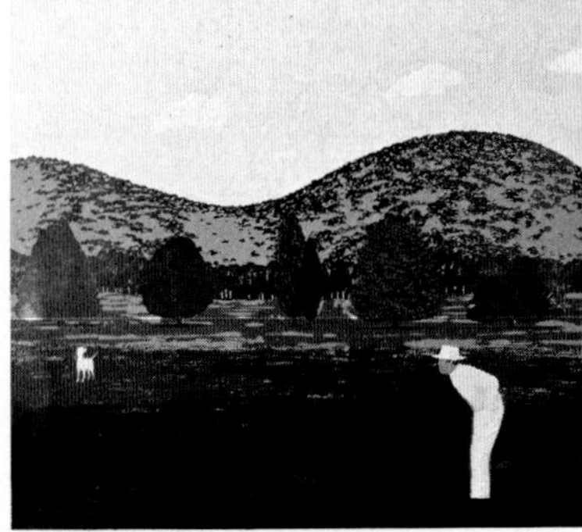

COWLAM, Keith
"A Man and his Dog"
440mm × 500mm
Edition: 50
Paper: Arches 88